W9-DAJ-980

Hungary

Structural Reforms
for Sustainable Growth

The World Bank
Washington, D.C.

Copyright © 1995
The International Bank for Reconstruction
and Development/ THE WORLD BANK
1818 H Street, N.W.
Washington, D.C. 20433, U.S.A.

World Bank Country Studies are among the many reports originally prepared for internal use as part of the continuing analysis by the Bank of the economic and related conditions of its developing member countries and of its dialogues with the governments. Some of the reports are published in this series with the least possible delay for the use of governments and the academic, business and financial, and development communities. The typescript of this paper therefore has not been prepared in accordance with the procedures appropriate to formal printed texts, and the World Bank accepts no responsibility for errors. Some sources cited in this paper may be informal documents that are not readily available.

The World Bank does not guarantee the accuracy of the data included in this publication and accepts no responsibility whatsoever for any consequence of their use. The boundaries, colors, denominations, and other information shown on any map in this volume do not imply on the part of the World Bank Group any judgment on the legal status of any territory or the endorsement or acceptance of such boundaries.

The complete backlist of publications from the World Bank is shown in the annual *Index of Publications*, which contains an alphabetical title list (with full ordering information) and indexes of subjects, authors, and countries and regions. The latest edition is available free of charge from the Distribution Unit, Office of the Publisher, The World Bank, 1818 H Street, N.W., Washington, D.C. 20433, U.S.A., or from Publications, The World Bank, 66, avenue d'Iéna, 75116 Paris, France.

ISSN: 0-0253-2123

Library of Congress Cataloging-in-Publication Data

Hungary : structure reforms for sustainable growth.
     p. cm. — (A World Bank country study, ISSN 0253-2123)
   ISBN 0-8213-3441-7
   1. Hungary—Economic policy—1989– 2. Hungary—Economic conditions—1989– 3. Hungary—Social conditions—1989–
I. International Bank for Reconstruction and Development.
II. Series.
HC300.283.H864 1995
338.9439— dc20

                                    95-33359
                                    CIP

iii

Contents

iv

List of Tables

List of Boxes

List of Figures

List of Acronyms and Abbreviations

APEH	Tax and Financial Audit Office
AVRt	State Holding Company
AVU	State Property Agency
BCU	Bank Control Unit
CAR	Capital Adequacy Ratio
CBI	Central Budgetary Institution
CMEA	Council for Mutual Economic Assistance
EBF	Extrabudgetary Fund
ECU	European Currency Unit
EFTA	European Free Trade Association
EPT	Enterprise Profit Tax
EU	European Union
FDI	Foreign Direct Investment
GATT	General Agreement on Tariffs and Trade
GDP	Gross Domestic Product
GNFS	Goods and Non-Factor Services
GYED	Cash Transfer for Family Support (Child Care Fee)
GYES	Cash Transfer for Family Support (Child Care Allowance)
ILO	International Labor Organization
IMF	International Monetary Fund
LBI	Local Budgetary Institution
MOF	Ministry of Finance
MOIT	Ministry of Industry and Trade
MTCWM	Ministry of Transport, Communications and Water Management
NBH	National Bank of Hungary
OECD	Organization for Economic Cooperation and Development
PIT	Personal Income Tax
SAO	State Auditing Office
SBS	State Banking Supervision
SIF	Social Insurance Fund
SOE	State Owned Enterprise
UN	United Nations
VAT	Value Added Tax

Currency Unit
Hungarian Forint (HUF)

Average Exchange Rates (HUF per US$)

1989	1990	1991	1992	1993	1994
59.10	63.20	74.75	79.00	92.00	105.1

Fiscal Year
January 1 - December 31

INTRODUCTION

The Hungarian economy is coming out of a severe four-year recession, having gone through important structural changes. Household incomes are growing in real terms for the first time since 1989. Industrial production has increased at significant rates for two consecutive years (2 percent and 8 percent p.a. in 1993 and 1994, respectively), leading the recovery of real GDP. Unemployment, while still high, is declining. Finally, the fact that such a recovery of economic activity has been driven by an expansion of investments by the private sector (which already generates 60 percent of GDP), would justify expectations of a new investment cycle and raise the prospects of a sustained growth of GDP.

Despite these positive developments, Hungary is also coming out of its "transformational"[1] recession with major weaknesses. The recent recovery has been accompanied by a very large current account deficit, itself reflecting a large imbalance in the fiscal accounts. These "twin deficits" are unsustainable. With a public debt to GDP ratio well in excess of 80 percent, Hungary cannot pursue growth unless the process of expansion is accompanied by a rapid reduction of indebtedness. Of course, if there is significant positive growth, then debt indicators will improve provided there is no increase in the real size of the stock of debt. This is the challenge facing Hungary: how to overcome the threatening twin deficits without giving up on enough economic growth to restore a sense of confidence in the future and foster the national cohesion needed to solve the difficult structure problems on the road to integration with Europe.

The first chapter of this report examines Hungary's macroeconomic performance in the first half of the 1990s, and shows how the emergence of severe external imbalances (as indicated by current account deficits of more than 9 percent of GDP in both 1993 and 1994) was essentially due to the appearance of large fiscal deficits after 1990 (around 6-7 percent of GDP). The potential impact of these fiscal deficits on the current account was initially offset by an impressive increase in household savings, primarily driven by precautionary motives, but was fully realized after household savings declined to the levels prevailing in the 1980s. Chapter I also argues that the emergence of large fiscal deficits in the early 1990s was, in turn, due to Hungary's failure to rationalize the role of the state and streamline transfer payments during the "transformational" recession. Although all countries in the region experienced that recession, Hungary is entering 1995 with public sector and current account deficits two or three times larger than those of other Central European countries.

Chapter I examines the stabilization package launched in March 1995, which has consisted of a fiscal adjustment, a small devaluation of the Hungarian Forint, and the announcement of a strict wage policy.[2] The chapter argues that, although these efforts to improve Hungary's macroeconomic situation are highly commendable, they will prove insufficient to eliminate the country's large macroeconomic disequilibria. The chapter indicates that such initial efforts will have to be followed by additional fiscal

---

[1]   Transformational was coined by Janos Kornai to describe the specific nature of the recessions in the "post-communist" economies.

[2]   At the time of publication, several measures of the stabilization package were declared unconstitutional by the Constitutional Court. The Government is proposing alternative measures, providing fiscal savings of a similar amount (approximately HUF 35 billion) which are still under consideration.

adjustments in subsequent years, in order to open room for a full recovery of investment and, at the same time, prevent further increases in Hungary's public debt. The chapter stresses that such additional fiscal adjustments will have to be focused on the expenditure side of the budget, involving primarily reductions in Hungary's system of transfer payments. This strategy would enable Hungary to reduce its fiscal deficit while also reducing the heavy tax burden imposed on the economy. The chapter suggests that only such overhaul of the public finances, combined with the completion of the enterprise and bank reforms, would allow Hungary to sustain the recent investment recovery, generate significant efficiency gains, and achieve the growth performance that it has been pursuing for so many years.

Chapter II examines the structure of fiscal revenues, and shows that Hungary's very large fiscal expenditures (around 60 percent of GDP) have resulted not only in large deficits, but also in a very heavy tax burden (as measured by ratios of revenues to GDP of 53 percent), and in very high tax rates. The chapter argues that these high tax rates have been imposing severe distortions on resource allocation, and have been one of the major explanations for the emergence of a very large informal economy (estimated at 30 percent of GDP). Chapter II also argues that any attempt to reduce the deficit by increasing these rates further would be self-defeating, because it would lead to further distortions in resource allocation, with negative effects on long-run growth, and possibly even more severe tax evasion. The chapter stresses that, while there is scope to reduce tax distortions through efforts to broaden tax bases, reducing public expenditures will prove critical to lowering the deficit and reducing the tax burden on the emerging private sector. Based on the assumption of appropriate expenditure reductions, the chapter proposes policy options to reduce tax distortions and the tax burden through a combination of lower tax rates, broader tax bases, and improved compliance.

The required reductions in the fiscal deficit and in the ratio of fiscal revenues to GDP define a broad envelope for reductions in fiscal expenditures. To implement these expenditure reductions, the Government will have to restructure the paternalistic, cradle-to-grave web of household benefits inherited from the former regime. Chapter III provides a detailed analysis of social expenditures in Hungary, and argues that a substantial reduction in household transfers is indeed achievable while maintaining the protection of the most vulnerable segments of the Hungarian society. It further argues that restructuring the system of household transfers is critical to restore the incentives to work, hire, and save. The chapter discusses four major categories of social expenditures, namely, old age pensions, employment-related benefits, health expenditures, and family allowances, as well as a menu of options for their reforms.

Chapter III considers the option of a serious pension reform, comprising immediate measures to improve the current pay-as-you-go system, and a more fundamental switch to a three pillar system. Such a system would consist of a flat basic pension, a mandatory, earning-related, and fully-funded second pillar, and voluntary pension plans. These reforms would allow Hungary to decrease the highly distortionary taxes on payroll and would most likely boost private savings, with positive effects on growth performance. The chapter also proposes a medium-run program for the health sector, designed to reverse the decline in life expectancy and maintain the nearly universal access to health services, whereas also reducing fiscal costs. Such a program would involve, *inter alia*, the intensification of health promotion plans, the restructuring of the hospital system, changes in the existing remuneration system, and a redefinition of the basic health insurance package. Finally, the chapter examines options to reduce family allowances while also meeting anti-poverty concerns. After considering options such as a negative income tax, administrative means testing, and taxation of benefits, the chapter recommends that Hungary adopts a heterodox approach, whereby the real basic allowance declines in line with inflation, and supplementary allowance is given according to family attributes, or with reference to an income ceiling.

Chapter IV examines the progress already achieved in reforming enterprises and banks, and argues that these reforms have not progressed enough. Indeed, despite the privatization of numerous enterprises, 65 percent of the initial State holdings of enterprise equity remains under State control, implying a low return on a substantial amount of the country's capital, with adverse consequences for long-run growth. The chapter also shows that, despite the progressive tightening of budget constraints, enterprise losses remain large (around 7 percent of GDP in 1994), indicating that substantial financial leakages remain, and that a significant amount of resources continues to be diverted from more productive uses. The Chapter shows further that, despite the entry of several new private banks into the financial sector, financial intermediation continues to be dominated by large State-owned banks. Furthermore, despite several rounds of bank recapitalization achieved at great cost to the public finances--payment of interests on recapitalization bonds amounts to 1.5 percent of GDP--these banks have not eliminated their relationships with loss makers, still suffer from bloated costs, and do not intermediate efficiently.

The report argues that there is urgency in completing the enterprise and bank reforms initiated in the late 1980s, in order to eliminate all the remaining loss-making activities, and maximize Hungary's growth potential for any given level of investment. The chapter also argues that the most efficient way to bring this about is to rejuvenate the privatization of enterprises and to accelerate the privatization of State-owned banks. For those enterprises that cannot be privatized in the short run, more transparent and stricter limits on any additional financial support from the State must be established, in order to tighten financial discipline and increase pressure for restructuring. Finally, the chapter argues that improvements in the general framework for bankruptcy and liquidation would stimulate restructuring activity and also contribute to the elimination of loss-making activities.

Chapter V examines the impact of macroeconomic stabilization and the recommended structural reforms on Hungary's growth. The chapter focuses on an adjustment scenario--labeled as the "high growth" scenario--which assumes full implementation of the fiscal reforms recommended in chapters II and III, and full implementation of the enterprise and bank reforms recommended in chapter IV. The chapter argues that these reforms would enable Hungary to grow at rates at least twice as high as the average EU growth rate, allowing the country to start catching up with EU member states by the turn of the century, and greatly enhancing the prospects for EU membership by the middle of the next decade. The chapter contrasts this rapid adjustment scenario with a downside scenario, which assumes no further fiscal adjustments, above and beyond those introduced by the March 1995 package, and less than full implementation of the enterprise and bank reforms. Under this scenario, Hungary would not be able to grow at rates higher than the EU average, and the large income gap with the EU would not be closed. The chapter also argues that the realization of this unfavorable scenario would make Hungary vulnerable to future balance of payments shocks, and would complicate and lengthen the process of EU membership.

This report does not underestimate the difficulties facing policy-makers in Hungary, as the pre-transition period provided Hungarians with a great deal of personal economic security. However, such security was only maintained at the cost of individual initiative, technological innovation, and income growth. Social security and solidarity should now become compatible with and supportive of competition and individual responsibility, as these are the driving forces of a market economy. This will prove a difficult challenge, because the full benefits of the reforms will not be immediate. It will take two or three years after the next round of structural reforms for an acceleration of growth to take hold. However, policy makers have on their side the population's eagerness to reverse the process of long-run economic decline, and to join the EU. Building on such strong popular sentiment, policy makers can adopt a bold growth strategy centered in a fast and deep transformation of the State. This strategy would also extract the country from the constant threat of a balance of payments crisis and greatly enhance the prospects of EU membership. These are the benefits of such a bold strategy, and they are worth the challenge.

This report is based on the findings of various economic missions that visited Hungary in 1994 and early 1995. The teams were led by Jean-Jacques Dethier and Roberto Rocha. The Department Director is Kemal Derviş, the Lead Economist Christine Wallich and the Division Chief Michel Noël. The Peer Reviewer was Richard Newfarmer. The authors would like to acknowledge the exceptional support provided by the Hungarian authorities during the preparation of this report, while taking full responsibility for its contents. The document was processed by Catherine Baumber, Dora Jankovics, Jennifer Smith and Laila Tushan.

CHAPTER I: HUNGARY'S SEARCH FOR GROWTH *

A.   Background

Hungary has been struggling for nearly two decades to achieve satisfactory growth. During the mid-1970s growth rates were still quite reasonable (around 4 percent a year), but very high investment ratios (above 30 percent of GDP) came at the cost of massive recourse to foreign borrowings, which increased the external debt to levels over 50 percent of GDP by the end of the decade. Growth faltered in the early 1980s and declined below 2 percent a year after 1982 with more restricted access to foreign finance and the resulting decline in investment ratios. As the severe inefficiencies of the economic system became visible, policy makers initiated a number of reforms in an attempt to restore growth and improve Hungary's creditworthiness in international capital markets.

Although a step in the right direction, the scope of the reforms was constrained by political factors, and did not fundamentally change the structure of Hungary's economy. At the end of the 1980s, the state continued to exert a strong influence over resource allocation through price controls, subsidies, and import restrictions. State ownership still largely predominated, and the CMEA markets still accounted for 40 percent of Hungary's trade. These limited reforms did not improve Hungary's economic performance; average growth rates fell further to around 1 percent a year in the second half of the 1980s. Attempts to stimulate output growth through expansionary demand policies did not produce a sustained recovery either, and led to financing difficulties and renewed doubts about Hungary's creditworthiness. As a result, Hungary ended the 1980s with a stagnant economy, a large current account deficit, and falling international reserves (Table 1.1 and Figure 1.1).

B.   Growth Performance Since 1989

To avert a foreign exchange crisis, the Government implemented a stabilization program in 1989, which included tax increases and expenditure cuts, tighter monetary policy, a devaluation of the forint, and tighter travel allowances. These measures produced a turnaround of the current account in 1990 (Table 1.1 and Figure 1.1) and pulled Hungary from the brink of default. The first democratic elections were held in the same year, marking the beginning of a new era in domestic policies and Hungary's international alliances. The change in the political regime allowed the new Government to implement a reform program that differed radically from earlier efforts in its clear vision of a market economy fully integrated into Western Europe. Since then, foreign trade has been substantially liberalized, prices freed, subsidies drastically reduced, legal restrictions on hiring and firing of labor removed, a substantial number of state enterprises privatized, and remaining restrictions to the entry of private-sector enterprises have been eliminated.

These reforms have led to an explosion of private enterprises—the number of private enterprises in the formal sector alone increased to almost 100,000 in 1994—and to a substantial increase in the share of the private sector in GDP—from 29 percent in 1989 to an estimated 60 percent in 1994. The increase in private-sector participation was partly due to an impressive increase in foreign direct investment, from negligible levels to around US$1.5 billion a year,[1] the highest among Central European countries. The reforms also contributed to a sharp initial increase in convertible exports. Finally, the authorities were able to implement these reforms while avoiding a slide into very high inflation. After accelerating in 1990

---

* Stijn Claessens, Bruce Courtney, Fabrizio Coricelli and Bart Kaminski contributed to this chapter.

[1]   The equivalent of 4 percent of GDP, or more than 20 percent of total fixed investment.

and 1991—partly due to the removal of subsidies—inflation was brought down to around 20 (CPI) and 14 (PPI) percent (Figure 1.1).

Unfortunately, the implementation of these reforms was accompanied by a sharp contraction of industrial output and real GDP—by 25 and 18 percent between 1989 and 1993, respectively. The number of resulting lay-offs was also dramatic, leading to an increase in unemployment from negligible levels to around 12 percent in 1993. The contraction of activity was accompanied by a pronounced decline in fixed investment from 24.7 percent of GDP before 1989 to 18.7 percent of GDP in 1993 (Table 1.1), despite the large inflows of foreign investment.

As elsewhere in Central and Eastern Europe, the initial contraction of activity (1990-91) was

Table 1.1: Selected Economic Variables, 1979-94						
	1979-89 a/	1990	1991	1992	1993	1994
Growth Rates (in %):						
GDP	1.5	-3.5	-11.9	-3.0	-0.8	2.0
Fixed Investment	-0.5	-5.2	-0.6	-2.7	1.7	11.5
Private Consumption	1.2	-3.6	-5.8	-0.5	1.3	1.3
Exports GNFS	4.5	-5.3	-15.3	2.1	-10.1	13.3
Inflation (CPI,Dec.)	8.9	33.4	32.2	21.6	21.1	21.2
Ratios to GDP (in %):						
Fixed Investment	24.7	17.8	20.7	19.7	18.7	19.7
Private Consumption	61.5	61.7	70.2	72.8	74.0	73.5
Exports GNFS	39.2	32.2	32.8	31.5	26.5	28.8
Current Account b/	-2.2	1.1	1.2	1.0	-9.0	-9.5
Gross External Debt c/	69.9	64.7	67.9	59.1	64.4	69.6

Notes: a/ Period averages; b/ 1982-89 average; c/ 1989

closely connected with the demise of the CMEA, and the resulting drop in exports (Table 1.1).[2] Exports also dropped sharply in 1993, due partly to other external shocks, such as the trade sanctions on the former Yugoslavia, and the recession in Western Europe, and partly to other factors, including a severe drought, the introduction of a tough bankruptcy law (which curtailed the activities of loss-making exporters), and some real appreciation of the forint. However, this second large drop in exports was partly offset by an expansion of domestic demand, resulting in just a moderate decline in GDP. As also shown in Table 1.1, the second important effect of this combination of falling exports and expansionary domestic demand was a sharp deterioration in the current account during 1993 (this issue is examined in more detail below).

Although adverse external shocks were clearly an important cause of Hungary's poor growth in the early 1990s, the absence of an earlier and more vigorous supply response also reflects severe structural problems that prevented faster private-sector expansion during this period. First, economic activity remained subject to heavy and distorting taxes, due to government failure to reduce its presence in resource allocation and cut its expenditures accordingly. Second, the persistence of loss-making activities and other structural bottlenecks at the level of enterprises and banks continued to drain scarce resources from the economy as a whole, hindering the growth of the most dynamic sectors.

---

[2] The ratio of exports to GDP did not drop in 1991, despite the sharp drop in the volume of exports, because the demise of the CMEA and the regional reorientation of exports also caused a sharp increase in the average price of exports.

3

Figure 1.1: Selected Macroeconomic Variables, 1988-94

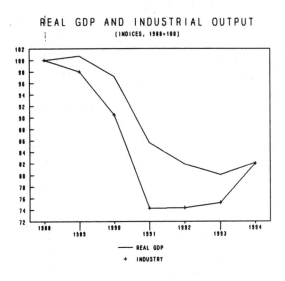

REAL GDP AND INDUSTRIAL OUTPUT
(INDICES, 1988=100)

REAL GDP
+ INDUSTRY

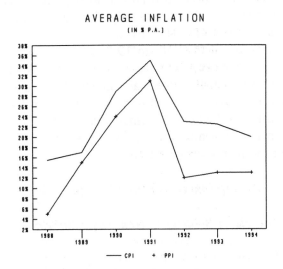

AVERAGE INFLATION
(IN % P.A.)

CPI   + PPI

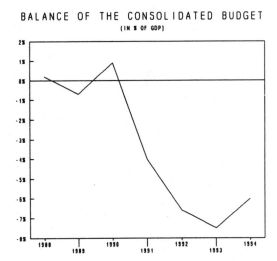

BALANCE OF THE CONSOLIDATED BUDGET
(IN % OF GDP)

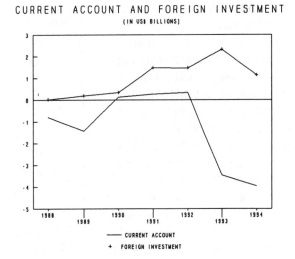

CURRENT ACCOUNT AND FOREIGN INVESTMENT
(IN US$ BILLIONS)

CURRENT ACCOUNT
+ FOREIGN INVESTMENT

RESERVES IN MONTHS OF IMPORTS (GNFS)

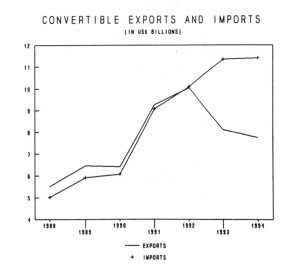

CONVERTIBLE EXPORTS AND IMPORTS
(IN US$ BILLIONS)

EXPORTS
+ IMPORTS

The recent recovery in economic activity seems to contradict the assertion that there are still serious obstacles to sustained growth in Hungary. Indeed, real GDP and industrial output increased by 2 and 9 percent in 1994, respectively (Figure 1.1), in good part due to an impressive 11 percent increase in fixed investment in 1994. This expansion in investment activity resulted in a significant increase in the ratio of investment to GDP (to 19.7 percent), and at first appearance justifies expectations of a new growth cycle. However, this recovery is hardly sustainable under present conditions. The resumption of investment and output has been accompanied by the emergence of large macroeconomic disequilibria, as indicated by fiscal and current account deficits of 7 and 9 percent of GDP (Table 1.1 and Figure 1.1). Severe structural bottlenecks remain and need to be overcome for Hungary to be able to grow rapidly without macroeconomic imbalances. The next two sections examine Hungary's macroeconomic and structural problems in more detail.

C.   Emerging Macroeconomic Disequilibria

The Fiscal Roots of Current Disequilibria

Hungary's current disequilibria have their roots in an overbroadened public sector and a large foreign debt. The fiscal deficits that have prevailed since 1991 (6 to 7 percent of GDP) are to some extent associated with the sharp drop in output and the rise in unemployment during this period, as these adverse developments contributed to decreasing revenues and increases in social expenditures. However, these fiscal deficits can also be attributed to the Government's failure to reduce its role in resource allocation and streamline social programs. Although increases in social transfers to mitigate the social costs of transformation are justified, the pace of the increase in transfers

Table 1.2: Operations of the General Government, 1988-94
(in percent of GDP) a/

	1989	1990	1991	1992	1993	1994
Revenues	56.0	54.4	51.9	55.2	54.9	53.1
Expenditures	57.2	54.0	54.0	60.6	61.5	59.5
Subsidies	11.4	9.0	7.4	5.5	4.3	4.5
Transfers	18.2	20.2	20.6	24.0	22.5	23.1
Pensions	8.6	9.2	10.5	10.4	9.7	10.3
Family Allowances b/	3.7	3.7	4.3	4.4	3.6	4.6
Sick Pay	1.2	1.1	1.2	1.0	1.0	1.0
Unemployment	0.0	0.0	0.8	1.6	2.1	1.1
Other Transfers	4.7	6.2	3.8	6.6	6.1	6.2
Interests	2.3	2.8	3.8	5.9	4.7	6.8
Other	25.4	22.0	22.2	25.2	30.0	25.1
Balance	-1.2	0.4	-2.1	-5.4	-6.6	-6.4
Adjusted Balance c/	-1.2	0.4	-2.1	-6.1	-6.7	-7.2

a/ GDP before 1990 adjusted for comparability.
b/ Includes child allowances.
c/ Excludes privatization revenues.

nearly offset the positive impact of the subsidy cuts on the budget (Table 1.1). Interest payments also continue on a rising trend. Thus, aggregate expenditures ended up increasing to around 60 percent of GDP, resulting in large fiscal deficits.

The shift of the general budget from a surplus to deficits in excess of 6 percent of GDP did not create immediate problems for macroeconomic stability, because it was initially accompanied by two offsetting factors. First, there was an impressive upward shift in the savings behavior of households at the turn of the decade, which seems to have been primarily driven by precautionary motives—the uncertainty generated by the change in the economic regime and the emergence of unemployment seems to have induced households to increase savings by nearly 8 percent of GDP (Table 1.3) to build a buffer stock of liquid assets. This increase in household savings translated into very strong real demand for financial assets, and a much greater scope for deficit financing, thus neutralizing the potential impact of fiscal deficits on the current account.[3] Second, in the early 1990s there was a significant depletion of the inventories accumulated by enterprises during the previous regime. This depletion was outweighed by increased enterprise losses during 1991, but generated an improvement in net savings in 1992 that helped offset the impact of the larger fiscal deficit (Table 1.3).

The very favorable environment enjoyed by the Government in 1991 and 1992 was turned completely around in 1993 and 1994, however. Exports collapsed due to various factors (para. 6), household savings ratios dropped close to the levels prevailing in the late 1980s, and enterprises started rebuilding their inventories and increasing capital formation. The collapse of exports and the increase in imports (resulting from stronger domestic absorption) resulted in an abrupt shift in the current account, from a surplus of US$0.3 billion to deficits in excess of US$3.5 billion in 1993 and 1994, the equivalent of more than 9 percent of GDP (Table 1.3 and Figure 1.1). The deficits were US$2 billion in excess of foreign direct investment, increasing gross and net external debt by 10 percent of GDP (to 69 and 46 percent, respectively).

Table 1.3: The Savings-Investment Balance, 1989-94 (in percent of GDP) a/b/						
	1989	1990	1991	1992	1993	1994
Gross National Savings	23.7	25.7	17.4	14.1	10.4	13.6
Households	7.5	8.6	14.9	12.4	7.7	9.3
Enterprises	11.3	12.4	-1.1	0.2	2.8	4.8
Government	4.9	4.8	3.6	1.5	-0.0	-0.6
Gross Investment	25.2	24.0	19.8	15.5	19.9	21.6
Households	4.9	3.6	5.4	4.4	4.7	4.5
Enterprises	14.7	17.0	10.2	5.0	9.8	12.1
Government	5.6	3.4	4.1	6.0	5.3	5.0
Savings-Investment Balance	-1.5	1.8	-2.4	-1.4	-9.4	-8.1
Households	2.5	5.0	9.4	7.9	3.0	4.8
Enterprises	-3.4	-4.6	-11.4	-4.8	-7.1	-7.3
Government	-0.6	1.4	-0.5	-4.5	-5.4	-5.6
Current Account Balance c/	-1.9	1.1	1.2	1.0	-9.0	-9.5

a/ Statistical discrepancies are inevitable, as the savings-investment balance is computed on a customs basis while the current account is computed on a settlements basis.
b/ GDP before 1990 was adjusted upwards for comparability.
c/ Convertible and Non-Convertible Currencies.
Sources: Ministry of Finance; Central Statistical Office; IMF staff estimates.

[3] The precautionary motive for savings has been more explored recently (see Deaton, A. (1992), Understanding Consumption, Oxford University Press), and may have been particularly relevant for Hungary during this period. Any Ricardian-based explanation for the increase in household savings should be ruled out, given the very limited evidence of the Ricardian equivalence theorem, and the fact that household savings collapsed in subsequent years. Finally, the simultaneous increase in nominal fiscal deficits and household savings in 1991 was also partly due to higher inflation in that year (see e.g., Cukierman, A. and Mortensen, J. (1983) "Monetary Assets and Inflation-Induced Distortions in the National Accounts", Directorate General for Economic and Financial Affairs, E.E.C., Brussels).

Hungary's fiscal situation is actually more complex than indicated by simple nominal ratios of General Government deficit to GDP, because these ratios do not capture the quasi-fiscal operations performed by the National Bank of Hungary (NBH) on behalf of the Government. Indeed, during the previous regime, NBH centralized foreign borrowings and rechanneled these resources to the budget and state enterprises through low-interest forint credits. As a result, NBH still holds more than 70 percent of Hungary's external debt and a large stock of low interest credits to the Government, and has also accumulated a large stock of foreign exchange losses. The Government has formally recognized this stock of losses as its debt to NBH, but does not pay interest on the stock. The Government has also not adjusted the low interest rate on its old forint liabilities to NBH.

When the central bank performs functions that really pertain to the Government, it is essential to consolidate the accounts of the Government and the central bank to obtain an accurate picture of the fiscal situation. Moreover, this consolidation of accounts has to be elaborated in real terms, as the operations of the central bank are essentially financial, and under these conditions nominal central bank surpluses can frequently disguise real deficits.[4] An estimate of the average real consolidated deficit is provided in Table 1.4, which also shows the average nominal and real government deficits for comparison (a more detailed analysis of the consolidated deficit is provided in Annex 1).

Table 1.4: Nominal and Real Deficits Average 1992-94 (in % of GDP)	
Nominal Government Deficit a/	6.8
Real Government Deficit a/	2.0
Real Consolidated Deficit b/	5.9
a/ General Government, without privatization revenues. b/ General Government and NBH.	

As shown in Table 1.4, the real government deficit averaged 2 percent of GDP over 1992-94, and was substantially smaller than the nominal deficit. This difference is not surprising, as the real deficit concept excludes the inflation component of interest payments, which has been large in the case of Hungary. Under reasonable assumptions, the real deficit concept may provide a more accurate indication of the true fiscal stance than the nominal deficit. Thus, real government deficits of 2 percent of GDP would suggest that fiscal pressures are not so strong as they seem at first sight. However, the consolidated real deficit averaged almost 6 percent of GDP during the same period, with the 4 percent of GDP difference capturing the real quasi-fiscal deficit of NBH.

The interpretation of this real quasi-fiscal deficit is straightforward. The average real interest rate on NBH's assets is still negative, because of the old stock of low interest credits to the Government, whereas the real interest rate on the stock of net foreign exchange liabilities is positive. Therefore, NBH has transferred a significant amount of real resources both abroad (to foreign creditors) and domestically (to the recipients of low-interest credits), and has resorted to seignorage and new foreign borrowings to generate these resources (Annex 1). The extent to which NBH depends on inflationary taxation to balance its accounts can be appreciated by noting that seignorage revenues averaged 1.8 percent of GDP over 1992-94, while the distribution of profits to the budget averaged only 0.3 percent of GDP during the same period.

---

[4]   See Van Wijnbergen, S., Anand R., Chibber, A., and Rocha, R. (1992); External Debt, Fiscal Policy and Sustainable Growth, The Johns Hopkins University Press, Baltimore.; and Rocha, R., and Saldanha, F., (1992); "Fiscal and Quasi-Fiscal Deficits, Nominal and Real: Measurement and Policy Issues", The World Bank, Policy Research Working Paper No. 919, (June).

One alternative and very simple way to assess the magnitude of NBH's financial imbalance is to examine directly the main components of its balance sheet. As shown in Figure 1.2, NBH's net foreign exchange liabilities are almost 50 percent higher than the stock of interest-earning assets (the negative net worth consists primarily of foreign exchange losses). This means that the average nominal interest on assets has to be at least 50 percent higher than the nominal interest on liabilities to prevent a nominal loss, which has been achieved primarily through high domestic inflation. Note also that NBH would not be able to balance its accounts if inflation was reduced to Western European levels, as that would also imply much lower nominal interest rates on its assets.

The solution to this quasi-fiscal problem is conceptually simple, lying in an increase in the stock of NBH's interest-earning assets, and an increase in the average real interest rate on these assets (both measures would increase NBH's net worth). In this regard, the gradual redemption of the old stock of credits to the Government, and its replacement by government securities paying market rates contributes to an improvement of NBH's financial situation. Also, an amendment to the NBH law introduced in 1994, through which the Government must securitize at least 5 percent of NBH's stock of foreign exchange losses every year, is another very important step in the right direction. However, if these additional resources are fully rechanneled to the budget as larger dividends, the stock of interest-earning assets may fail to increase, and NBH may remain dependent on high inflation (and on new foreign borrowings) to balance its accounts. A faster increase in the stock of interest-earning assets will probably require less distribution of profits to the Government, and ultimately a fiscal adjustment by the latter. Therefore, the real deficit of the Government understates the severity of Hungary's fiscal situation, and the need for a fiscal correction. The true underlying fiscal situation is revealed through the consolidation of the government and NBH deficits.

The Initial Policy Response

The abrupt shift of the current account into a large deficit in 1993 was not counteracted by a well-articulated adjustment effort by the Government, even after it became clear that the deterioration of the current account was more than just temporary. Indeed, fiscal policy remained expansionary, and there was even further deterioration, if one excludes privatization revenues from general revenues (Table 1.1). Also, aside from some larger devaluations in 1994, there was no willingness to undertake a sharper correction of the exchange rate and offset the real appreciation that had occurred since 1990. Although the extent of the real appreciation is not obvious—as it depends on the indicator used to measure competitiveness—it is clear that some loss in competitiveness occurred after 1990, due primarily to the periodic use of the exchange rate as an anti-inflation device (especially in 1991). This real appreciation probably contributed to the shift in the current account and should have been corrected earlier. In addition, a permanent adverse shock to the current account would have called for a more aggressive exchange rate policy, irrespective of the extent of the real appreciation in previous years.

The initial policy response to the deterioration of the current account was effectively limited to a tightening of monetary policy by the National Bank of Hungary (NBH). Indeed, the realization that household savings and the real demand for financial assets had started declining, and that the current account was shifting into a large deficit, prompted the NBH to tighten monetary policy significantly in mid-1993, resulting in a sharp increase in interest rates on government securities (Figure 1.2). Real interest rates on T-bills increased to 8 percent a year in 1994, and increased further in early 1995, well above real GDP growth rates, and generating an adverse debt dynamic. Nominal and real interest rates on deposits and credits also increased, albeit with a considerable lag (Table 1.5 and Figure 1.2).

Although NBH had no alternative but to tighten monetary policy, given the absence of adjustments in fiscal policy and other policy instruments, this policy mix proved highly problematic for several reasons. First, monetary policy was not very effective in curbing aggregate demand and improving the current account, initially because of the lags between the increase in NBH rates and bank interest rates (Figure 1.2), and subsequently because of the access of the best enterprises to foreign credits at more favorable terms. Indeed, net foreign borrowings by this group of enterprises (mostly joint ventures and multinationals) amounted to US$1 billion a year (2 percent of GDP) in 1993 and 1994, opening room for an expansion of fixed investment and a continued increase in imports during 1994.[5]

Table 1.5: Nominal and Real Interest Rates, 1992-95[a] (in percent)					
		1992	1993	1994	1995[b]
Deposits	Nominal	24.4	15.7	9.7	23.0
	Real[c]	2.6	- 0.5	1.4	-
Credits	Nominal	33.1	25.4	27.0	29.0
	Real[c]	16.5	15.5	13.0	-
T-Bills	Nominal	22.7	17.2	25.8	33.0
	Real[c]	1.1	0.9	8.0	-

a/ Average of Monthly Rates, real rates are ex-post.
b/ January and February.
c/ Deposit and T-bill rates deflated by CPI,
  Credit rates deflated by PPI.

Second, the increase in real interest rates produced by the combination of tight monetary and easy fiscal policies generated strong endogenous increases in real interest payments, tending to complicate further the fiscal situation (Table 1.2). Third, the policy mix imposed a great burden on most Hungarian enterprises, especially of medium and small size, as they did not have access to foreign finance, and remained severely deprived of credits. As shown in Figure 1.2, domestic credits to enterprises declined significantly after 1992 in real terms, as a share of total domestic credits, and as a share of M3. This impressive decline in domestic credits may have been initially due to bank reluctance to accept further credit risk—state banks became more risk averse after realizing their state of insolvency in 1992—but more recently it has been primarily due to crowding out in the classical sense.

Hungary faces, therefore, a highly complex macroeconomic situation, which is rooted essentially in the Government's failure to maintain control of public finances during the last four years. Although the recent recovery of investment activity is in itself a welcome development, this recovery seems excessively concentrated on enterprises with access to foreign credits, and in any case cannot be sustained for long, as it is happening at the expense of large current account deficits and further increases in Hungary's external debt. Maintaining the policies that characterized the 1993-94 period would inevitably draw Hungary into a balance of payments crisis, reduce access to foreign markets, and ultimately force it to undertake a harsh macroeconomic adjustment, thus aborting the new investment cycle in its early stages. Therefore, policy makers face a formidable stabilization challenge, which is to maintain the recovery momentum while simultaneously averting further increases in indebtedness.

---

[5]   Hungary seems to have followed a decision-variant crawling peg in 1993-94, with relatively frequent devaluations, but without explicit commitment to a formula (see Williamson, J., "The Crawling Peg in Historical Perspective", in Williamson, J. (1981), Exchange Rate Rules, The Theory and Performance of the Crawling Peg, St. Martin's Press, New York). However, a crawling peg does not allow full independence of monetary policy under the increasing capital mobility experienced during this period (see, e.g., the early analysis of Black, S. , "The Analysis of Floating Rates and the Choice Between Crawl and Float", in Williamson, J. (ibid)).

Figure 1.2: Money, Credit, and Interest Rates, 1988-94

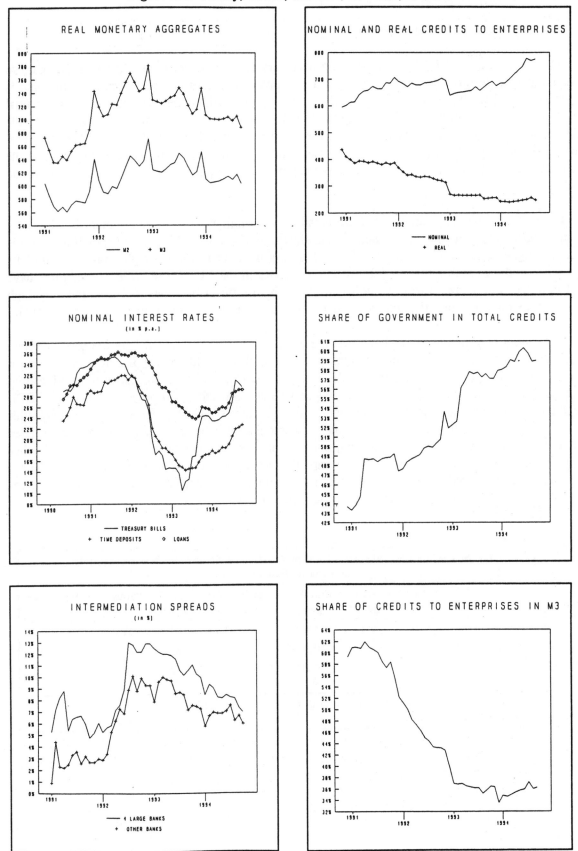

D.   Unfinished Structural Reforms

The Large Size of the Public Sector

Macroeconomic stabilization will prove a necessary but not sufficient condition for Hungary to improve its growth performance, however. Once the country reduces its current account deficit and is forced to count relatively more on its own resources, growth will depend critically on substantial improvement in the allocation of those resources. For this reason, the Government also needs to tackle long-standing structural bottlenecks and finish the reforms initiated in the 1980s. These structural bottlenecks originate partly in the public sector itself, more specifically in the massive presence of the state in the allocation of resources, as indicated by the persistence of public expenditures at levels around 60 percent of GDP.

Hungary's ratio of expenditures to GDP is indeed very high by international standards, especially taking into consideration its per capita income. As shown in Table 1.6, Hungary's expenditure ratio is significantly higher than the ratios of other Central European countries, much higher than the OECD's average ratio, and also higher than middle-income countries in the EU. These large expenditures have resulted in a very heavy tax burden, as indicated by the high ratio of revenues to GDP, and very high and distorted tax rates (Chapter II), with detrimental effects for resource allocation and long-run growth.

The extent to which tax rates have become excessive is best exemplified by the case of social security contributions. The contributions of employers and employees add up to approximately 60 percent of wages, suppressing private-sector activity, discouraging employment in the formal sector, and leading enterprises to operate in the hidden economy (whose size is estimated at 30 percent of official GDP). Although the development of a large hidden economy is sometimes seen as beneficial, because it provides jobs to the officially unemployed labor force, it may also entail large efficiency costs. Informal enterprises congest some public services without contributing to them, and do not have access to several other important public services (e.g., courts) or the capital market, because of their illegal nature. These features imply an atomized structure of operations, suboptimal capital-labor ratios, and low factor productivity, with adverse effects on growth (see Chapters II and V).

Table 1.6: Size of the General Government in Selected Middle Income Economies, 1994 (in percent of GDP)									
	Hungary	Poland	Czech Republic	Slovak Republic	Slovenia	Croatia	OECD average	Portugal	Spain	Turkey
Expenditure	59.5	49.6	49.5	54.6	47.3	43.6	41.3	52.2	44.6	25.8
Revenue	53.1	46.2	46.4	50.6	47.1	43.3	37.5	47.5	40.1	21.5
Government Employment a/	26.0	21.4	15.5	20.8	18.3	22.0	na	na	na	9.2

a/ Employees of the general Government as a percent of total employment in 1993.
Source: World Bank staff estimates.

Unfinished Enterprise and Bank Reforms

In addition to the problems created by a very large state sector, Hungary's economic performance continues to be adversely affected by a number of problems at the level of enterprises and banks. Despite the significant development of the private sector since 1989, 65 percent of the initial state holdings of enterprise equity remain under state control, implying a low return on a substantial amount of the country's capital. The persistence of enterprise losses provides an even more clear indication that reforms may not have progressed enough. Indeed, although the tightening budget constraints and the recovery of economic activity have resulted in a general improvement in enterprise financial performance in recent years, gross enterprise losses still remain large—around 7 percent of GDP in 1994 (Chapter IV). These losses effectively imply that budget constraints have not been tightened enough, and that a substantial amount of scarce resources continues to be diverted from more productive uses, with adverse consequences for long-run growth.

Banks face similar obstacles to better growth. Despite the entry of several domestic and foreign private banks since the start of the reforms, large state-owned banks continue to play a dominant role in mobilizing and allocating financial resources. Moreover, although the Government has spent a great deal of resources to recapitalize these banks—recapitalization bonds already issued amount to 7 to 8 percent of GDP, and the related interest costs amount to 1.5 percent of GDP—it has not obtained satisfactory results from these efforts (Chapter IV). Indeed, although the recapitalizations have restored solvency, averted a potential liquidity problem, and probably contributed to the decrease in intermediation spreads (Figure 1.2), state-owned banks have not eliminated completely their relationships with loss-makers, still suffer from bloated costs, and are still not fully able to identify the best combinations of risk and return among potential borrowers.

E.   First Steps Toward a Full Recovery

The Government elected in mid-1994 intends to implement a program of reforms aimed at eliminating macroeconomic disequilibria and removing Hungary's long-standing structural problems. The macroeconomic component of the program was announced in March 1995, and includes an immediate reduction in the fiscal deficit, to be followed by additional reductions in subsequent years, devaluation of the forint, and a restrictive wage policy. The structural component of the program (parts of which are already under implementation) includes a medium-term reduction in the size of the public sector, an ambitious program of enterprise privatization, and privatization of state-owned commercial banks.

The March 1995 Package

The March package should generate savings of approximately 3 percent of GDP relative to the original 1995 budget through a combination of revenue increases and expenditure cuts of 2.2 and 0.8 percent of GDP, respectively. Full implementation of the package would lead to a reduction in the general deficit excluding privatization revenues (the relevant definition to assess the impact of fiscal policy on the current account), from 7.2 percent of GDP in 1994 to around 5.5 percent of GDP in 1995. The package contains more revenue-enhancing measures than expenditure cuts, thus contradicting to some extent another objective of the reforms— public-sector retrenchment. However, the ratio of revenues to GDP should actually decline (from 52.3 percent in 1994 to 50.8 percent in 1995, excluding privatization revenues), because of larger than anticipated inflation and nominal GDP (resulting partly from the devaluation of the forint), and revisions in major revenue items. Indeed, the share of payroll taxes in GDP should decline as a result of real wage compression, and the VAT should have a weak performance for the same reason. The ratio of expenditures to GDP should decline faster (from 59.5 percent in 1994 to 56.3 percent in 1995) as a result of a larger nominal GDP and the expenditure cuts, which include reductions in family and child allowances, sick pay, and cuts in personnel expenditures.[6]

The package announced in March also included a 9 percent devaluation of the forint relative to the foreign currency basket and institution of a pre-announced crawling peg for the remainder of the year. The pre-announced devaluations imply an overall devaluation rate of 28 percent during 1995, and an expected real devaluation of 8 percent (defining the real effective exchange rate with the relative PPIs). To avoid these nominal devaluations triggering a wage-price spiral and diluting the initial devaluation, the Government has instituted a very restrictive wage policy for employees of state enterprises and the public administration. Average nominal wages in state enterprises should grow by only 15 percent in 1995, and those of public employees by an even lower rate. There is no binding incomes policy guiding wages in the private sector, but the Government expects that the contraction of wages in the public sector will produce a demonstration effect and help constrain wages in the private sector as well.[7]

The March 1995 package should lead to a reduction in the current account deficit and reduce inflation, after the initial increase produced by the devaluation and other measures.[8] However, the initial fiscal adjustment will have to be reinforced in subsequent years, as it is not sufficient to reduce the current account to the level of foreign direct investment and avoid further increases in the net external debt, especially taking into account the need to accommodate further increases in fixed investment (Chapter V). Although a medium-run fiscal program has not yet been formally announced, the Government has indicated its intention to undertake further fiscal corrections, and has also indicated that these corrections would be implemented primarily on the expenditure side of the budget.

Structural Reforms Under Implementation

Whereas the macroeconomic component of the Government's program has only recently been announced, some structural components have been under elaboration and implementation since 1994. In December 1994 the Government submitted a new privatization law to Parliament designed to broaden the scope of privatization and lead ultimately to the divestiture of approximately 80 percent of enterprise equity held by the state. The new privatization law was finally approved by the Parliament in May 1995. Also, by the time of the completion of this report, the privatization of four smaller state-owned banks was

---

[6] The original 1995 budget contained a target deficit, excluding privatization revenues, of 8.5 percent of GDP. The fiscal measures announced in March 1995 and submitted to the Hungarian Parliament a few weeks later as a supplementary budget, represent a substantial improvement over the original budget, and have been fully incorporated in this report. However, the March package was still under Parliamentary debate at the time of the completion of this report. Therefore, final approval of the supplementary 1995 budget by Parliament could involve some changes and revisions relative to the first version proposed by the Government.

[7] Although there is no guarantee that this demonstration effect will work in Hungary, the combination of controls on public wages and moral suasion on the private sector, has been successful in reducing inflation in other cases (see Dornbusch, R., and Fischer, S., (1993), "Moderate Inflation", The World Bank Economic Review, June).

[8] The introduction of a temporary 8 percent import surcharge and a sharp correction in energy prices earlier in the year should also contribute to an increase in inflation to 30 and 22 percent in 1995, as measured by the CPI and PPI, respectively.

very advanced, and the Government had also initiated the privatization of the National Savings Bank—Hungary's largest financial institution. Again, these are very important steps in the right direction, although they will have to be followed by privatizing the largest state-owned commercial banks—the most problematic institutions in the financial sector—and by many other measures required to improve financial intermediation (Chapter IV).

Completing the Reform Agenda

The macroeconomic package announced by the Government in March 1995, and the structural measures under implementation, are important initial steps toward macroeconomic stabilization and the elimination of Hungary's long-standing structural bottlenecks. However, the March package will have to be followed by additional fiscal efforts, and the structural reforms fully implemented, for Hungary to achieve the growth it has been pursuing for so many years. The purpose of this report is to contribute to such efforts by providing an analytical discussion of key reform issues, and recommendations for the successful completion of Hungary's transformation. Chapter II examines Hungary's tax structure and revenue performance, and identifies measures to reduce tax distortions and improve tax administration. Chapter III provides a detailed analysis of social expenditures, and identifies the reforms that must be implemented to reduce further the fiscal deficit and decrease the size of the public sector. Chapter IV assesses the progress already achieved in restructuring enterprises and banks, and provides recommendations for the successful completion of these reforms. Finally, Chapter V attempts to integrate all these chapters into a consistent macroeconomic framework, and assesses the likely impact of these reforms on Hungary's future growth.

CHAPTER II: LOWERING TAX PRESSURE AND IMPROVING THE TAX STRUCTURE *

A.   Introduction

The development of Hungary's tax system in recent years has not been positive, as it has occurred in the context of large and increasing fiscal expenditures (Appendix Box 2.1 provides a summary description of Hungary's tax system). The Government's efforts to finance these large expenditures through tax revenues and avoid an even greater increase in the deficit have resulted in an unstable and contradictory tax policy. Tax policy instability is evidenced by frequent legislative activity across all taxes, and by the magnitude of the changes involved. Revenue losses induce the Government to periodically adjust tax rates upward and create legal measures to curb evasion. Increases in the rates are self-defeating, because they lead to reduced compliance and to further loss of revenues, and because they reduce the incentives to save and invest of those who continue to comply. Tax policy is also contradictory, because the combination of high nominal rates with targeted (and often open-ended) preferential treatment engenders a multiple system of intractable tax distortions. Finally, tax institutions are weak and lack the expertise to deal with the problems created by taxpayers (e.g., evasion, arrears). The very high tax rates and other characteristics of the tax system result ultimately in a hostile environment for private-sector development, and an inadequate solution for budgetary revenue requirements.

The deterioration of the fiscal situation during 1994 again prompted the Hungarian Government to introduce a number of tax measures at the end of the year (Box 2.1). These measures increased indirect taxes (VAT and some excises), redefined the taxation of business, and modified several aspects of the personal income tax. The same motivation led the authorities to introduce an 8 percent import surcharge and to decree new excises on automobiles in March 1995. These measures did little to improve the efficiency of the tax system, as they were motivated primarily by the need to obtain an immediate increase in revenues. As a result, tax rates remain very high, perpetuating evasion and distortions.

Box 2.1: Tax Measures Introduced at the End of 1994

The Government of Hungary issued a number of tax measures at the end of 1994, mainly on VAT, corporate income tax (CIT) and excises. Changes in personal income tax (PIT) were relatively minor.

•   The VAT base was broadened and rates were increased. Selected pharmaceutical products started being taxed at 12 percent, and the rates on telecommunications and household fuel were changed from 10 to 25 percent. The 10 percent rate was changed to 12 percent. This means that the average effective tax rate will be closer to 25 percent (the rate at which most goods are taxed).

•   CIT rates were defined differently. Instead of having a single rate (36 percent) on company profits, from 1995 a reduced (18 percent) rate is applicable at the corporate level and a supplementary tax of 23 percent is applicable on distributed profits. With this strategy the Government dismantled in practice most existing preferential tax treatments, although it also introduced an incentive for reinvestment of profits of questionable effectiveness.

•   Excises payable in a fixed HUF amount were adjusted to offset the Tanzi-Olivera effect.

---

* Mark Lutz and Jaime Vazquez-Caro contributed to this chapter.

B.   The Tax Burden Must Be Reduced to Support Growth

The problem of high and distorted tax rates exists across the whole spectrum of taxes. First, payroll taxes are extremely high (nearly 60 percent of wages), discouraging employment and leading enterprises to shift operations to the informal sector. Second, the marginal income tax rate on individuals also remains high, and a large proportion of the tax base remains untaxed. Third, despite the 1994 changes in the corporate income tax regime, distortions in the rate of return of investment across sectors remain, resulting in sub-optimal investment allocation decisions. Finally, the differential between the low (12 percent) and high (25 percent) rates of VAT remains large, leading to distortions in production and consumption decisions. These tax-induced distortions are probably depressing Hungary's growth potential in a significant way, as they happen in the context of a very heavy tax burden.[1] Indeed, Hungary's tax burden (as measured by the ratio of tax revenues to GDP) remains very heavy compared with fast growing middle-income economies outside the EU, and is also significantly higher than the middle-income economies inside the EU (Table 2.1).

Table 2.1: Tax to GNP Ratios in Selected Countries in 1992	
Hungary	40.8
Ireland	40.1
Portugal	34.8
Greece	32.3
Spain	29.0
Uruguay	28.5
Chile	21.4
Mexico	14.4
Sources: MoF, WDR, 1994.	

Table 2.2: Hungary: Tax Structure in 1994	(% of GDP)	% of Total
Tax Revenues	39.3	100.0
CIT	2.1	5.5
PIT	7.1	18.1
VAT	8.0	20.3
Excises	4.0	10.2
Trade	3.4	8.7
Social Security	12.7	32.3
Employers	9.5	24.1
Employees	3.2	8.2
Source: Ministry of Finance.		

Any tax reform aimed at reducing distortions and increasing the efficiency of the economic system needs to involve an effort to reduce tax rates and broaden the tax base. Hungary is not an exception to this general rule, but its very high ratio of revenues to GDP indicates that tax reform in Hungary cannot be revenue-neutral. Although there is scope for base broadening in Hungary, and a broader tax base can certainly contribute to a reduction in tax rates, the reduction in tax rates in Hungary must be primarily associated with a reform of the expenditure side of the budget to enable a substantial reduction in the overall tax burden.

---

[1]   Recent research indicates a significant negative correlation between the size of the public sector (and the tax-induced distortions associated with it) and growth performance. See, e.g., Barro, R. (1991), "Economic Growth in a Cross-Section of Countries", Quarterly Journal of Economics, pp. 407-444; and Barro R., and Lee, J. (1993), "Losers and Winners in Economic Growth", in the Proceedings of the 1993 World Bank Conference on Development Economics, World Bank, Washington D.C.. The negative impact of large informal sectors on growth is examined in Loayza, N. (1994), "Taxation, Public Services, and the Informal Sector in a Model of Endogenous Growth", processed, The World Bank, Washington D.C.

Options to reform the expenditure side of the general budget are presented in Chapter III, while this chapter identifies the major corrections needed on the revenue side. The next section examines each tax, and provides options for reducing the rates and broadening the base, in the situations where base-broadening is feasible. The final section provides recommendations for improvements in tax administration. Chapter V combines the recommended reforms in the revenue and expenditure sides of the budget in a consistent macroeconomic framework.

C.   Measures to Reduce the Tax Burden and Increase Efficiency

Social Security Contributions. Contributions are currently earmarked for the Health Insurance Fund (health care, pharmaceutical subsidies, sick pay, maternity leave, and invalidity pension for people of working age), the Pension Fund (old age, survivors and disability pensions) and the Solidarity Fund (unemployment compensation). The total contribution rate levied on employers amounts to nearly 50 percent (Table 2.3), which is much higher than in other economies in Western and Eastern Europe—about 31 percent in Western Europe, 26 percent in the Czech Republic and 32 percent in Poland.

Contribution rates have increased as a share of both employer costs and employee wage (Table 2.3).

Table 2.3: Social Contributions and Tax Wedges, 1989-94				
	1989	1992	1993	1994
Employer pays	143.0	149.0	151.0	149.3
o/w Social security	43.0	44.0	44.0	44.0
o/w Solidarity fund	--	5.0	7.0	5.0
o/w Wage Guarantee Fund	--	--	--	0.3
Worker gross wage	100.0	100.0	100.0	100.0
o/w Pension contribution	10.0	10.0	10.0	10.0
o/w Personal income tax	14.6	18.0	20.9	19.7
o/w Solidarity fund	--	1.0	2.0	1.5
o/w Net wage	75.4	71.0	67.1	68.8
Total wedge	67.6	78.0	83.9	80.5
as % of employer cost	47.3	52.3	55.6	53.9
as % of gross wage	67.6	78.0	83.9	80.5
as % of net wage	89.7	109.9	125.0	117.0
Source: Ministry of Finance.				

Coupled with real wage rigidity, these high rates have several associated effects. The first is the high incidence of tax evasion by the private sector, as employers seek to avoid labor taxes. The second—more specific to transition economies—is large arrears by state-owned enterprises (SOEs), leading to increasing financial commitments from the central budget and budgetary pressures. Indeed, budgetary contributions for social security and unemployment were at least 12 percent below projected revenues for 1993. The gap is largely due to arrears, primarily by large SOEs. High contributions rates are also a disincentive for hiring in an economy where employment in the formal (i.e., taxed) sector has declined substantially. Contribution rates should be lowered by base broadening, reforming the pension system, and other measures (Chapter III).

As shown in Table 2.4, the combination of broadening the tax base to include non-wage cash earnings (fringe benefits), and a reduction in average contribution rates (from 44 to 36 percent, and 10 to 8 percent for the HIF/Pension Fund; 5.2 to 3 percent, and 1.5 to 1 percent for the Solidarity Fund, employers and employees contributions respectively) could be roughly neutral in the short run. Note that in the three scenarios, pre-tax wages net of contributions remain broadly constant, but the average employer contribution rate drops (the figures use the original 1994 budget estimates). The calculations exclude labor demand effects and formal/informal sector effects. To the extent that lower contributions lead to more employment in the formal sector, the benefits to public finances could be significantly higher. In the medium term, the Government could also envisage shifting the financing of health expenditures to general budgetary revenues and away from payroll taxation to decrease the rates further.[2]

Personal Income Tax (PIT). There is still scope for lowering tax rates and reducing distortions in the PIT, probably without losing revenue from this very important source. Provided that base erosions and tax allowances are removed from the PIT system (see below), tax rates should be reduced consistent with the overall reduced revenue target. Currently, taxation at 20 percent starts at HUF110,000 income per year (less than the minimum wage) and increases in five brackets to 44 percent for income above HUF550,000. This scale would undoubtedly imply a very progressive and high

Table 2.4: Reducing the Payroll Tax - Three Scenarios (1994 Budget Data - in HUF million)			
	Current Rates Narrow Base	Current Rates Broad Base	Lower Rates Broad Base
Employer Contributions:	613	748	678
Employer Rate:	49.2%	49.2%	39.0%
Worker Contributions:	143	175	157
Worker Rate:	11.5%	11.5%	9.0%
Pre-tax wage bill (net of contributions):	1376	1344	1365
Source: World Bank calculations.			

marginal tax rate in the case of a broadly defined income tax base. The design of the scale should be made a multiple of the average wage. For instance, the first bracket should be 2 or 3 times the average wage, the second bracket, 4 times, and so on. To avoid bracket creep, all forint-denominated numbers in the PIT law should be adjusted for inflation at least once a year. Thus, PIT progressivity would only capture increases in real income.

The PIT statute excludes a sizeable proportion of its base through explicit exclusion of specific income items from the taxable bases, or allows reductions from the tax itself. A complete review of exempted incomes should be undertaken, with a view to increasing the share of household income that is taxable. This should include non-wage cash benefits, income from intellectual activities, rental income, alimony income, and income from small-scale farming. The present situation in which employee-paid contributions into the pension fund are deductible, and pension incomes subsequently received are exempt from taxation, should be amended. Two immediate reforms should be envisaged. First, including pension income in the PIT tax base. Second, placing public and private pensions on a comparable footing from a tax point of view.

Corporate Income Tax (CIT). Many changes in the rules have occurred since the enactment of the tax. Most of these changes aimed either to reduce the general burden of the tax (open-rate reductions), to provide tax incentives to particular groups, or to curb observed loopholes in the law. These three objectives are conflicting in many cases, and tend to define a contradictory legal system. In this process, the tax became complex, and has not been a major source of revenue. Recent reforms of the CIT were in the correct direction, and took care of some of the concerns identified during the preparation of this report. In spite of their controversial nature, the changes introduced in December 1994 balance tax obligations between former beneficiaries of incentives and newcomers, and reduce the pressure from new

---

[2] Although the very high contribution rates and the magnitude of Hungary's hidden economy (estimated at 20- to 30 percent of GDP) might define a Laffer curve for the Hungarian case, the attempt to increase revenues just by reducing contribution rates would entail unacceptable risks. The best policy package would probably involve reductions in rates, coordinated with reduced expenditures, shifts to other forms of taxation, improvements in tax administration, and possibly a set of regularization measures designed to promote entry/re-entry of taxpayers. This package could attract a substantial number of firms to the formal sector, increase revenues, and perhaps allow a second round of reductions in contribution rates.

investments to obtain conditions comparable to those of former preferred investors. However, international experience suggests that the split of CIT rates into a preferential rate for retained earnings and a higher one for distributed profits has a questionable impact on investment decisions. Profitable firms with good prospects should be willing to re-invest their profits in their firms without tax incentives. If the concern is more broadly about a high user-cost of capital, since capital income is taxed twice (as profit under the CIT and as dividend under the PIT), consideration should be given to eliminating the double taxation and replacing it with tax integration, either through an imputation system or partial shareholder relief or deduction schemes. Finally, the elimination of the minimum tax is a measure in the right direction. As trade margins vary widely across sectors, the same 2 percent assessment rate on modified revenues results in very different effective tax rates. Clearly, the preferable alternative would be to introduce higher standards of accounting, auditing, and tax administration.[3]

Indirect taxes. In the case of the Value-Added Tax (VAT), the historical tendency to unify rates at 25 percent has reduced distortions somewhat and broadened the base. However, the level of the rate is too high and encourages the "informalization" of production. In addition, the remaining differential between the two VAT rates, at 13 percentage points, is still high by international standards, and distorts consumption and production patterns. As the performance of VAT revenue critically depends on the behavior of VAT rebates, increases beyond certain perceived tolerable levels may induce further abuses with rebates. Therefore, consideration should be given to aligning the upper rate with levels similar to those found in many EU countries to prepare for integration with the tax system of the EU. Withholding by the seller (formal) of a proportion of the VAT rate that the buyer is supposed to pay upon his subsequent sale, could be established to curb evasion by unregistered purchasers. This strategy was successfully implemented in Argentina in the early 1990s. In addition to promoting registration by informal traders, it generated substantial revenue in the short term.

Import surcharges. In addition to being distortive, import taxes tend to be "addictive". Although the recently enacted 8 percent import surcharge was announced as a temporary measure, budgets that depend on import taxes have the risk of being "forced" to keep them more permanently than expected. This was the case of many Latin American

Table 2.5: VAT Effective Rates and Rebate Rate				
	1991	1992	1993	1994
VAT/Private Consumption	8.6	8.2	10.2	10.6
VAT/Imports	12.5	17.7	17.6	19.0
Rebates/Gross VAT	56.2	55.9	50.4	51.7

countries during the last decade. In Hungary, the VAT revenue statistics suggest that there is a *de facto* higher average rate of VAT on imports than on internal consumption (Table 2.5). The ratios should be analyzed with caution due to the very large percentage of rebates that may be attributable to both internal production and imports—including capital goods. The 8 percent surcharge aggravates existing distortions, and should be removed as allowed by progress in reducing expenditures.

Property taxes. The Government is envisaging the introduction of real estate taxes as a way to develop a less distortionary tax structure. Although the Government has not yet announced a concrete proposal, some general notions about this type of tax should be borne in mind. First, they are not a major revenue source, although they may become an important solution for local government financing. Second, as real estate property rights are not totally clear in Hungary (in terms of registered owners with clear

---

[3]   See the Appendix Box for a description of the minimum presumptive income tax.

titles), introduction of this tax would require a major effort in land registration and valuation. For this reason, it would be advisable to check institutional capacity for implementing the tax before its introduction.

D. Improving Tax Administration

Simplifying and Stabilizing Tax Rules

A compliance-based system is one in which the taxpayer is the active party and the tax administration responds in different ways to taxpayer actions. Currently in Hungary, over 96 percent of revenue comes from compliance actions—declaration and payment of tax obligations by taxpayers and related third parties. However, the proper functioning of Hungary's compliance-based system depends on a greater simplification of tax rules. Although simplification is generally associated with lower rates and broader bases, it must also include a reduction in the number of taxpayers with no fiscal interest— it does not make much sense to keep minimum salary taxpayers declaring without payment. Also, the option of joining tax and social security collection in one agency should be explored, given the access of social security to budgetary transfers and the resulting lack of incentives to fully enforce its system.

A second condition for the sustainability of a tax system is stabilizing the expectations of taxpayers. Hungary does not fare well in this respect. Taxpayers have difficulties in planning their economic decisions, as every year a number of tax measures are implemented. An environment that combines high rates with high uncertainty, negatively affects economic agents in their investment decisions and attitudes to compliance. To promote stability, the revenue strategy should not be as short-sighted as in the recent past. A revenue package should offer the guaranty of at least two to three years of stable rules, and the expectation of marginal, not radical, changes if circumstances force government to change the rules.

Reduction of Non-compliance

The actual preparation of taxpayers compliance (design of tax forms, reception sights, data processing, etc.) is a major line of development—and permanent function—of tax administration. The Hungarian tax administration was capable of implementing the initial steps for establishing a compliance-based system for both income taxes and VAT for over 4 million registered taxpayers. Tax payers were registered, tax forms issued, and finally received together with the tax payments. These measures may explain the initially high compliance levels (as evidenced by the high rates of collection (as percent of GDP of PIT, CIT and VAT). However, compliance has gradually diminished, forcing the Government to act repeatedly on the system.

VAT payers responded positively to the implementation of the tax, as shown by the increase in gross VAT revenues—from 14.6 percent of GDP in 1991 to 16 percent in 1993 and 1994.[4] However, VAT actual net payments—i.e., those after rebates—have been between 6 and 8 percent of GDP, in spite of rate increases. This is because Hungarian authorities are reimbursing over 50 percent of the tax

---

[4]   Gross VAT is total VAT paid. It includes those credits that make taxpayers eligible for a tax rebate.

collected (Table 2.5). This seems to be a very high level when the VAT base is relatively broad, and a very limited range of goods and services are zero rated.[5]

In 1993 the Government became aware of fraudulent rebate requests (counterfeit receipts) and improved the controls somewhat. Rebates increased less (22 percent over the 1992 level) than the gross base (which grew by 35 percent) when most of the system moved to the 10 or 25 percent rates. Nonetheless, the final outcomes for 1993 and 1994 are still worrisome, as the level of rebates is still very high by international standards. A detailed study of the situation should be started immediately to clarify whether the origin of the problem derives from legal flaws or from administrative incapacity.

The increase in tax rates beyond certain limits induces civil disobedience by taxpayers and promotes the underground economy. Clearly, today in Hungary, economic agents have major incentives to evade tax payments (particularly Social Security, PIT and VAT). Initially, to reduce the income tax of the employee, tax exempt payments in kind flourished. As these attitudes derive from legal design flaws, tax administration is very difficult in such an environment, as it can do little to control the problem. Corrective legislation made payments in kind taxable at the highest PIT rate, which formally closed the loophole. But, in doing so, this created an additional incentive to "go informal". Acceptance of taxes by the community should be promoted first on the base of a reduced tax burden that makes the cost of informality higher than the cost of taxation. In parallel, a major enforcement capacity should be developed on the side of the Government. Improving compliance and the estimation of both tax under-reporting and the number of unregistered taxpayers are important priorities for the medium term. During the first years of the transition, the focus of APEH, understandably, was to capture tax returns and payments. While this needs to continue, it must establish a parallel system that ensures compliance and minimizes tax evasion.

Small taxpayers' regimes are a double-edged sword. On the one hand, they lighten the burden of tax administration. But, on the other, they can break the VAT chain and may become a shelter for disguised large taxpayers that decide to split into several small tax-paying entities. A better long-term approach would be to discriminate among taxpayers using discretional administrative criteria, not rigid legal rules. In the short term, Hungary should maintain its small taxpayer presumptive taxation approach, at least for the sake of stability in the rules. Two years appear to be the time necessary to completely organize the administration of large and medium taxpayers. At that point, the presumptive regime for small taxpayers would become superfluous, and should be eliminated. If presumptions were to remain, they could be defined as a general safeguard (fall back position) of the system and, hence, include all taxpayers within their coverage.

Tax Audits

Under a compliance-based system, ex-post tax audits are necessary. Minimum technical features are required to monitor compliance, and accurately target evasion and prevent future non-compliance. While APEH has a clear vision of what the system should look like, actual institutional development of the audit/inspection function leaves much room for improvement. Currently, APEH performs many "audits" and requests large amounts of information from taxpayers. Most audits are based on formal and/or arithmetic errors, without any hypothesis about the type of evasion they are looking for. The tax

---

[5]   The gradual increase of tax credit on imported capital goods initially taxed at entry point may explain in part this situation.

administration is not making significant efforts to estimate tax base under-reporting or to determine the number of unregistered taxpayers. There is also a lack of understanding of economic processes associated with different sectors. Finally, the indicative audit plans issued by APEH can be executed in many ways. Without objective audit rules and internal controls, tax administration can become highly discretionary and prone to corruption.

Resources are managed with little economic rationality. Selection of individual taxpayers is at the discretion of field offices. Local audit staffs are trying to establish audit selection and operational methods. However, collection-biased data capture will not allow the provision of good information for structured checks of the VAT. The only possible check is the VAT/Turnover Ratio, which could be a good starting strategy, but one taxpayers could quickly understand and counteract. As actual returns to be audited are selected under a very subjective method, there is no ex-ante hypothesis to be checked, nor a tax revenue expectation. Taxpayers complain about excessive arbitrariness of tax agents on matters that are unclear under the law, and for which there is no official interpretation. High penalties are used as an intimidation weapon. In addition, when APEH's system detects a mistake and generates clarification letters, corrections are not made in the system, the letters continue to be generated, and the compliance cost is increased unnecessarily.

Hungary's tax system is still in its formative years. The quality of tax policy and administration remains below European standards mainly because the initial need to invest in capturing tax returns and payments has diverted the attention of the authorities from fighting tax evasion. Currently, information management comprises the processing of all payments made by incorporated business, and the processing of different tax returns and business financial data. In 1993, there were 7.5 million tax return documents and 9.5 million items related to massive controls on employee declarations prepared by employers. Given the growing volumes of tax returns and data problems, "data management"—in contrast to "information management"—has dominated the efforts of the Hungarian tax authorities. In spite of this, fundamental processing problems make it impossible to integrate and manage a unified taxpayer tax account. The information captured when tax payments are registered cannot be matched with that of the returns, because payment data does not include the name of the tax being paid. As a result, a current account by tax and taxpayer cannot be produced. In addition, the information registered when tax payments are made cannot be matched with that of the returns, because payments data do not include the tax concept. The lack of a current account makes the collection task much harder and inefficient. The standard collection, audit, and internal control functions of a tax administration are still being carried out at very low managerial, technological, and automation levels.

It is not clear to what extent data about the different tax bases and the different factors that erode them actually feed back into the political decision process. The available quantitative information would enable the development of analytical models to estimate the impact of legislative initiatives. These estimates could support more objectively the targeting of taxpayers that evade and the type of evasion. For instance, at the present time the information on beneficiaries of VAT rebates due to capital imports is captured in the accounting system, but nobody in the administration checks if this is consistent with aggregate data on imports. No systematic efforts have yet been seriously attempted.

The Hungarian tax authorities perceived the need and advantage of establishing a unified procedural framework for all taxes. A common procedural code was enacted soon after the enactment of individual taxes. This systemic approach contrasts with that of some neighboring countries, where each procedural route was defined as part of the definition of the individual tax. The most serious flaw of the code is its definition of penalties, as they are subjectively imposed from 0 to 50 percent, at the agent's discretion. There is no gradation of penalties differentiated by the nature of offenses.

A recent ruling issued by the Constitutional Court on privacy rights weakened tax administration. The court's interpretation forbids the use of citizen identification numbers for tax purposes. This limit constrains the Government in carrying out basic functions like cross-checking. In addition, the Constitutional Court has forbidden the systematic exchange of information between revenue agencies, precluding possible synergy between APEH and Social Security. As a result of this interpretation of the constitution, APEH will have to generate its own registration numbers, and find acceptable ways to share information with other agencies.

24

Appendix Box 2.1: Evolution of the Revenue System, 1990-95

The evolution of the main taxes in Hungary has been the following:

Personal Income tax. Introduced in 1988, its revenues are shared with local governments. It is levied on all personal incomes for residents in Hungary. Withholding and advanced payments are mandatory. It is withheld at the source for wage income at the effective rate consistent with annual income tax. Minimum exempt income and other brackets have been adjusted retrospectively to account partially for inflation. Marginal rates are 20, 25, 35, 40 and 44 percent (for incomes greater than, respectively, HUF 110,000, 150,000, 220,000, 380,000, and 550,000); general schedular flat rates of 10 percent on interest on fixed-term deposits and dividends. In 1994 the curve was made more progressive by raising the marginal rate from 40 to 44 percent. Deductions are allowed for local taxes, social security contributions (introduced in 1993), charitable contributions as well as for housing payments and some other deductions. Tax-free incomes need not be reported.

Corporate Income Tax. Introduced in 1989 and substantially modified in 1992, Hungary's CIT may be considered a relatively modern and well structured tax. Levied on all legal persons (whether state-owned, cooperative, or private). Specific rules exist for financial institutions. The rates have been decreased several times from their original maximum of 50 percent. From 36 percent in 1994, the rate was reduced to 18 percent for undistributed profits and 23 percent additional on distributed profits. The original tax was considerably narrow- based due to numerous targeted incentives that have been reduced over time. However, the basic definition of the tax limited interest deductions, depreciation, and loss carry-forward. Depreciation is based on historic cost. Interest deductions for investment were first allowed in 1993. Initially, useful lives of assets were too large and the 1992 reform made them more realistic. (Implicit useful life for depreciation: buildings 17, 33, and 50 years, equipment 7, computer products 3 years; in the case of high technology assets fiscal and accounting depreciation are equal). Loss carry-forward was initially set at two years in 1989 and modified to five years in 1992; initial three-year losses can be carried forward indefinitely. The reform of 1994 virtually eliminated the incentive to use the "acquired" rights of the pre-existing incentives.

Small taxpayer turnover presumption. A small taxpayer presumptive tax was initially introduced in 1993 and eliminated in 1994. With the reforms of end-1994 a new version of presumptive taxation for small entrepreneurs was enacted. The original turnover presumption was applicable to both entrepreneurs and corporations. If the calculated profit of the last year represents less than 2 percent of gross income, 2 percent was presumed as taxable income. After the 36 percent rate is applied all tax benefits are deductible from the presumed tax. The new presumption, established starting in 1995, is a lump-sum tax to be paid by small entrepreneurs that qualify. The target group is different from and much more narrow than the one initially selected in 1993.

Value Added Tax (VAT). Hungary introduced a multiple rate VAT in 1988 following EC directives. VAT base is the sale price before tax of goods traded domestically; on imports VAT base includes import taxes and fees to customs value. Special exemptions are available to imports of capital goods. VAT allows the refund of payments on investment goods. This possibility has been gradually increased from 20 percent in 1988 to 80 percent in 1991. The rates have been increased over time by increasing the lower rates and reclassifying products into the higher ones. Currently, 25 percent is the general rate (applicable to 58 percent of consumption), 12 percent (public utilities, therapeutic products, transport and communications and some services) and 0 percent (exports and some associated services). Rebates are available in the case of credit balances.

Excises. Excise taxes have been applicable to a number of "sin" and luxury goods, and to petroleum products. Rates and values have been discretely adjusted over the years, after some revenue erosion due to inflation. Starting May 1995 a differential ad valorem excise tax (rates between 10 and 32 percent of the value) was introduced.

Import tax. Rates are on average 17 percent. In addition, there are statistical, permission and customs clearance duties that amount to 6 percent. A broad based import surcharge of 8 percent was introduced in March 1995.

Social Security Contributions. Based on salary with a maximum of HUF 2,500 per day. Comprises health, retirement, unemployment and solidarity contributions. Employer's contribution comprises remuneration in kind; employees' contribution excludes it and is limited to HUF 2,500 per day. Employers' rates total 48.5 percent and employees' rates 11.5 percent for 1995 after having been, respectively, 51.5 and 11.5 percent for 1994.

CHAPTER III: TOWARD A NEW SOCIAL CONTRACT: OPTIONS FOR REFORMING THE WELFARE SYSTEM *

A.   Overview

Growth is the key to fiscal sustainability, and changes in the level and composition of public expenditure are needed to promote faster growth. That is the essence of Hungary's macroeconomic challenge as laid down in Chapter I. As Hungary's welfare system absorbs a large share of public expenditure, its restructuring is unavoidable if resources for growth are to be released. This, in turn, will help sustain Hungary's welfare system in the future.

International comparison shows that Hungary spends a far larger share of its resources on welfare than other market economies at similar stages of development. Indeed, Hungary's system of transfers and entitlements is only emulated in the most redistributive OECD economies, such as Sweden, the Netherlands and France, all of which have considerably higher per capita incomes (Table 3.1). To a large extent, this level of spending in Hungary is an inheritance of the past, but, if Hungary is to join the ranks of high-income countries, reforming its welfare system is a *sine qua non*.

Promises of a better tomorrow justifying austerity today are plentiful in Hungarian history. Voters know that prosperity in the future hinges not on the state, but on the actions of millions of individuals who work, save, and pay taxes. Microeconomic public-sector reform, which is as important as macroeconomic reform, hinges on the incentive signals public-sector behavior sends to individuals, households, and enterprises. This is particularly true for Hungary's welfare system, which is the major focus of this chapter.

Table 3.1: Social Expenditures in an International Context (share of GDP)				
	Public Health	Aged	Non-aged a/	Total
Hungary (1993)	6.2	9.8	9.3	25.3
EU Average	5.4	8.5	7.7	21.8
OECD Average	5.7	9.2	7.7	22.3
Selected Countries:				
Sweden	6.9	11.9	14.4	33.1
Netherlands	6.0	9.9	13.1	29.0
France	6.8	12.2	8.3	27.3
Italy	6.5	15.3	3.2	25.0
Austria	5.6	15.0	4.0	24.5
Germany	6.1	9.7	7.2	22.9
Spain	5.5	7.9	6.6	20.0
USA	5.2	5.8	3.5	14.6
Australia	5.6	3.8	3.6	13.0
Japan	4.8	5.0	1.8	11.6

a/ Non-aged includes invalidity/disability pension for those of working age, maternity and all family benefits, unemployment benefits (passive and active), housing, sick pay and social assistance.
Source: OECD (1994) for OECD countries and World Bank calculations for Hungary using same OECD definitions. OECD data refer to 1991.

* Christine Allison, Simon Commander, Csaba Fehér, Teresa Ho, Mark Lutz, Robert Palacios, Andrew Rogerson and Dimitri Vittas contributed to this chapter.

Increased Dependency

What accounts for this increasing overhang of welfare-related spending? There have been several powerful Hungarian and international diagnoses and reform prescriptions[2] since 1990. They converge on the idea that the former system's paternalistic, cradle-to-grave web of benefits and services, predicated on compressed wages and high labor force participation, remains essentially intact today in a different political and economic context.

Box 3.1: Changing Expenditure Patterns

The composition of public expenditure shifted considerably between 1989 and 1994, a period in which GDP fell by some 16 percent and real public expenditure by about 11 percent. Within public expenditure, subsidies fell by 66 percent, and public consumption by 18 percent, while transfer payments increased 8 percent, and interest payments rose nearly 154 percent, all in real terms. The share of transfer payments and interest payments in the total has therefore risen appreciably, whilst that of subsidies has fallen sharply (see Figure 3.1). This is true both of subsidies to industry and of some major reductions in housing and consumer subsidies.

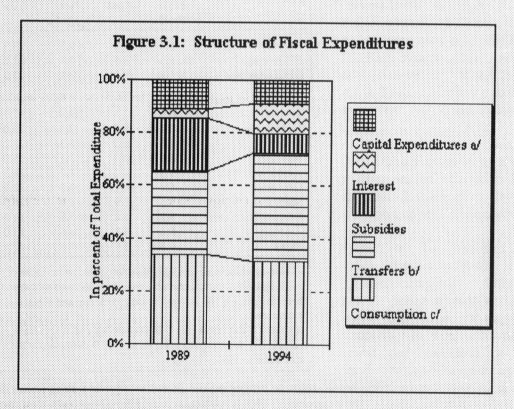

Figure 3.1: Structure of Fiscal Expenditures

a/ Includes Fixed Investment + Capital Transfers.
b/ Includes "in kind" and "in cash" transfers to households, but excludes consumer price and housing subsidies.
c/ Includes wages and salaries and expenditures on other goods and services.
Source: Ministry of Finance and World Bank staff estimates.

---

[2]   Major reports include "Social Security Reform in Hungary", prepared by the IMF (Kopits, Holzmann, Schrieber, Sidgwick), 1990; "Hungary—Reform of Social Policy and Expenditures" World Bank, 1992; "Review of Labor Market and Social Policy of Hungary" final draft report, OECD, September 1994; "Reforming Social Policy in Hungary—Policy Study #3", Blue Ribbon Committee, July 1993.

Onto this base, eroded by inflation but unreconstructed, whole new "western" categories of benefits have been overlaid, such as unemployment benefits and new categories of social assistance, to help face the unprecedented strains of transition. The uptake of existing benefits also increased sharply, as a coping mechanism. The shock of massive job losses—1.4 million between 1990 and 1994—was partly absorbed by a sharp rise in early retirements. About 600,000 other unemployed, though statistically counted as employed, are sheltered in various long-term leave and work/training programs at public expense. *About 40 percent of the population aged 15-59 (15-54 for women) is now dependent on the wages of others and on social transfers, double the dependency ratio of 1990.*

Insufficient Incentives

Incentives to work, in the formal sector at least, are undermined by these benefits, which replace a relatively high share of average net wages, in an earnings distribution profile that is still much flatter than in most OECD countries. At the same time, significant taxes on declared employment, even at relatively low income brackets, imply very high marginal tax rates, a classic welfare trap situation (Section C below).

Moreover, the bulk (57 percent) of social transfers in kind and in cash are financed by payroll taxes. Contributions currently account for 61 percent of gross wages and 33 percent of total compensation costs.[2] The latter is one of the highest rates in Europe. Only a small fraction of this is notionally identified as employee contributions. This has no bearing on the ultimate incidence of wage taxes, since whether they are passed on to consumers, absorbed, or passed back as reduced net wages depends on the competitive position of the firm and its employees in product and factor markets. (Given significant wage rigidities in the Hungarian formal sector, the burden of payroll taxes is probably falling on the firms in competitive sectors). In any case, employees are not even provided with statements of what is contributed on their behalf, which hardly encourages them to monitor how these funds are deployed.

The disincentives are even stronger on the employer side, where **evasion** is rampant, with or without the collusion of employees. The most obvious form of evasion is outright non-registration of grey economy activities, which has reached grave proportions in Hungary (see Chapter II), with potential effects going well beyond the insolvency of the insurance funds. Even more frequent is the (usually quite legal) avoidance of contributions, through under-reporting of wages or shifting to tax-exempt wage-like remuneration. This leads to the proliferation of inefficient side benefits, manipulation of salaries at critical stages in the career cycle, and other distortions with both direct financial and long-term economic costs. *Systemic reforms aimed at reducing wage tax rates, and tapering off net penalties for welfare recipients who openly return to work, are therefore critical policy targets in their own right, even if achieved in a budget-neutral way.*

Capital market development also suffers, to the extent that very large potential pools of savings are not tapped for investment through efficient financial intermediaries, but instead redistributed between and within generations through the pay-as-you-go pension plan, which is the largest single component of public consumption. As with all mature PAYG plans, rates of return to the contributions of younger

---

[2] Employers pay 24.5 percent of gross salaries for pensions, 19.5 percent for health, and 5 percent for unemployment insurance and 0.5 percent for a wage guarantee fund (related to bankruptcies), totaling 49.5 percent. They also withhold 6 percent, 4 percent, 1.5 percent and 0 percent respectively from employee wages for the same coverage. Therefore social contributions amount to 49.5/149.5 or 33 percent of employer costs.

cohorts are low and falling. At the extreme, this creates the risk of a giant "Ponzi" scheme in which the last to join are sure to lose their stakes: the more this risk is perceived, the greater the incentive to avoid or evade, closing the vicious circle. *Section B argues that significant internal reforms can and must be made to the PAYG system. However, only the opening of a complementary, publicly sponsored fully funded retirement plan based on professional institutional investors provides both a long-term mechanism to correct this fundamental incentive problem, and a stimulus for savings in the economy.*

Fairness and Realignment

The *equity* dimension of welfare policies is examined in section E below and Box 3.2. With the transition has come a progressive widening of the earnings distribution, and rising incidence of absolute poverty. This worsens the "fairness" of the welfare state system in two ways. On the revenue side, proportional payroll taxes, subject to contributions ceilings, tend to reinforce the relative position of the new higher earners, compared to reliance on broad-based and progressive direct taxes. On the benefits side, a dominant combination of universal assistance benefits (family allowances) and current-income-weighted insurance payout formulas (pensions), appropriate for an era when real incomes varied little across households or life cycles, reinforces rather than corrects inequalities. And despite the very heavy tax burden carried, a growing number of households, including many headed by younger workers, slips into chronic poverty every year. *Reforms are also needed to correct this perverse redistribution.*

Box 3.2: Poverty in Hungary

Poverty measured in absolute terms as the share of the population receiving less than the subsistence minimum income calculated by the CSO affected between 1.5 and 2 million people, about 15 percent of the population in 1992. The incidence of poverty appears to have increased quite dramatically since the late 1980s, possibly doubling. But the CSO subsistence minimum, which lies between 50 and 70 percent of the average net wage, is set high and may not be an adequate indicator of poverty. However, other poverty lines and other data sets may vary in their estimation of poverty, but none dispute the general trend of an increasing poverty incidence. On a more positive note, poverty in Hungary is relatively "shallow"—the average income of the poor is not substantially below any given poverty line (about 20 percent below). This has important policy implications.

With regard to essential characteristics and key correlates of poverty, analysis to-date of the various household data sets indicates the following types of households are most vulnerable to poverty:

- single-parent families
- households with elderly heads (>70 years of age)
- households containing unemployed persons
- households where the working-age head is inactive
- households where the head has low (primary) education
- households having four or more children
- gypsies

Although generally shallow, there is some variation in the depth of poverty with household characteristics. Of note is the strong concentration of single-parent families, households headed by an unemployed person and families with four or more children among the very poorest (less than 50 percent of the median income). By contrast, over-represented among the poor (defined as the poorest quintile), but less poor, are pensioners and single female households. Overall, there has been a shift in poverty from the rural old to urban families with young children, away from specific occupation to family circumstances (especially unemployment), and away from inactive households to households with active earners.

The following sections concentrate on four categories of social expenditure, and a menu of options for their reform: *old age pensions; employment-related benefits; health; and family allowances.*[4] In most cases, arguments are presented for redirecting expenditure to improve incentives for work, savings, self-reliance, and participation in the open economy, and to protect the weaker sections of the community more effectively. In the last case, the analysis shows that significant net savings can be generated over time at improved performance levels; in the case of health, the challenge is to contain real spending at today's levels, but obtain for this level of effort clearly improved health outcomes and better regional distribution of services; in the case of pensions, the analysis shows that aggregate expenditure of the PAYG scheme can fall significantly relative to GDP.

Unfinished Business

A more comprehensive coverage of social expenditure reform would have included, at least, housing and education. *Housing* is not included because, relative to other transition countries and other expenditure heads, Hungary is well advanced along the reform road in this area. It now absorbs less than 1 percent of GDP in the form of state assistance. Private ownership of the housing stock is high (80 percent) overall. Two cautionary notes are appropriate. Management of public housing, concentrated in Budapest, remains a problem. Labor mobility into the high-growth metropolitan areas would benefit from a greater supply of private rental units. This is a function both of rent deregulation and the availability of long-term finance, itself dependent on resolving title and collateral constraints beyond this paper's scope. Secondly, the remaining housing subsidies are mainly in the form of first-time-buyer grants and interest subsidy entitlements. Since these are proportional to the value of transactions, which require large down payments, they are inherently untargeted, indeed regressive. They could also grow explosively from the present low base if construction activity picks up rapidly.

The report does not contain a review of options for *education expenditure reform* because school curriculum, finance, and management are largely a local government prerogative in Hungary. Thus any serious approach towards realignment challenges fundamental equilibria. A draft new constitution is expected to enter public debate in the coming months, but a consensus on major shifts of center-local responsibilities within it is not likely. The further dimension of church-state relations is inescapable, as parochial schools and their relationship to government(s) need to be considered as part of any systemic reform. International experience in this regard is not encouraging. The techniques of reform, on which the Bank is ready to assist, are not as problematic as is the political gestation period and risk of reversal of such a complex undertaking. This question merits a separate in-depth assessment. Box 3.3 merely introduces the debate.

---

4   The second and fourth categories, combined, comprise the third column "non-aged" in Table 3.1. The health and pensions (= "aged") categories are self-explanatory, but see Box 3.5 for distinctions between "pension" and "pension fund" expenditure.

Box 3.3: The Education Sector

By most standards, Hungary can claim a well developed and well-functioning education system. Participation rates for both pre-school (3-5 years) and the core school aged population (6-16 years) are very high, and Hungary's performance in international assessments (especially mathematics and science) is outstanding. Although access to higher education is still limited, compared to many EU countries, Hungary has wisely improved its tertiary education and research base since 1989, recognizing the importance of human capital investment as a key engine of economic growth. As Hungary continues the transition to a market economy, the importance of education grows apace: its central role underpinning a successful democracy, a functioning and growing market economy, and in ensuring social equality is widely acknowledged.

But the system is not without its problems. Spending between 6 and 6.5 percent of GDP on education, Hungary cannot afford to address the shortcomings of the country's education system simply by allocating more public resources to it. Modernizing the system, improving its quality and relevance, maintaining nursery education, and increasing access to upper secondary and higher education will have to be achieved through more efficient use of existing public resources and by mobilizing other resources.

One of the most striking indicators of potential inefficiency relates to the deployment of teachers and other school staff. Compared to many OECD countries, pupil/teacher ratios are generous (low), especially at the pre-primary and primary level. In higher education (for which directly comparable figures for these countries are not available), the ratio is very low indeed. In attempting to make better use of scarce public resources, the appropriate strategy would be to re-deploy teachers and use them more effectively by addressing the three underlying causes of under-use: low teaching loads, over-specialization of subjects offered, and over-reliance on single-subject teachers at lower school levels. Increased salaries could accompany these measures.

Pupil/teacher Ratios in Hungary and in Selected EU Countries

	Hungary	Austria	Netherlands	Denmark	Ireland
pre-primary	10.8	20.9	21.2	13.6	28.3
primary	11.6	10.8	19.7	11.1	26.9
secondary	13.5	10.0	15.9	10.7	17.2

Source: OECD (1993)

Other priority areas for reform at the school level include modernization of the curriculum and the introduction of companion textbooks and learning aids, less heterogeneity in school structures but greater diversity in school provision (in particular church-based schools), and the removal of skill-specific vocational training from all schools prior to 11th grade. But although these are in the end also national priorities, only independent local authorities who have jurisdiction over schools may chose whether or not to adopt them.

Significant inefficiencies exist in higher education and result in very high student unit costs. In meeting the objective of increasing access to higher education the Government will be obliged to address these inefficiencies otherwise the expansion will not be sustainable. Key areas are: the rationalization of the institutional network, further integration of research institutions, reorganization of teaching programs and teaching staff, and flexible learning arrangements— shorter, evening and correspondence courses. These changes can in part be brought about by the introduction of "normative financing". Higher education, because of the substantial private returns to be gained from it in the evolving market economy, is also a target for cost sharing with its consumers. There are various ways to achieve this: reducing student stipends and charging tuition fees, with appropriate funding mechanisms for students from poor families is one approach; another is the levying of a proportional "graduate income tax" on the beneficiaries of publicly-funded higher education once they enter the labor market and begin to reap the benefits (higher incomes) from their education.

B.   Pensions and Old Age Security

Toward a Three-Pillar System

The role of the state in providing the framework for income security in old age is changing at an accelerating pace in Europe and worldwide. The starting conditions that underpinned the world's major social protection systems (Bismarck to Beveridge) between the late 19th century and the 1950s have evolved. Moreover, as age profiles and systems mature, massive financial strains in state-managed systems are forcing painful reappraisals in many countries, most recently in France, Sweden, and Italy. This global concern is amply documented in a leading World Bank publication.[4]

The basic case for public involvement remains strong: many individuals who are not poor while working, left to their own devices, can under-provide for their future and become a burden on society. Others will suffer chronic poverty because of the insufficiency of their lifetime earnings. Information gaps and various deficiencies of private insurance markets, such as adverse selection and failure to address "cosmic" risks such as hyperinflation, strengthen the case for some state intervention; the critical question being how much.

The design of every pension system (consisting of both public and privately managed activities) thus has a built-in conflict of objectives. Ideally one would want to enable everyone to reconstitute a target share of their own career earnings in retirement. At the same time, civilized societies want some floor to be placed below everyone's living standards in retirement, regardless of what they actually earned and contributed. Any attempt to achieve both objectives—intertemporal insurance and interpersonal distribution—in a single "pension pillar" involves messy and dynamically unstable compromises. Simplifying greatly, a single pillar scheme cannot fulfill both the savings insurance objective and the redistribution objective (see Box 3.4).

This is why, in Hungary and elsewhere, a consensus[5] has emerged that a more transparent combination of three distinct "pillars"—formal arrangements involving public regulation—is needed for old-age security. One form this multi-pillar arrangement could take is the following:

- *a Citizen's Pension*, providing a more or less flat benefit to those who reach old age;

- a transparently *earnings-related mandatory retirement savings plan*, which could take many forms, and,

- *voluntary pension plans*, prudentially regulated and tax-assisted.

The following analysis assumes, as a first approximation, that the three aim to replace on average, respectively, 30 percent, 30 percent, and 10 percent of average net earnings. Until 1993, only the single-pillar, pay-as-you-go option existed in Hungary, providing a benefit linked only very loosely to past earnings (see Box 3.4).

---

[4]   "Averting the Old Age Crisis: Policies to Protect the Old and Promote Growth", a World Bank Policy Research Report, Oxford University Press, 1994.

[5]   See Resolution (60/1991) of the Hungarian Parliament.

Box 3.4: Equity Considerations in the Context of Pension Reform

Public pension schemes usually look to redistribute to those who were too poor during their lifetimes to support themselves during their old age. "Progressive" benefit formulas, which promise higher "replacement rates" for lower income workers than for higher income workers are used in many countries including the United States and Hungary. While this rule nominally favors the low income worker, the final redistributive outcome depends on several more subtle factors which may offset the progressive formula.

One such factor is the advantage in terms of life expectancy held by higher income workers over lower income workers. Empirical evidence in the U.S. and the Netherlands for example, has found that differential mortality rates can produce a significant bias in favor of high income workers, increasing their rate of return from the pension system. Some studies even found that this differential alone completely offset the lifetime redistribution from rich to poor which had originally been thought to occur.

Another factor which may counteract any intended redistribution toward the poor arises from the tendency observed in many countries, including Hungary, to use the final or last few years' salary to calculate the pension. This practice has the effect of giving a higher rate of return to those which steeper age-earnings profiles, typically, those with higher education and skill levels. As a result higher income workers will be favored by the use of final earnings in the pension benefit formula.

This regressive feature can become particularly acute during the course of a transition away from centrally-determined wage structures. Wage data has shown that age-earnings profiles since 1989 have begun to resemble those found in market economies where high skilled, high income workers have a steeper age-earnings profile than manual workers. These changes, combined with the pre-transition benefit formula, favor higher versus lower income workers in a way never intended by policy makers.

The table below shows the internal rate of return simulated for high and low income workers in Hungary taking these two factors into account. The high income worker has an age-earnings profile which reflects a sudden wage increase during the last 3 years of his career resulting in a final year salary of 80,000 monthly 1993 forints. The low income worker meanwhile, experiences a constant age-earnings growth of only 1 percent and retires with a base salary of only 16,000 monthly 1993 forints.

Intragenerational Redistribution in the Hungarian Pension Scheme

Type of Worker	Low Income %	High Income %
Internal Rate of Return	.54	.73
Internal Rate of Return w/mortality differential	.30	1.55

The results show that even with a formula which replaces a higher portion of the salary of the lower income worker, the age-earnings profile combined with the method used to calculate the base salary favor the higher income worker and all but wipes out the intended redistribution. As the second row shows, if income levels are strongly correlated to life expectancies as in other countries, the high income worker receives a much higher rate of return. Reducing the pensions of higher income workers is not necessarily "unfair", in that these high benefits may not be based on past contributions but on special circumstances linked to the transition.

The low (absolute) rates of return to all categories of workers also illustrate the strong incentive to evade and the poor performance of the system as a method of savings. In the end, the scheme does not perform either function—redistribution or savings—in a satisfactory manner and, in the confusion, any concept of an actuarial relationship between contributions and benefits is completely lost.

The Third Pillar

The first concrete step towards a three-pillar scheme was taken in November 1993 with the passage of the *Act on the Voluntary Mutual Benefit Funds*. The intention was to provide a **true third pillar**, that is, a regulated vehicle for optional retirement savings, for an additional contribution cost of course, beyond the mandatory national PAYG scheme. In the first year, about 40,000 members formed/joined plans, currently taking in an average 8.4 percent of the members' wage base. Participation is developing rapidly among higher-earning, white-collar, mainly middle-aged contributors, who see the risk of erosion in their PAYG pensions, and/or whose earnings are above the cap used to establish PAYG benefits. Myopia—the risk of chronic undersaving by certain individuals—cannot of course be solved by the third pillar, which is self-selected for its very foresight. Also, some of the voluntary groups may not reach the critical mass needed for adequate life insurance risk pooling, and may need reinsurance guarantees. But a very promising start has been made nonetheless.

Two possible improvements in the third pillar's legislative framework deserve to be considered soon, even absent other systemic changes. First, voluntary pension fund managers are now completely barred from investing in foreign securities. This does not allow adequate risk spreading, especially in the present embryonic phase of Hungary's capital market development. And second, tax treatment (after the 1995 budget) is still inconsistent and costly, with the third pillar getting the windfall of **both** tax credits on contributions (at varying rates) **and** tax-free pensions, whilst first-pillar contributions are tax-deductible and its benefits, though tax-exempt, are counted in determining income tax brackets. Broader pension tax treatment realignment is discussed below.

The real challenge and controversy on modernizing the system, however, lies in the choice of the **second pillar**, and in the transition arrangements that would enable a shift out of the present single mandatory pillar to a more transparent and efficient arrangement. *To develop these options, it is essential to start with a detailed analysis of the problems facing Hungary's first-pillar PAYG system, and the reforms required under any circumstances for the sake of fiscal sustainability, with or without a more comprehensive systemic reform goal.*

The Crisis in the Hungarian PAYG Scheme: Unemployment, Evasion, and Early Retirement...

It is not true that the pension crisis in Hungary is due to the aging of the population. That bomb is, alas, still ticking. The **age/dependency** ratio is still only .36, actually less than in 1990 (.38), thanks to two baby-boom blips working through the pyramid. It will start rising again only after 1998, reaching the 1990 level in 2003 and peaking at around .42 in 2015. This mature demographic structure is essentially similar to many OECD countries (horizontal axis, fig. 3.2) and, of course, a parameter beyond the reach of policy makers in the next two decades.

What is much more striking is that the **system dependency** ratio in Hungary (.66), on the vertical axis, is one of the highest in the world.[6] It is far out of line with Hungary's age structure, as measured

[6] **System dependency ratio** is the number of pensioners (including under retirement age disability pensioners) divided by the number of contributors; **Old age/dependency ratio** is the number of people over age 60 divided by those aged 20-59. Whereas the old age/dependency ratio can be easily calculated from demographic statistics (which are readily available in Hungary), the system dependency ratio is based on the number of employed persons in Hungary, since there is no information on the number of contributing individuals. The social security account-holders are legal entities (such as enterprises) and not individuals.

by the distance from the 45 degree line. This indicator measures those drawing pensions as a proportion of current contributors. It rises when formal sector jobs are lost (because the activity ceases or it goes "underground"). And it rises when pensions are awarded to those under 60. The ratio has deteriorated from 0.50 in 1990. Most of this deterioration was due to unemployment and grey economy/evasion effects, though a smaller share is due to excessive early retirement, mainly in the form of disability pension awards. Both phenomena **are** subject to policy remedies and need to concern policy makers urgently.

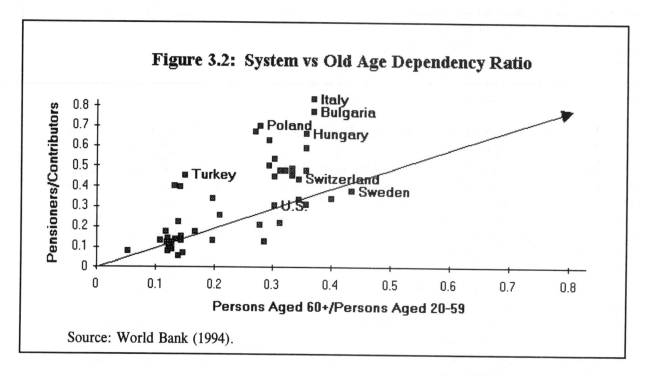

Figure 3.2: System vs Old Age Dependency Ratio

Source: World Bank (1994).

The early retirement effect combines both legislated entitlements and administrative behavior. "Normal" statutory retirement age for women is still 55, among the lowest in Europe, despite repeatedly delayed government aims to raise it to the male equivalent, 60.[7] Though certain occupational groups enjoy preferential early retirement options, the **low system-wide effective retirement age** (53.3 years in 1993) is overwhelmingly the result of excessive use of disability pensions as a form of early retirement.

The transition brought about an explosive growth of new **disability pensioners**. In 1993, 27 percent of all pensioners received benefits originally awarded on "disability" grounds. Disability pensions are still growing at twice the rate of 1989. There is no independent medical evidence of morbidity rising this rapidly: the additional disability pensions are largely a function of "soft layoffs" and collusion between employers and employees.

---

[7]   Normal retirement age for men is a minimum, i.e. there is no provision to retire earlier, even at steep, actuarially fair discounts, thus disability is an especially attractive option. Women, used to have to retire at 55 (minimum and maximum age), but from 1995 are free to continue to work, register and contribute until reaching 56, though they get no added benefit from such contributions.

... Leads to Unsustainable Expenditures

The payroll tax rate (P) needed to balance expenditures and revenues on pensions is simply the product of the system dependency rate (SD) and the system replacement ratio (SR)— what the average pensioner gets as a share of the average contributing wage in the same period. Using gross covered salary definitions, these numbers were in 1994 approximately: SD = .66, SR = .53, so P = .35. Thirty-five percent of gross payroll would therefore be required to cover current expenditure **on all pensions** (as opposed to the expenditures of the Pension Fund (see Box 3.5).

Box 3.5: Implicit Tax Rates, Social Security Budgets

Approximately 88 percent of public pension **expenditures** are managed by the Pension Fund, 12 percent by the Health Fund in the form of under retirement age disability pensions. The Pension Fund also pays a health insurance contribution on behalf of pensioners and the Health Fund pays the pension insurance contribution on behalf of disability pensioners below retirement age and many others. While pension expenditure is therefore easily defined as total spending on benefits for old age, survivors, and disability pensions, no symmetrical **revenue** figure exists. Disability insurance, moreover, is not linked to a defined portion of either the health or pension contribution, so its notional share must be inferred from the benefit side.

The budgets of the two Funds also regularly show items which can be best labeled as **"ghost revenues"** or claims of varying merit on the State budget. Some relate to payments for special groups-the unemployed, conscripts, and students especially-which the State has pledged by law to make good on the contributors' behalf, with varying justifications. Less clear-cut revenue categories (which include items such as "returns on assets (not yet) transferred by the State", "revenues (needed) for replenishing the liquidity reserves", etc) rarely materialize as foreseen: at best they account for how the deficits of the funds may be financed, not what they are. Finally, **contribution arrears** do not feature in the official financial statements. The outstanding receivables of the Social Insurance Funds (HUF180 billion at end 1994) have been partly financed by bonds issued by the State, whose servicing cost is not yet charged back to the funds.

As a first approximation, we estimate that 1994 expenditures on health, pensions, and sickness benefits, (net of contributions paid by the State on behalf of the unemployed), were equivalent to about 57 percent of the covered wage bill, or about 0.5 percent of GDP more than the combined contribution revenues of the two funds. That is, spending on pensions and health by the Social Security "self-government" would have required a break-even payroll tax of 57 percent given the effectively taxed wage bill. A 35 percent payroll tax would have been required for pensions alone.

(The rest of this section uses the yardstick of "Implicit Contributions Rate", a notional payroll tax rate required to balance expenditures on pensions, as defined above, which is free from many of these complications. It cannot, however, be directly compared to the legally prescribed contribution rate (24.5 and 6 percent) flowing from employers and employees, respectively to the Pension Fund).

How does this translate in terms of deficits today? Box 3.5 takes us through some of the arcana of social security budgeting. There are offsetting flows between the health and pension funds and large claims on the central budget on behalf of both funds. *A transparent third-party assessment of the true state of social insurance finances, and objective, actuarially sound projections of the likely evolution of the deficit, if delivered to Parliament every year, could greatly enrich public debate and democratic scrutiny.*

How is this situation likely to evolve through the year 2000 and beyond if no radical corrective steps are taken? In the next few years, this will depend on the employment situation in the formal sector. Some further deterioration of the system dependency ratio (SD) through further job losses is likely to occur. The continued shrinkage of the formal/covered sector as a percentage of the workforce is a serious risk, though this is not factored into our projections.[9] After 1998, as we have seen, the deterioration of the age/dependency ratio will increasingly drive up the SD also.

Another way of assessing the extent of the crisis is to estimate the present value of the pension rights already been earned by workers and pensioners in the system. This "implicit pension debt" comes to 118 percent of GDP for current pensioners and 145 percent of GDP for current workers, for a ***total implicit pension debt of 263 percent of GDP.*** This is based on a discount rate of 2 percent, but even if we use a higher discount rate—say 8 percent—the pension liabilities are still greater than the explicit domestic debt. *The assumptions can be debated, but the order of magnitude is sobering. It is also more than 20-40 times the amount of state assets pledged to the Pension Fund as "reserves".*

The need to significantly raise retirement wages before a current middle-aged cohort begins to retire in ten years is not seriously disputed by Hungarian analysts. While raising political support has proven a problem, the technical arguments behind this measure are clear and compelling. Here, we assume that to avoid crisis retirement ages must increase.

Figure 3.3 shows the result of this indispensable reform using the "muddle though" macroeconomic scenario (see Chapter V). The figure shows the Implicit Contribution Rate (ICR) rising through 1997 from its very high current levels. The positive impact of the reforms begin to show in 1998 as the ICR falls slightly to 34 percent by the year 2000 stabilizing at 32 percent in the long-run.[10]

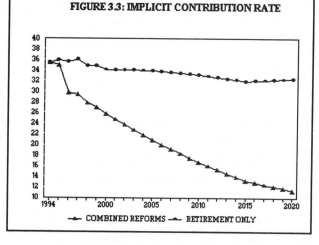

Leading Reform Options for the Existing Mandatory Pensions Scheme

The main policies that could enable the existing PAYG scheme to survive well into the next century without becoming an intolerable burden on public finance are well known. They have been the object of several well-researched studies[11] whose recommendations are remarkably consistent, even

---

[9] Other countries, at the same level of income, have a coverage ratio 10-15 points lower than Hungary.

[10] It is interesting to compare these implicit rates to those projected by Kopits, Holzmann et al (IMF) in 1990. They assumed a fall from 30 percent in 1990 to 27 percent in 1996 even without reforms. The age/dependency windfall was not then expected to be nullified, as unfortunately proved the case, by unemployment and the early retirement boom. However, after 1996 the implicit contribution rate was to rise sharply without reforms, reaching 42 percent by 2020.

[11] Refer to the footnote at the beginning of the chapter.

if increasingly urgent, as corrective actions are repeatedly deferred. There are three main categories of actions, briefly revisited in Box 3.6, that could have major effects:

- Increasing the effective retirement age;

- Broadening the tax base, and,

- Changing the indexation formula.

Box 3.6: Key Reforms of Hungarian Public Pension Scheme

- Raising effective retirement age has three components. The first is raising the normal retirement age for women to 56 in 1996, 57 in 1998 and so on, until it reaches 60 in 2004. The second is to raise retirement age for both men and women, starting at 60 in 2004, to 61 in 2006 and so until it reaches 65 in 2012. The third is to reduce the rate of new disability pension awards back to 1989 levels, approximately 80 per 10,000 workers: some of this reduction could be achieved by reviewing previous awards, as well as by the measures in section C.

- Including pension income in the income tax base for all those with pensions above 75 percent of the average net wage. This clawback, of about 2 percent of total pension expenditure, could be achieved by alternative tax methods, such as grossing up pension benefits at the basic rate then taxing at full marginal rates, etc. On the revenue side, broadening the tax base would reduce the share of monthly remuneration not subject to payroll tax to pre-1990 levels, equivalent to capturing 10 percent of the wage bill, mainly in the form of wage-like remuneration, which is not currently subject to payroll tax.

- Changing the basis of indexing benefits from nominal wages to the CPI, from 1996 onwards. An alternative would be to pass only part of the wage increase, on to pensioners (e.g., only real wage growth above 2 percent).

Annex 2 illustrates the impact of the three above stand-alone actions using the MoF medium-term framework instead of the "muddle-through" and "fast adjustment" macroeconomic scenarios used here. However, only the combination of these three measures produces significant savings before 1998, and therefore deserves careful attention. In the longer run, it is the increase in the effective retirement age and the change in the indexation formula which produce the greatest savings. The disability pension reduction is the most effective single spending measure in the very short term, compounded if one assumes that a sizeable fraction of those who are deemed ineligible will remain in the formal labor force rather than leave it (see Annex 2).

The **retirement age** measure is indispensable for the long term, especially beyond 2004, where it just "catches" the otherwise progressive worsening of the age/dependency ratio. But it does not achieve a return to the situation of the early 1990s until, at best, 2005, and scarcely does more than that thereafter. Before 1999 it has a small effect, of course, given the very gradual reduction of the flow of new retirees, compared to the existing stock. **Indexation to the CPI** pays off cumulatively in an impressive way—it is the only measure that can actually bring tax pressure in the outer years, assuming the wage bill grows faster than pension spending.

Results. Figure 3.3 shows the combined effect of all three sets of measures, under the "fast adjustment" scenario. It illustrates that the current implicit contribution rate can be reduced below present levels, in the face of unfavorable demographic trends, to 25 percent in 2000, 21 percent in 2005 and 11 percent in 2020. It does so without undermining the purchasing power of current benefits and with a long lead time for current contributors to adjust to higher retirement ages.

Accelerating the Second Pillar: A Complementary Approach

The above are "standard" reform options designed to build down the first pillar gradually to a tolerable fiscal pressure, with the least possible damage to genuine pensioner interests. They update, but diverge little from reforms considered already by successive Hungarian administrations. And yet very little action has been taken on them since 1989. Why?

Pensioners are a very large single-issue constituency. They account for some 40 percent of the electorate, and many more are in their "affinity group"—those within several years of retirement, or relatives who would be obliged to complement insufficient retirement income. They have a single clear issue to focus on: the maintenance (at the same level and timing) and, preferably, improvement of real pension benefits. The mechanism by which benefits are financed, on the other hand, is obscure in the extreme, and the link between contributions and benefits remote, if it exists at all in contributors' minds. Thus those who stand to lose most from the single pillar's crisis— the younger generations—are among the least aware of it. As a result, there is a great imbalance between the public support enjoyed by organizations and individuals promoting change and those resisting it.

A **systemic** change, involving **splitting the current single public scheme into two mandatory pillars**—a flat citizen's pension and a transparently earnings-related scheme—could, therefore, have broader appeal. It could also have much stronger dynamic effects than protracted struggles to pass "austerity measures" seen as needed to prop up the old system. The new *first* pillar would fulfill an overriding distributional commitment and improve the lot of those now on inadequate benefits. We assume here it would be a nearly flat, universal benefit paid at 65, administered by the Pension Fund and funded by a specific payroll contribution.[12]

The new *second* pillar, while still mandatory, should offer a clearer link between one's own actual (cash) contributions and the returns obtained on this sum. The second pillar can be arranged in variety of ways. The main options are whether (i) the plan should be **PAYG**, as now, or **fully funded**,[13] and (ii) whether it should be managed as a public **monopoly**, or by **competitive tender** among alternative managers, public or private, who meet regulatory requirements. *While other combinations are theoretically arguable, the only ones we consider here as serious alternatives are 1) PAYG monopoly versus 2) fully funded, competitive tender.*

---

[12]   There are many variants. One pragmatic formula, drawn from the Estonian 1992 reform, is :

Pension= (0.6*Subsistence level) + (A* years of service)

where A is an accrual factor, for example: .01(Subsistence level). In the rest of this chapter, we shall also assume this to be financed from payroll taxes and not means-tested. Alternative options could be considered.

[13]   In a pure pay as you go scheme, annual contribution revenues are equivalent to annual pension spending whereas a fully funded scheme accumulates assets the value of which is equivalent to all outstanding pension liabilities.

The PAYG option is similar in spirit to the present system, and carries most of its strengths and weaknesses. The only difference lies in restructuring the benefit formula, so that individual benefits are more accurately "scaled" by how the individual's actual contributions in each period compare to the average from all members for that period. The individual benefit can then be related to the system average retirement benefit via index numbers, appropriately adjusted for inflation. Record-keeping and computing requirements are heavy, but by no means insoluble. Switzerland is a typical example of these arrangements, although the modest size of its public pillar still allows room for a mandatory fully funded occupational plan.

The second solution involves transferring some part of payroll contributions to individual accounts with pension funds that invest these savings in the capital market, and pay annuities on retirement. Government, which tightly regulates these funds, like other financial intermediaries, to avoid fraud and bankruptcy, may however insure some minimum pension level for participants. A variety of instruments, including index-linked Treasury bonds and foreign securities, can be used to hedge against inflation.

Fund management is provided on a competitive basis: one of the bidders for contributors could be a branch of the present PAYG Pension Fund. Collection from wage bills (which has a strong element of automatic compliance, since contributions and gains remain escrowed in the individual's name) can be subcontracted, for an agency fee, to Social Security, the tax agency, or other collectors. Contributors are free to shift savings between funds, at minimum intervals, without penalty. The most comprehensive cases of such second pillars exist in Latin America (Chile, Argentina, Colombia), as well as occupational pension plans in Europe (UK, Switzerland, Netherlands) and Australia.

In comparing the pros and cons of each solution, there are several dimensions to be considered. These are summarized in Table 3.2.

The most obvious is the **capital markets** impact. Channeling progressively large sums into a whole new generation of institutional investors, with very long-term investment horizons and relatively low liquidity needs in the short and

Table 3.2: Features of Alternative Second-pillar Schemes		
	PAYG	Funded
Labor Market Distortions	High	Low
Intergenerational Transfers	Yes	No
Capital Markets Stimulus	None	Strong
State Budget Guarantee	Full	Partial
Administration Costs	Low	Moderate
Accountability of Managers	Low	High
Impact on Savings (compared to present PAYG)	Negative or Neutral	Positive

medium terms, would be a major boost to stock and bond markets. It would also spur investment and potential output growth. Under plausible scenarios developed below, such individual retirement savings plans would accumulate some 5 percent of GDP by the year 2000 and thereafter grow exponentially—which has been international experience. (PAYG contributions are, by definition, consumed in the year they are collected).

Transparency and savings incentives are also much stronger in the fully funded case, as the contributions-benefit link is clear to all. PAYG earnings-related pillars invariably involve some element of compression of benefits and capping of contributions, both being politically determined. The actual average benefit, to which the individual benefit is pegged, is also fixed in advance as a function of past earnings that the individual is powerless to affect.

Governance, accountability and administrative cost implications are quite different. There is a tradeoff between choice and cost. Competitive-account contributors can vote, ultimately, by moving their money between funds. They would also have a larger stake in the "self-government" of one of several medium-sized competitor organizations than they can in a single giant public monopoly. Administrative costs might be higher in the competitive system, given economies of scale and the additional need for meticulous prudential accounting. However, the direct costs of a PAYG earnings-related pillar would also rise sharply from present levels. Individual contributions data are still not collected from employers and are virtually impossible to reconstitute accurately for pre-transition years. And compliance incentives, translating into lower arrears and enforcement costs, would be much stronger in the fully funded case.

In Hungary's present economic situation, there is much to argue for the creation of a fully funded second pillar—especially the incentives for greater savings, and the dynamic effect on capital markets. There is also merit in diversifying the risks that those who save for old age will face by offering a balance between the dangers of state management and those of market-based returns. But the ultimate choice is quintessentially political, shaped by the assessment by both pensioners and contributors of whether the essence of the social contract is maintained, or even improved, by the new system.

The Transition from a Single Public PAYG to a Multi-Pillar System

The design and implementation of a well-articulated transition from a public PAYG system to a multi-pillar system lies at the core of successful pension reform. The new system should be able to generate some efficiency gains, even in the transitional period, and at the same time prove acceptable from the fiscal point of view. This is not an easy task, as an aggressive reform strategy may stretch public finances in the short run beyond an acceptable level, whereas an excessively gradualist strategy may yield very few benefits in the first years of implementation, and even open room for policy reversals. Any strategy must obviously take into account initial country conditions, which in the case of Hungary are unfortunately quite adverse, including high contribution rates, a high general tax burden, substantial evasion, high budget deficits, and a large public debt.

Due to Hungary's adverse initial conditions, some strategies might create serious problems in the very first stages of implementation. For instance, an aggressive strategy could involve transferring all workers to a new fully funded pillar, while also honoring current pension obligations and the accumulated entitlements of current workers to future pensions. Although the net present value of current and future entitlements under the old system—the implicit pension debt—could be reduced by prior reforms in the old system (such as increases in the retirement age), the Government would still face a financing problem, as these expenditures would no longer be financed from payroll contributions. Instead, the contribution rate would be substantially lowered from the present 30 percent to 10-15 percent, and the proceeds would be channeled toward financing the second pillar under the new system. To finance both pillars and avoid an unbearable tax burden on wages, the Government would have to introduce a substantial increase in other taxes, or accept a much larger deficit and finance it through bond issues.

Tax or bond financing at the required scale could prove a problem. General tax finance would not contribute to the reduction of the very heavy tax burden in Hungary. In addition, it would imply increasing the marginal rates of income and consumption taxes to even higher levels, as the tax bases can only be broadened gradually. Therefore, the gain in efficiency would be questionable. Bond finance would imply increasing significantly the public sector deficit in the short run, and recognizing a huge implicit public debt.[14] Although the demand for government bonds from the new pension funds would in principle facilitate the financing of the deficit, the explicit acceptance of a public debt of this order of magnitude could introduce an element of risk in the perception of savers, and greatly complicate the issue of government bonds.

At the other extreme, an excessively gradualistic strategy would avoid additional up-front fiscal problems but could easily stall before its full implementation. For instance, the second pillar could be introduced only after a significant reduction of contribution rates, engineered by prior reforms in the public PAYG system. A reduction in contribution rates to levels below 20 percent would indeed allow the introduction of a second pillar without large initial deficits or excessive increases in the overall contribution rate. However, it would take at least ten years for the reform measures to decrease contribution rates to reasonable levels. The probability of policy reversals (a politically-driven return to the public PAYG system) during this relatively long period would be very high, as the PAYG would be dismantled very slowly, without the parallel introduction of an alternative or complementary system.

One possible intermediate solution would involve an irreversible switch to a fully funded second pillar, but combined with a gradual implementation. Under this solution, all workers below a certain age, say 25 years (and all new labor market entrants, irrespective of their age), would be forced to move to a new mandatory retirement plan with two components. All of their employee contribution and about half of their employer contributions (adding to a contribution rate of 18 percent) would continue to be channeled to the National Pension Fund. They would be entitled regardless of contribution history, to a citizen's pension at age 65. This would deliver a flat or semi-flat benefit replacing, on average, some 30-50 percent of today's net wage, indexed to an appropriate cost-of-living index. Half of the employer contributions for these workers (a contribution rate of 12 percent) would go to the fully funded scheme, enough to buy at least another 30-35 percent of net wage at 65, with flexible decrements for early withdrawal.

The implementation of this solution would involve greater pension financing requirements in the very first stages of its implementation. This is because the loss in revenues generated by the diversion of contributions from the youngest generations to a private scheme would initially outweigh the reduction in pension expenditures generated by the reforms. The shortfall in the PAYG scheme would warrant financing from the central budget and should be ideally accompanied by offsetting decreases in other expenditures, to avoid an increase in the consolidated deficit. As reforms took hold, these deficits would taper off and eventually turn into surpluses, allowing a decline in the transfers from the budget to the National Pension Fund, and, in a subsequent stage, a reduction in the contribution rate. Indeed, all workers under 50 would have joined this scheme by 2020, with the first citizen's pensions payable in 2036.

Application of these measures would, therefore, allow the immediate introduction of the second, fully funded pillar (although at a gradual pace), and generate a constituency for the full implementation of the pension reform. It would also avoid a serious fiscal problem in the first stages of implementation. The major shortcoming of this solution lies in the fact that the average payroll tax in the economy would remain high in the first stages of implementation, generating only minor efficiency gains during this

---

[14] The gross consolidated public sector debt (the consolidated Government and the NBH) amounts to 85 percent of GDP, and the implicit pension debt amounts to as much as 250 percent of GDP (see Para. 89).

period.[15] However, a payroll tax that remains initially high is the price that may have to paid, at least until the Government is able to implement a fiscal reform to reduce the consolidated deficit and broaden the base of income and consumption taxes. At this stage, the projected decline in the payroll tax could be anticipated through further recourse to general taxation. That would imply permanent transfers from the Central Budget to the National Pension Fund, but these transfers would be justified by potentially larger efficiency gains.

Tables 3.3 and 3.4 compare the "muddle-through" scenario where only the retirement age is increased with this gradual but fundamental reform of the system under "fast adjustment" parameters. Raising the retirement age results in a gradual reduction in pension spending as a percentage of GDP but without sufficient savings to allow for either a reduction in the payroll tax or the introduction of a funded pillar. In contrast Table 3.4 shows a rapid decline in pension spending as well as a dramatic reduction in the ICR. The overall impact of the "fast adjustment" parameters and the combined package of reforms allows for gradual introduction of the second pillar while the portion of the wage bill required to finance both pillars (see Table 3.4, line 6) continues to decline. At the bottom of Table 3.4 the accumulation of private pension funds is shown reaching 5 percent of GDP by 2000 and 11 percent of GDP by 2010. This new source of long-term savings would have a positive effect on capital market development with important implications for long-term growth.

Table 3.3: Slow Adjustment, Raising the Retirement Age Only (Percent of GDP)								
	1994	1995	1996	1997	1998	1999	2000	2005	2010
Pilar I Spending	10.13	10.45	10.41	10.56	10.09	10.06	9.84	9.37	8.61
Implicit Contr.Rate Pillar I	35.41	35.86	35.60	36.05	34.83	34.79	34.08	33.90	33.09
Financing Gap (Line 3-10.1)	0.00	-0.32	-0.28	-0.43	0.04	0.07	0.29	0.76	1.52

Note: The last line refers to the difference between the pension financing requirements for both pillars as a share of GDP in 1994 and the current year.

An **accelerated** variant of this strategy is likely to become more attractive as the system starts growing and the Government consolidates the fiscal reform. There could be some provision for **voluntary** opting-out by current contributors who are above the mandatory joining age but below, say, 45. This could involve a swap of their implicit claims on the existing National Pension Fund for recognition bonds, offering a very moderate real rate of interest and payable upon retirement (as has been done in pension reforms in several Latin American countries). Such a swap would be offered, presumably, at a deep discount to present value, reflecting the greater tangibility, loan-collateral, and other advantages of the new plan. The emergence of an explicit pension debt could be partly offset by putting all the enterprise assets already pledged to the Fund (which owes the implicit debt) into professionally managed escrow accounts, and also opening room for swaps of enterprise shares for recognition bonds before the retirement date. This variant is indeed attractive, as it would allow a faster implementation of the second pillar. However, the fiscal consequences of this variant would have to be examined in detail. This variant should be accompanied, ideally, by the generation of surpluses in the central budget, opening sufficient room for servicing the pension debt and avoiding a large consolidated deficit.

---

[15] The increase in the share of young workers in the overall working population would decrease the average payroll tax, as the 12 percent contribution to the second pillar is not really a tax, but a contribution to an individual retirement account.

Table 3.4: Fast Adjustment, Combined Reforms a/ (Percent of GDP)									
	1994	1995	1996	1997	1998	1999	2000	2005	2010
Pilar I Spending	10.1	10.0	9.8	9.6	9.0	8.7	8.2	6.3	4.4
Pillar II Contributions	0.0	0.0	0.7	0.9	1.0	1.1	1.2	1.7	1.9
Pillars I+II	10.1	10.0	10.5	10.5	10.0	9.8	9.4	8.0	6.3
FinancingGap (10.3-line 3) b/	0.0	0.3	-0.2	-0.2	0.3	0.5	0.9	2.3	4.0
Implicit Contr.Rate Pillar I	35.4	35.0	29.8	29.4	27.8	27.0	25.7	20.8	16.7
Implicit Contr.Rate Pillar II	0.0	0.0	2.3	2.7	3.1	3.5	3.8	5.5	7.3
Implicit Contr. Rate, Both Pillars	35.4	35.0	32.0	32.0	30.9	30.4	29.6	26.3	24.0
Pillar II Contrib. Accumulations	0.0	0.0	0.7	1.6	2.6	3.9	5.2	12.8	14.7

a/ Including the introduction of second pillar for workers with 25 years of age and below.
b/ The financing gap is defined here as the difference between the pension financing requirements for both pillars as a share of GDP in 1994 and the current year.
Source: World Bank staff projections.

C.   Getting People Back to Work

Between 1990 and 1994 the economy lost around 1.4 million jobs (net). In part this reflects a necessary adjustment to the artificial "full employment" policy of the past, but it also reflects the macroeconomic downturn of the past few years. Although declining as a result of the job losses, Hungary's labor-force participation rate for the working age population (at 79 percent in 1993; see Table 3.5) is still quite high by OECD norms, especially for women. This stems in large part from the low official retirement age. When adjustment is made for this, Hungary's labor-force participation rate (defined on the basis of the 15-64 year old population) is fairly average (73 percent compared to 71.5 percent for OECD), and tending on the low side for men (75 percent compared to 81 percent). Because of relatively high unemployment, the employment rate for the working age population is also on the low side by OECD norms (again especially for men).[16]

Rising unemployment, women on paid child-care leave together with increased uptake of disability pensions and early retirement, growing numbers of students of working age, and withdrawal of discouraged workers from the labor force, have led to a dramatic rise in the dependency ratio for the working age population. From a situation of almost four working (formally employed) persons to one non-working person of working age in 1990, the ratio deteriorated to only 1.5 in 1993 (Table 3.5). Add to this the burden of children and the elderly, and the dependency problem becomes extremely serious.

Hungary's tax base is already narrow, and the funding of almost 60 percent of social transfers (almost 20 percent of GDP) by ear-marked payroll taxes levied on those in formal-sector employment places an even heavier burden on a few. Expenditure reduction to lessen this burden is a key message of this report. But getting people back to work and off welfare is also a key policy goal.

The reduction of these labor market imbalances mainly depends on the resumption of economic growth and the accompanying increase in labor demand. But the experience of OECD countries in recent years suggests that economic growth alone may not generate sufficient jobs to return unemployment rates

---

[16]   For women this statistic is somewhat misleading because the Hungarian definition of employed includes women on extended child-care leave (GYED and GYES).

Table 3.5: Changes in the Composition of the Working Age Population (thousands of people)				
	1990		1993	
Population 15-54, 59 yrs ('000)	5957	100.0%	6057	100%
Active in labor market	5011	84.1%	4792	79.1%
Inactive	946	15.9%	1265	20.9%
Active in labor market:	5011	84.1%	4792	79.1%
Employed	4742	79.6%	3657	60.4%
Unemployed (passive support)	24	0.4%	663	10.9%
Unemployed (active programs)	0	0.0%	210	3.5%
Child care leave	245	4.1%	262	4.3%
Inactive:	946	15.9%	1265	20.9%
Students	483	8.1%	565	9.3%
Disability/early retirement	251	4.2%	365	6.0%
Supported family member	212	3.6%	335	5.5%
Dependency ratio: Employed: inactive+ Unemployed+child care		1:0.26		1:0.66

Source: Frey (1994).

to low single-digit numbers. Policies that make working more attractive and being dependent on welfare less attractive, and policies that make the unemployed more employable are increasingly considered important. A major recent OECD report[17] recommends a number of policies to reduce unemployment. Among the major recommendations are: increased wage and labor cost flexibility, reduced non-wage labor costs, improved labor force skills and competence, more emphasis on active rather than passive labor market measures, and reformed benefit systems to increase work incentives. These policies are of equal relevance to Hungary. Of particular importance are the following:

- *reduce non-wage labor costs*: high payroll taxes have at least three negative effects—evasion and avoidance of taxes, serious tax arrears, and (given competitive product markets and relatively rigid wage rates) a negative effect on hiring. Reductions in payroll taxes can be revenue neutral by broadening the tax base and lowering rates (see Table 2.3), and be fiscally neutral by accompanying reductions in both contributions and expenditures (for instance, on unemployment benefits and on sick leave);

- *rearrange unemployment benefits to encourage take-up of new jobs, including low-paid jobs*: in Hungary as in many countries, welfare systems discourage the unemployed from accepting new jobs which offer wages close to—or even below—the level of benefits paid

[17] The Jobs Study (OECD, 1994).

to the unemployed.[18] The OECD study recommends that further, partial "unemployment" benefits should be paid to people who take up low-paid jobs, to ensure that they are clearly better off in work than on welfare alone.[19] Such a measure could be financed in Hungary by reducing the duration of unemployment benefit entitlement to six months, making it more strictly a job-search allowance, and subjecting it to a stricter job-search test;

- *introduce a re-employment premium*: for job-seekers who find paid employment and exit from unemployment before their benefit entitlement has been exhausted. It could work in conjunction with a subsidy paid to employers for hiring certain groups of unemployed. With appropriate checks and balances, such a scheme could act as an incentive to job search and to job creation of a durable nature;

- *place more emphasis on active labor market measures*: although no panacea for solving unemployment, programs that improve the education and skills of the unemployed can help their re-employment chances. In times of high unemployment, public works schemes that keep people active and in the habit of working can also be important. In general, early intervention with active measures, well designed and targeted at particular groups of unemployed, are preferable to passive income support.

Hungary has a particular reform challenge that differs from most OECD countries. In addition to measures that are needed to get the openly unemployed back to work, Hungary has one-tenth of its working age population on paid child care, and on disability and early retirement pensions, costing the country around 2 percent of GDP. These programs have served an important role as part of the social safety net and as a "political buffer" during the past few years that saw rapidly rising unemployment. But because of their lengthy duration and the relatively generous nature of the benefits (the child-care allowance, GYED, for example is paid at a higher replacement rate than unemployment benefit), these programs are typically more expensive for the welfare state than unemployment benefit. Measures to reverse past decisions to withdraw from the labor force, and avoiding further excessive use of these schemes, should be adopted.

For the array of child-care programs (GYED, GYES and GYET),[20] the preferred approach would be to abolish them. The rationale for this would be that they were no longer appropriate as instruments to encourage women to participate in the labor market, and that if women choose to take extended maternity leave it should not be at the cost of the budget. At the same, steps to encourage the provision of creche and nursery care, and more efficient and better targeted poverty prevention/poverty alleviation

---

[18]   Lowering benefits is, of course, an alternative. But in a society where the notion of a state guaranteed minimum income exists, lowering (say) unemployment benefit would only push more people on to social assistance. There would be minimal expenditure saving, and minimal incentive effect.

[19]   The UK has introduced a scheme (the Family Credit) whereby an additional benefit is paid to low-paid workers with children. Tax credits subject to an earned-income test are used in the U.S. and elsewhere.

[20]   These programs provide, in the case of GYED, 65-75% of salary (non-indexed) for 84 weeks, GYES at a fixed amount (but less than the minimum pension) for a further 52 weeks, and GYET, for only the third child, at the minimum pension to youngest child's eighth birthday.

programs should be taken. A less harsh transitional measure would see the administrative consolidation of the various child-care programs (since they are now all funded from the same source), the payment of a flat-rate benefit that was unrelated to past wages, and a shortening in maximum benefit duration (say to two years, still quite generous by international standards). Some of these transitional measures were adopted in the 1995 budget (e.g., compression of GYED payments).

Disability pensions and early retirement have been used extensively in the past few years as ways of dismissing people and avoiding unemployment (so-called soft layoffs). The scope for early retirement funded by either the Solidarity Fund or the Employment Fund has been severely curtailed, but opportunities for disability pension remain. Until such time as the incentive system for employers, workers, and doctors (who do the certification) changes, there is little hope for reversal. There are possible routes to attack this problem, and the experience of other countries (e.g., the Netherlands) could be valuable. Aggressive re-certification of the very large stock of those on "temporary" disability awards, whose cases can be re-examined formally at periodic intervals, should be done as a matter of priority. If necessary, active labor-market programs could be used to help get some of these people back to work. Other suggestions include shifting more of the cost onto the employer in the case of disability, or early retirement (a severance payment in favor of the insurance funds), and using some of the work-incentive schemes discussed in Para. 153 above.

There is one further program that Hungarian employers and employees make extensive use of— that is sick pay. Hungary continues to have one of the highest numbers of compensated sick days per insured worker in the western world—averaging between 25 and 30 days (compared to the West European average of around 18 days). In part this reflects the genuine poor health status of the population, but it also allows both employers and employees to use it for other purposes. In an attempt to curtail abuse of social insurance-funded sick pay, greater responsibility was given to employers at the beginning of 1992. There has been no obvious significant improvement in the situation. Further measures to reduce expenditures and to increase contributions were taken in the 1995 budget (e.g., working retirees no longer have any sick pay entitlement, the effective replacement rate has been reduced by paying only on wage as strictly defined, an increase in the number of employer-responsible days to 15, and a broader tax base). Additional steps are still needed. Emulating the experience of other countries, the general direction should be one of shifting full, or at least primary, responsibility for sick leave provision to the employer (25-30 days), as part of the employee compensation package. In addition, to make employees more health conscious the first sick days (typically 1-3) should be borne (at least in part) by the employee. To gain employer acceptability of an increased liability on their part, an equivalent decrease in the payroll contribution is recommended, so this measure should be fiscally neutral.

D.   Health Care

A Hungarian man aged 45 can expect to live nearly six years less than his Austrian counterpart. This scandalous statistic suggests avoidable human tragedy on a massive scale, and huge economic costs—through foregone output and intensified catastrophic health care needs.[21] Hungary's unfavorable health status can largely be attributed to socio-economic factors such as unhealthy lifestyles, overwork

---

[21]   Life expectancy at birth in 1991 was 65.1 years in Hungary (not significantly better than in the late 1920s) and 72.6 in Austria: in the early 1960s both countries' figure was around 67. The overall gap has narrowed recently, but the relative situation of adult males (24.8 years life expectancy at 45, compared to 30.6 in Austria) has not improved.

and related stress, and occupational and environmental hazards. Hungary's health system has failed until recently to evolve in response to these changing needs, building perhaps on the false assumption that medical care alone, without corresponding changes in individual behavior, would solve all or even most of the problem of deteriorating health status.

The health sector can also be indicted for the generally poor quality of care offered in health facilities, resulting in a low level of consumer satisfaction, and inconsistent effectiveness in reducing illness—results that are not evident from mortality statistics but have significant effects on the overall welfare of the population. Despite the almost universal access to care that was achieved over the last few decades, the quality of care and range of services available to individuals is unequal, remaining more a function of chance or of influence than a guaranteed universal entitlement.

Recent Developments in the Health Sector

Starting in the late 1980s when Government openly acknowledged the growing crisis in health and health care, important changes have taken place in the health sector. These changes can be summarized as follows:

- *Changes in the financing system.* Financing of recurrent health expenditures was shifted from the state budget to a compulsory health insurance system. New methods of paying health facilities were introduced based on the following principles: for family physician services, capitation-based pay; for outpatient specialist care, relative-tariff fee-for service ("point" system); for inpatient care, DRG-type[22] payment. Spending caps were built into payment formulas for family physician services, outpatient care and hospital care. Incentives for increased output are thereby modulated by resource limitations. Subsidies on pharmaceutical retail sales were also transferred to the health insurance system. Contrary to widely-held belief, the creation of a Health Insurance Fund (HIF) to channel public resources for health care does not of itself constitute significant health reform. It is the shift to payment systems based on performance rather than on inputs (number of beds, staff, etc.) that lies at the heart of health financing reform. If properly designed, these new payment systems could provide the incentive signals needed for efficient production of health care and health outcomes.

- *Changes in ownership arrangements.* Ownership of public health facilities was transferred from central to local governments, and autonomous private practices, including private health service enterprises, were legalized. The first steps are being taken to introduce modern methods of management in health facilities, particularly through computerized management information systems.

- *Start-up of a National Health Promotion Program.* The program was initiated to increase awareness on the importance of health-promoting behavior and develop programs to help individuals make these changes and train health professionals to offer such help. The earliest steps were institutional: the creation of a National Public Health Center whose main tasks include oversight of the National Health Promotion Program and professional supervision and quality control. Subsequently, a ban on cigarette advertizing was

---

[22]   "Diagnosis-related groups", a technique for standardizing and aggregating treatment outputs.

introduced. Community- and school-based health promotion programs have started, all on a pilot scale. There are plans to start a nationwide anti-smoking campaign and develop pilot hypertension control programs in 1995.

- *Upgrading of Primary Care and the Family Physician Service.* This service consists of the network of (former) district doctors and newly established private family physician practices, with access to the new capitation-based remuneration system. Free choice of family physician was introduced. In addition, most cases at the specialist care level now require written referral from the family physician. New training programs have been developed for primary care physicians and "model" practices established on a pilot scale.

Increased Real Health Budgets. Developments in health expenditures since 1989 are shown in Table 3.6. Public-sector health expenditures increased significantly as a share of GDP, from 4.6 percent in 1989 to 6.3 percent in 1993. *In real terms, public sector health expenditures increased by 7 percent while real GDP decreased by 22 percent, making health the only major social expenditure category to increase in real terms during the early transition period.*[23] However, all the increase in real expenditures took place between 1989 and 1990, at the time of the creation of the HIF; they have remained almost unchanged from 1990 to 1993.

Table 3.6: Health Expenditures in Hungary, 1989-93 (in million HUF)					
	1989	**1990**	**1991**	**1992**	**1993**
Health Insurance Fund					
(1) Personal Services	48,400	74,376	96,059	113,241	132,623
(2) Pharmaceutical	19,264	21,500	34,100	42,962	54,233
Government					
(3) Ministry of Welfare	2,123	2,842	4,284	6,148	7,668
(4) Investments by central and local government	9,099	10,375	15,130	17,984	26,751
I. Total Public Sector Expenditures on Health a/ (1)+(2)+(3)+(4)	78,886	110,093	149,573	180,335	221,275
(as percent of GDP)	(4.6)	(5.2)	(6.0)	(6.1)	(6.3)
(in real terms, 1989=100)	(100)	(108)	(109)	(107)	(107)
II. Private expenditures (Pharmaceuticals)	3,600 b/	5,140	7,730	11,648	15,267
Total Health Expenditures (I+II) c/	82,466	115,233	157,303	191,983	236,542
(as percent of GDP)	(4.8)	(5.5)	(6.3)	(6.5)	(6.6)
(in real terms, 1989=100)	(100)	(108)	(110)	(109)	(109)
($ equivalent per capita, at current exchange rate)	(134)	(175)	(202)	(236)	(250)
a/ Public expenditures does not include administrative costs and other local government support for current costs. b/ Estimate. c/ Excludes "gratitude money".					

Total health expenditures, including private co-payments on drugs, increased from 4.8 percent of GDP in 1989 to 6.6 percent in 1993. It is estimated that "gratitude money" amounted to around 0.6 percent of GDP in 1993; this would raise total health expenditures to 7.4 percent of GDP. The share of

---

[23]   Excluding unemployment compensation and social assistance which were almost insignificant at the start of the transition.

health expenditures in GDP, whether measured in terms of total expenditures or public sector expenditures, is high for Hungary's level of income.

In the next 20 years, health care funding will be subjected to serious strains similar to those faced by the pension system. International patterns suggest a strong correlation between health spending and an aging population. In Hungary, public spending rises sharply by age group: spending on the average 60-year old is three times that on a 30-year old; at 85, the ratio rises to 5:1.

An Action Program for the Medium Term

Hungary's health sector faces three major challenges today: to reverse the declining trend in life expectancy that started in the late 1960s; to improve the standards of services offered to the public, thus improving health outcomes as well as consumer satisfaction, and to maintain the almost universal access to services. These three objectives must be attained in an environment of greatly restrained financial resources. The Government believes that these objectives can be attained— partly in the long-term, but to some extent more immediately—if radical but low-cost changes are adopted both in health-related behavior of individuals, which could reduce a large part of the avoidable mortality, and in the efficiency with which health resources are used. The Ministry of Welfare (MOW) is working on defining precise actions to promote health-enhancing behavior and to further the structural reform needed to induce cost-effective behavior on the part of providers and their clients. The proposed medium-term program described below offers some suggestions. Given these rising claims on resources, and the relatively privileged position health expenditures have occupied in the last few years, the key focus of health reform must be on reallocation within this real resource envelope to obtain improved outcomes and better distribution of health care within it. Health expenditure relative to GDP would therefore start to fall slowly, as growth picks up in the late 1990s.

The proposed action program consists of five parts focused on: (i) intensifying the National Health Promotion Program; (ii) putting the financial reform back on track; (iii) defining clearly the limits of the publicly-funded health insurance package; (iv) enhancing the autonomy of managers of health facilities, and (v) restructuring the hospital system. The program is complex and politically sensitive, with each important change (e.g., in the price of drugs) directly touching the lives of every individual in the country. It will require strong leadership to balance the many conflicting interests within and outside the sector, as well as high-caliber analytical expertise to sort out the complex medical, economic, and other technical issues involved in health sector reform.

Intensify the National Health Promotion Program. Though still in its early stages, this program is getting on track after a slow start-up. Pilot experiments undertaken under the program will be replicable throughout the country. Anti-tobacco legislation is to be vigorously enforced. Most importantly, the country's health status is being given a prominent place on the national political agenda: stopping the unnecessary deterioration in health is an overriding objective not just of health policy but of general economic and social policy. People, and politicians, need to be made aware that Hungarians are getting ill and dying in unusually high numbers compared to their peers in the rest of the world, and that the solution to this problem does not lie in more expensive health care services but in a combination of actions involving a cross-section of sectors: education, food production, industry, taxation, local government, and health care.

Put the Financial Reform Back on Track. The new payment systems, to be fully effective, must build the right incentives. Further correction is needed in remuneration systems, including: (i) eliminating the historically based element in the DRG and point systems for hospitals and outpatient specialist services, which tend to reward facilities with historically high unit costs; (ii) including high-tech services in the spending caps for inpatient and outpatient services to encourage providers to evaluate more carefully their value relative to less expensive interventions, and (iii) restructuring pharmaceutical expenditures by limiting full coverage to a core package of essential drugs and basing the level of subsidy on the price of the lowest-cost equivalent drug. Measures have recently been proposed in that direction. It is critical that cost-effectiveness concerns, alone, not extraneous concerns such as industrial protection, guide the specification of which drugs will be paid for by the HIF and what level of co-payments will be set;[24] and (iv) introducing financial incentives for performance of preventive services by primary care physicians. These changes in financial incentives will not have the desired impact without training and information for providers, to enable them to respond to the incentive signals. This includes, for example, training in improved prescription practices and on preventive medicine. Information programs aimed at the general public, explaining how their taxes translate into outputs and what the system can and cannot deliver, will also be essential.

Reform of budgeting and contracting processes can also produce valuable improvements. The principal aim would be to eliminate the vast differences in regional allocation of resources, which translate into a perverse situation of waste and duplication in generously endowed areas existing in parallel with large under-served areas. Specifically, **regional allocation of budget resources, on a capitation basis**, would force a more equitable distribution of care and reduce inefficiency. Contracting procedures under the insurance system should be made to represent the interest of the insured population rather than providers. Specifically, the current legal provision that obliges the HIF to contract with every existing publicly owned facility must be eliminated. The contracting process could also be brought down to the regional level, once the necessary institutional capacity can be built within the HIF system. With the above changes in budgeting and contracting, the budget-capping mechanism could gradually migrate from one based on national-level caps for different types of services, to global budget caps at the regional level where the choice of type of service (e.g., outpatient vs. hospital) is determined by cost-effectiveness comparisons at the local level.

Define clearly the limits of the Publicly-funded Health Insurance Package. Except for the most obvious "non-essential" services such as cosmetic surgery or private hospital rooms, the health insurance system theoretically guarantees access to all medical care that is deemed necessary. In reality, resource constraints make obligatory the rationing of services, and the practical limits of entitlement are fuzzy and subject to non-medical influences. Hungarians may need to come to terms with the fact that the full range of medical technology known today cannot be guaranteed universally in all cases of "need", with per capita public budgets at around $250 per year. The technically complex and socially difficult exercise of

---

[24] The recently proposed Health Insurance Fund's is new drug policy would lead to a significant reduction in the level of coverage of drug costs covered by the HIF: for 1995, the drug purchase price (patients' co-payments) would increase by 55-200% depending on whether or not the structure of drug consumption changes, as it is expected, in response to the different levels of coverage by the HIF. As a result, drug expenditures (drug subsidy) covered by the HIF could be kept in 1995 at the same nominal level as in 1994 (HUF62 billion), i.e. decrease of about 20% in real terms. To further curb the high level of health expenditures on drugs (currently 30% of total health expenditures), additional measures would accompany the increase in patients' co-payments: a strict review based on cost-benefit analysis for new drug registration as well as for already registered drugs; a reduction in the number of physicians authorized to prescribe drugs paid for by the HIF; monitoring of prescription practices and analyses of drug use profiles; and a reduction in the number of diagnoses for which drugs are fee.

determining the package of services that can be guaranteed, and the specific (medical) circumstances under which each service will be covered, needs to be started immediately. This would require extensive analyses of the relative cost-effectiveness of alternative interventions for specific diseases, and of the extent to which the system can afford to pay for various alternatives. This exercise, which would result in the preparation of standard protocols to guide medical practice and to define the limits of the insurance package, will take time—although there is much technical expertise to build on. It should start immediately for the major disease groups (cardiovascular disease, cancers, traumas) and service packages (MCH care, periodic checkups for different age and sex categories). Once again, education and information programs for health providers and the general public will be essential to disseminate results and gain widespread acceptance.

A clearly defined basic insurance package, and the reduction considered in the drug coverage will also facilitate the development of private health insurance (theoretically available under the 1993 law on mutual benefit funds, see Para. 79). At present private insurers can only compete on "quality" differentials that are of dubious objective merit.

Enhance the autonomy of managers of health facilities. Managers of health facilities need and deserve to be granted greater autonomy—and bear corresponding accountability—to run health institutions as independent economic units, responding to the signals offered under the new financing system. This includes the freedom to hire and fire staff and set salary levels on the basis of performance. For example, managers and governing boards should be able to take local decisions to cut down on staff numbers and, with the savings, increase overall salary levels, which at present are too low to elicit the quality of service expected from health workers. To this end, the current laws that cover health workers under public service employment laws would need to be revised. Transferring ownership of health facilities to non-profit organizations would be an alternative solution; however, this could also involve complex and costly procedures covering termination of public service employment for the thousands of health workers involved. There is no credible long-term solution for improving the quality of health care (or other social services for that matter) in Hungary that is likely to leave the issue of civil service status untouched.

Investment decisions should also be largely decentralized, although limits will have to be set by Government or a designated regulatory agency on investments in expensive high-tech services or on major expansion projects (see the following section). This would require changes in the way investments are currently financed, moving away from the current practice of financing investments through the state-funded MOW budget towards a system where the cost of depreciation of equipment is included in payments made by the HIF.

Restructure the hospital system. The persistence of excess capacity in the health service system, and particularly in acute hospital care, continues to be a major cause of inefficiency, of financial shortages, and ultimately of poor quality services. In Hungary in 1993, there were 33 physicians and 101 hospital beds (78 acute beds) per 10,000 population; the averages for EU countries, where per capita budgets for health are significantly higher than in Hungary, were 25 physicians and 90 beds (55 acute) per 10,000 in the same year. Reducing excess capacity is a *sine qua non* for successful health reform, and the government's program recognizes this. Based on a comparative analysis of existing normative and effectively used hospital capacities, the HIF plans to revise its "contracts" with hospitals. The objective is to allocate hospital expenditures toward the best-performing facilities. This should, in turn, constitute a strong incentive for hospitals to reduce capacity. However, it is also the most politically sensitive element of the strategy. Fear of adding to already large numbers of unemployed, especially among the influential class of specialist physicians, has stalled attempts to correct this problem in the past.

Correcting the structure of financial incentives is therefore a necessary but not sufficient condition for hospital sector reform. These incentives will most likely generate slow, marginal adjustments on the part of health facilities, but would take too long to bring about the more radical reductions in overall capacity needed to make the system function efficiently. For this, a global view of the entire network of facilities is needed, a view that individual facilities do not take. The Ministry of Welfare will need to initiate a review of the current structure of the health facilities network, and the distribution of functions among facilities, comparing key indicators of performance (admissions, length-of-stay, occupancy rates, doctor-to-bed ratios, staff cost per admission, income-expenditure flows), the physical conditions of sites, and the distribution of technology and skills. It would then identify potential cost savings to be generated either through changes in clinical practice or in organization of services. Early results of cost-effectiveness analysis used to define the basic insurance package could be used for this purpose. Actions to streamline the network of hospitals (reductions in size, merging facilities or functions, reallocating functions, closing facilities) and recommendations for changes in clinical practices (reductions in admissions or length-of-stay, increased use of outpatient services, increased use of day-surgery, separation of chronic care services, etc.) would then be made. Part of the acute care capacity should be converted to long-term care (nursing homes) to fill gaps in the latter.

With few exceptions, this exercise could best be carried out not at the national level but at the regional level (ideally covering reasonably homogenous populations of 700,000 to 1,000,000, not necessarily along county boundaries) where local needs and local facilities are better known. Demographically based regional budget allocations would be the binding constraint on the exercise and would ultimately determine the level of services that would be affordable. As owners of hospital facilities, local governments would be the key actors in implementation of hospital restructuring, with the participation of all concerned parties (local government, managers of local hospitals in region, representatives of employers and employees).

The proposed overall objective could be to attain an average of around 25 physicians and 50 acute care beds per 10,000 population at the national and regional levels within the next five years. Reductions in numbers of physicians should affect specialists—and especially hospital staff— rather than primary care physicians.

Over time, *clear guidelines for allocation of investment resources must be developed*, especially for high-tech equipment. A greater share of investment resources should be set aside for replacing outdated basic equipment before introducing new high-tech equipment. Major investments with implications for the overall structure of services in the country (new hospitals, major expansions, purchase of expensive technology) would require approval at the national level.

E.   Family Allowance

Hungary has many benefits available to families with children. The most important in financial terms is the family allowance. The orientation of family benefits continues to reflect the objectives that were established for them in the past: to support the well-being of mothers and children, ease the employment-child care dichotomy for mothers, and—together with income tax deductions for children[25]—boost fertility. While recent years have seen a quite dramatic shift in the structure and dispersion of household incomes, and in employment and unemployment, there has been little realignment

---

[25]   These have been abolished with effect from January 1995.

in family benefits. Indeed, the family allowance has become more regressive, as market incomes have become more dispersed and, most seriously, it has failed to prevent substantial numbers of families with children from falling into poverty. The fact that high public spending on family benefits (3.0 percent of GDP for the family allowance in 1993) is coexisting with increasing poverty among children clearly points to the need for a fundamental overhaul of the system. However important the objectives of encouraging fertility, supporting all parents during the years of early childhood, and assisting all families to help meet the costs of child-raising, no country in the world can afford to stand back and watch increasing numbers of its (young) citizens fall into poverty when it can prevent it. Poverty prevention and poverty alleviation are therefore considered, in what follows, the overriding public policy objective for the family allowance. We recognize that this implies a strong value judgement.

Without a fundamental reform of the family allowance system the expenditure effort needed to reduce poverty incidence would be beyond reach. To increase the transfer across the board to a level sufficient to prevent poverty among the most needy would be prohibitively expensive. The approach has to be one of greater selectivity and targeting. Targeting can be achieved through a number of ways: (I) *means testing*; (ii) *bringing the transfer within the framework of income taxation*, and (iii) *providing payments to families exhibiting certain characteristics, known to be closely correlated with poverty*. We examine each alternative approach in turn. For various reasons the third, "indicators targeting" approach seems most promising for Hungary in the next few years. Ongoing Bank-supported work on poverty will soon be able to indicate the family characteristics most closely associated with poverty and simulate the distributional effects of targeting with different family attributes.[26]

In 1993 the family allowance was paid to the parents of 2.28 million children, costing HUF103 billion, 3.0 percent of GDP. This level of expenditure places Hungary on a par with the most pro-family countries in Europe, for instance France (2.7 percent of GDP) and Netherlands (2.1 percent of GDP).[27] Although the family allowance is declining in real terms (since it has not been fully indexed for years, and not at all since January 1993), its value in relation to the average wage is still very favorable by Western European standards. In 1994, the family allowance for two children accounted for around 25 percent of the average gross wage (down from 34 percent in 1990). In Western Europe—where admittedly wages are less compressed—few countries cross the 10 percent threshold. In this way, it remains a very important source of income for Hungarian households, especially those at the lower end of the income spectrum (where it accounts for around 10 percent of net disposable income).

In terms of benefit incidence, recent household data for 1992 and 1993 indicate that about one-third of all households benefit from the family allowance. Households throughout the income spectrum are found to benefit from similar amounts of family allowance (see Table 3.7). If there is any concentration of benefit in terms of amount, it is in the middle income ranges.[28] This pattern occurs

---

[26]   A Poverty Assessment, by the World Bank in collaboration with TARKI and the CSO, was produced in draft form in May 1995.

[27]   These countries also have tax-based allowances for children so that the overall fiscal effect is larger.

[28]   Benefit incidence is sensitive to the adjustment of household income for household size, an adjustment which reflects economies of scale when more people live together as one family (fixed costs such as housing, utilities, even food expenses). In the analysis reported here an adjustment for household size is made (the equivalence elasticity, e, is 0.73). If this adjustment were not made, the benefit incidence of family allowance would be somewhat more concentrated in the lower income groups, but one would still see benefit incidence throughout the income spectrum.

because the family allowance is targeted at all children, irrespective of the overall family income situation, parental employment, or other factors.

As with many other social transfers where there is no automatic indexation, under-indexation of the family allowance has

Table 3.7: Distribution of Family Allowance by Income Groups Households Ranked by Income Level					
	Poorest 20%	Next 20%	Middle 20%	Next 20%	Richest 20%
Distribution of family allowance receipts	16.4%	19.1%	22.5%	23.5%	18.6%
Share of family income from family allowance	8.2%	6.2%	5.8%	4.8%	2.5%

Source: TARKI. Toth et al. (June 1994).
Note: Household income adjusted for household size using an equivalence elasticity of 0.73. See footnote 28.

resulted in a significant real expenditure decline (down from 3.5 percent of GDP in 1991 to an estimated 2.5 percent of GDP in 1994). But the generosity of the Hungarian family allowance in terms of coverage and benefit amounts remains striking by international standards (including comparison with other Central European countries). Moreover, under current arrangements, this large public expenditure benefitting a wide cross-section of the population coexists with increasing poverty (See Box 3.2). This clearly points to the merits of redirecting larger per-family transfers at families most in need, in order to ameliorate and prevent poverty. Conversely, it suggests it is time to withdraw benefits from families that can manage quite well without them.

The negative income tax approach. Within the broad "focus on the needy" framework, there are a number of reform options. In the ideal world one would configure a system under which only those below a certain income threshold would receive transfers—and those transfers would be sufficient to bring them up to the desired threshold income. This would be fiscally most efficient. Such perfect targeting would be best achieved through the income tax system (*the negative income tax idea*), and would have the major advantage of allowing for flexibility and irregularity in income levels. However, in few countries does the income tax system in reality allow for such a sophisticated mechanism. In Hungary, the current structure of individual (as compared to family-based) personal income taxation presents a major obstacle to this approach, as does the serious under-reporting of incomes. There is also the problem of those people outside the tax system, often the poorest of all.

Administrative means testing. As alternative to the negative income idea is means testing of benefits through some other administrative structure (such as local governments). But means testing as an instrument of targeting also faces many problems, in Hungary and worldwide. Besides the obvious concern for the high administrative and distortionary costs, and stigma of this approach, there is the lack of accuracy in assessing household income. With many people engaged in multiple activities, some in the grey economy, and the well-developed art of hiding income, there is little scope in the foreseeable future of successfully extending the administrative means-testing approach. The experience in 1994 with the family allowance supplement bears witness to this problem: the number of families who presented themselves with an income less than the designated income threshold was considerably more than expected from household survey data. In addition to the problem of inefficiency in targeting through inclusion of people "cheating the system" there is also the problem of exclusion of the really needy from non-declaration or administrative bias. A further problem with any system that attempts to target the transfer only to the poor is the lack of political support that the poor typically enjoy. In this respect, the middle class are often needed as an important advocate for the poor.

Taxing benefits. As an alternative to ex-ante means testing there has been considerable discussion over bringing various social transfers, including the family allowance, within the framework of the personal income tax base. The taxing of family allowances is another form of targeting, as lower-income families would not be concerned, while the value of family allowances would be decreased for higher income groups. As with the negative income tax idea, one of the major advantages of this approach is that it allows for flexibility and irregularity in income levels. However, there are similar shortcomings with the income tax system in Hungary as an instrument of "post transfer clawback", most importantly that of individual-based taxation. It is understood that the system of personal income taxation is likely to be changed, with "split taxation" being a possible alternative to the present arrangements. In this eventuality, bringing the family allowance within the catchment of personal income taxation could be a major step forward, but tax evasion and tax avoidance, and the progressivity of the system would need to be assessed.[29] (In this regard the recent abolition of tax allowances for children should be commended as a positive development from a vertical equity perspective.) Attention would also be needed to avoid the "poverty trap".[30]

Categorical targeting is probably the best approach for Hungary. Indeed, some would argue that this is precisely the system that exists today, with all children under the age of 16 years being considered the desirable target, and given the correlation between household (per capita) income and number of children it is not an entirely ineffective instrument of targeting. More precise incidence calculations that use the notion of equivalency change the picture somewhat. But under either calculation, there is the question whether more poverty alleviation and poverty prevention could be achieved with a constant, or, preferably, reduced, level of expenditure, organized in a different way.[31] One preliminary option is to concentrate the family allowance on families with larger numbers of children, preferably three or more. Currently with the family allowance there is a differential in the per child payment, rising with larger numbers of children, but this differential has fallen since 1990, and was much more substantial in the past. Maintaining the family allowance in nominal terms for one and two child families and increasing it substantially for families with three or more children is one way of achieving better targeting from an anti-poverty perspective. This approach, however, will generate no significant savings and could even increase overall spending on family allowances. A more radical option would be to abolish the universal family allowance for one- (and possibly two-) child families, and increase the allowance for families with three or more children (or other specific groups). Since the situation of single-parent families is particularly acute, different treatment of their situation might be appropriate. They could, for example, continue to receive some family allowance for first and second children.

Heterodox approach. A mixed approach would build on the scheme introduced in 1994, so that the basic family allowance is gradually reduced for all children (in real terms by inflation) and a

---

[29]   See Jarvis and Micklewright (June 1992), for a good discussion of family allowance and taxation issues. This report concludes the following: "we do not believe that this [taxing family allowance] would be a good policy change....the unit of assessment in the Hungarian income tax system and the degree of progression in this system are not those which are most suited to the use of taxation as a targeting mechanism."

[30]   If benefits are income tested or clawed back in such a precise way that for every extra $1 earned, families lose an equivalent $1 in benefits, this can act as a serious disincentive to work (in the formal sector) and to earn declared income.

[31]   Van de Walle, D., M. Ravallion, and M. Gautam. "How well does the Social Safety Net Work?", LSMS Working Paper # 102, World Bank 1994.

supplementary family allowance is available for a more limited category of families, whether defined by family attributes (which is likely to be preferred if well chosen) or with reference to a ceiling income which is then means tested. This general approach has been used in a number of Western European countries undergoing reform, as it combines a solution that requires no overt political "retrenchment" on what is perceived as an acquired right, yet at the same time enhances the targeting and poverty-alleviating capacity of the family allowance. The rate at which a reduction in the universal payments can occur is of course limited to the rate of inflation. One possible scenario, with inflation around 20 percent, would be to save approximately 0.5 percent of GDP in the first instance, through a continued nominal expenditure freeze, but redirect 0.1-0.2 percent of GDP out of the savings to increase specific benefits aimed at poverty reduction.

CHAPTER IV: REFORMING ENTERPRISES AND BANKS *

A.   Introduction

As stated in the previous chapters, Hungary must decrease the size of its deficit and reduce the tax burden imposed on the private sector to achieve sustainable growth. However, sustained growth will also require eliminating loss-making activities generated in other areas of the economy, and ensuring that the resources released by the retrenchment of the state and the elimination of loss-makers are allocated to the most dynamic enterprises and sectors. Despite the overall progress in transforming its economy, Hungary needs to make additional efforts in all these reform areas. Indeed, despite the significant development of the private sector since 1989, 65 percent of the initial state holdings of enterprise equity remain under the control of the state, which still generates 40 percent of GDP. Moreover, although budget constraints have been tightened, enterprise losses remain large, and continue to divert scarce resources from more productive uses. Finally, despite the entry of several domestic and foreign private banks in the financial system, state banks continue to play a dominant role in mobilizing and allocating financial resources.

This chapter assesses the progress already achieved by Hungary in transforming enterprises and banks, examines the remaining structural bottlenecks in the two sectors, and identifies the measures required to successfully complete the reforms initiated in the late 1980s. The second section examines Hungary's progress in reforming enterprises, and the third section provides a similar analysis for the banks. The final section proposes an agenda for completing enterprise and bank reforms, which coincides to a significant extent with the program being implemented by the Government that came to power in mid-1994.

B.   The Enterprise Sector

Private-Sector Development

Significant development of the private sector began in 1988, with the enactment of the Company and Transformation Laws. Initially, Hungary saw widespread spontaneous privatization of parts of state-owned enterprises as profitable assets such as workshops and other ancillary units were spun off into new limited liability companies.   Over 1989-90, 9,000 new companies were established in this way. Subsequently, greenfield investments provided the main drive in private-sector development. Between 1990 and 1994, private capital in incorporated enterprises grew by HUF1.5 trillion, of which two-thirds was accounted for by new investments and one-third by the acquisition of state assets. Foreign direct investment accounted for about 50 percent of the increase in private capital. At the end of 1994 the number of enterprises in the formal segment had increased to nearly 100,000, of which more than 98 percent were in the private sector.[1] Private enterprises in the formal segment accounted for more than 50 percent of GDP and employment in the same period. Taking into account the informal segment, the share of the private sector had increased to 60 percent of GDP in December 1994.[2]

---

* Mihaly Kopanyi contributed to this chapter.

[1]   The formal sector consists of untransformed state enterprises, limited liability companies, joint stock companies, cooperatives, and other non-social enterprises with legal status and double entry bookkeeping.

[2]   The informal segment comprises 120,000 unincorporated entities and 780,000 individual entrepreneurs.

In part to check the perceived abuses of spontaneous privatization, the State Property Agency (AVU) was established in March 1990 to exercise ownership on the state's behalf, and manage the privatization of virtually all state enterprises. In August 1992 the State Holding Company (AVRt) was set up to manage holdings in enterprises in which the state opted to retain a minimum ownership. After its establishment, AVRt received 172 enterprises from AVU, which also transferred 64 enterprises to other State Asset Managers (SAMAs) during the same period.

AVU's portfolio is characterized by many small and medium holdings, while AVRt's portfolio is characterized by a much smaller number of large companies in energy, infrastructure, industry, agriculture, forestry, and finance. AVRt started exercising control over more than half of the value of state equity immediately after its creation, despite the much smaller number of companies in its portfolio (Table 4.1). Although privatization has always been a principal activity for AVRt, the Government initially mandated that the institution retain minimum shareholdings in its enterprises, which ranged from 1 percent to 100 percent.

AVU has had a reasonable record in privatizing state assets since its creation in 1990. Total divestitures by AVU have amounted to HUF844 billion, or roughly 75 percent of its initial holdings of enterprise equity (HUF1,098 billion), after transfers to AVRt and other SAMAs (Table 4.1). This amount includes HUF353 billion sold to foreign and domestic investors, primarily for cash, but also through credit schemes, installments, leasing, and compensation coupons. HUF322 billion was transferred via liquidation proceedings to new owners, who are generally private. In addition, asset sales negotiated by enterprises and approved by AVU amounted to around HUF168 billion. This leaves HUF254 billion (or 25 percent of its initial holdings, after transfers to AVRt) in the remaining 665 enterprises available for sale.[3]

AVRt's record in privatizing state assets has been much less impressive. Restrictions on the privatization and liquidation of its companies and operational delays, resulted in divestitures of state equity of HUF135 billion, or only 9 percent of its

Table 4.1: The Progress in Privatization		
	Number of Enterprises	Value of State Equity (HUF billion)
Ownership of State Equity before privatization a/		
AVU	1,841	1,098
AVRt b/	171	1,477
Others	86	200
subtotal	2,098	2,775
Divested by AVU as of 12/94		
liquidation	523	322
sold 100 percent	653	206
sold partially	248	147
subtotal	1,424	676
Divested by AVRt. as of 12/94		
liquidation	13	15
sold 100%	-	-
sold partially	23	138
subtotal	36	153
Total Asset Sales Approved by AVU + Equity Reduction as of 12/94	-	168
Total Divested as of 12/94	-	997
State Equity Portfolio managed by AVU and AVRt as of 12/94	823	1,578
AVU	665	254
AVRt	158	1,324
a/ After last transformations and transfers. b/ Excludes AVRt shares in 10 financial institutions. Source: AVU and AVRt.		

---

[3] All the numbers refer to the book value of enterprise equity owned by the state, where equity is defined to include share capital, reserves, and retained earnings. State equity was calculated by multiplying the percentage of enterprise share capital owned by the state to total equity.

initial holdings. The bulk of divestitures has taken place through partial sales of enterprises, and there has been very limited privatization through liquidation. None of the enterprises initially held by AVRt has been entirely sold to the private sector. Even the celebrated sale of shares of the national telecommunications company (MATAV) in December 1993 resulted only in a partial privatization.

Because of the Government's reluctance to sell the larger companies, by the end of 1994, AVU and AVRt together had divested the equivalent of only 35 percent of initial state equity holdings. As indicated above, most of the progress in privatization was achieved by AVU, which by that date had sold the bulk of its attractive enterprises. AVU's remaining portfolio consists mostly of small and medium enterprises in precarious financial conditions that may prove difficult to sell as ongoing concerns. On the other hand, AVRt's remaining portfolio includes large enterprises in the energy, infrastructure, pharmaceutical and financial areas which would be highly attractive to foreign and domestic investors.

Enterprise Financial Performance

The privatization of Hungarian enterprises has been taking place against a background of adverse economic conditions, including the collapse of CMEA, the war in the former Yugoslavia, and slow growth in Western European economies. These external shocks implied a sharp contraction of enterprises' traditional markets, and were accompanied by the opening of the Hungarian economy to imports and a substantial reduction of production subsidies. Although the last two policy measures were essential ingredients of the reforms, they aggravated the impact of the external shocks on enterprise finances, resulting in a drastic increase in gross losses, from 0.6 percent of GDP in 1988 to 14.2 percent of GDP in 1992—the worst year. The net enterprise balance also deteriorated at a commensurate speed, from a surplus of 17 percent of GDP in 1988, to a deficit of 6.1 percent of GDP in 1992, the year where practically all formal enterprise subsectors reported losses. Losses have declined steadily since then, but continue very large as a share of GDP (Table 4.2).

Table 4.2: Financial Performance of the Enterprise Sector, 1988-1994 (in percent of GDP)							
	1988	1989	1990	1991	1992	1993	1994[a]
Net Losses (Losses-Profits)	-16.9	-16.2	-13.3	-4.1	6.1	3.4	- 1.0 to 1.0
Gross Losses	0.6	1.4	2.6	8.4	14.2	10.1	7.0 to 7.5

Sources: Central Statistical Office, Ministry of Finance.
a/ Estimated Range.

The emergence of large enterprise losses after 1990 raises the question of how these losses were financed. The first point to note is that enterprise losses may be somewhat overstated because of efforts to evade high tax rates. Shifting capital expenditures to current expenditures and under-invoicing exports are two examples of creative accounting utilized for this purpose. The second point to note is that losses are to a large extent "financed" by decapitalization by non-replacement of depreciated capital and asset sales. However, it is also apparent from enterprise liability structures and the situation of Hungarian banks (see next section), that in the first three years of the reforms banks were very accommodating to enterprise financial needs, ultimately absorbing a large share of losses in their books. Arrears to other enterprises and to the state were also sources of financing, although apparently to a smaller extent.[4] Finally, both AVU and AVRt recycled a share of their privatization revenues to loss makers, through guarantees on bank loans that were ultimately unpaid, and through new equity infusions.

After 1992 the possibilities for loss makers to shift their imbalances to their creditors became more restricted with the introduction of a tough bankruptcy law and increased reluctance of banks and other creditors to continue financing losses, in part due to the emergence of a large stock of unpaid claims and the threat to their own survival. The recent slowdown in privatization also limited the amount of resources that could be recycled to loss makers by asset managers. Losses have decline since then, although they still remain large—estimated roughly at 7 to 7.5 percent of GDP in 1994—raising again the question of how these enterprises have managed to finance their losses and keep themselves afloat.

Although it is difficult to determine with accuracy current sources of loss financing, it is possible to make a broad assessment of the current situation by resorting to independent information from different sources. Depreciation by loss makers is estimated roughly at 2 percent of GDP in 1994, leaving 5 to 6 percent of GDP in "cash" losses to be financed. Budgetary subsidies that can be related with the financing of these losses amounted to 0.8 percent of GDP.[5] "Automatic" financing by banks, in terms of accrual of interest on unpaid loans is estimated at 2 percent of GDP in 1994,[6] while accumulation of arrears to the customs authority and the Social Security Funds amounted roughly to 1 percent of GDP that year.[7] Finally, transfers from asset managers in various forms amounted to 0.5 percent of GDP. That leaves an "unexplained" residual of 0.7 to 1.2 percent of GDP to be financed from other sources, such as new bank loans, asset sales, and arrears to other enterprises and the tax authority (APEH).

Asset sales by managers with and without the direct involvement of creditors must still be common practice, given the growing number of "shell" companies— firms that have been stripped of their assets while retaining most of their original debts—which account for a significant share of enterprise

---

[4]   In 1992, debts to banks accounted for 43 percent of total liabilities of large loss-making enterprises, whereas debts to the state and to other enterprises accounted for 27 percent and 29 percent of total liabilities, respectively. There is no information on the liability structure of loss-makers for the other years.

[5]   Includes subsidies to agriculture of 0.2 percent of GDP, subsidies to the railway company (MAV) of 0.3 percent of GDP and payments on guarantees of 0.3 percent of GDP. Subsidies to finance *reported* losses are substantially lower than total subsidies to enterprises (2.3 percent of GDP) for two reasons. First, subsidies that are clearly accounted for as revenues by the beneficiaries effectively reduce reported losses, and cannot be interpreted as financing the final balance. Thus, in the case of MAV, only subsidies to finance the final balance are included. Of course, losses would be commensurately larger if all subsidies to MAV were computed as a "below the line" financing item. Second, some subsidies do not necessarily finance losses (e.g., agriculture exports).

[6]   Obtained by the multiplication of the average stock of bad and doubtful assets (HUF250 and 100 billion respectively) and an average lending rate of 25 percent. Accrued interest is included in "other expenses" of enterprises and added to the loss figures. Note that banks are allowed to include accrued interests in their revenues, but have to make 100 percent provisions in their expenses. The absence of an interest income on the loans was largely replaced by the interest income on the recapitalization bonds issued in 1993 and 1994.

[7]   Changes in capital arrears amounted to 0.3 percent in the case of the customs authority and to 0.7 percent in the case of the Social Security Funds. Changes in total arrears amounted to 1.5 percent of GDP, but it is not clear that enterprises included accrued penalty interests explicitly in their expenditures.

losses today. In 1993, 24 percent of the losses generated by the large loss makers consisted of enterprises with less than 50 employees—*prima facie* evidence of a shell company—and 9 percent of losses were generated by companies with no employees at all. Banks do not seem to be providing new loans to loss makers to any significant extent, a conclusion supported by the significant decline in real bank credits to enterprises after 1992 (chapter I). As to There is no reliable information to assess the importance of inter-enterprise arrears and arrears to APEH as financing sources.

Whatever potential sources finance this loss residual, the persistence of large losses indicates that there are still important leakages from the state and other creditors. As shown above, financing from the state alone, either in the form of budgetary subsidies, transfers from asset managers, and condoning of tax arrears, amounts to more than 2.5 percent of GDP, and probably a significantly larger amount, taking into account unidentified sources of finance (such as APEH).[8] In the case of banks, although there is no evidence of significant new lending to loss makers, the accrual of interest on classified loans not accompanied by a more aggressive collection policy implies an automatic source of finance that allows several loss makers to remain unchecked. Therefore, further reduction of losses will depend on tighter enterprise budget constraints by the state and other creditors.

Initiatives for Resolving Debts and Losses

Bankruptcy and Liquidation. Hungary has made efforts to develop a working bankruptcy system as a main vehicle for enterprise restructuring. A tough bankruptcy law was passed by the Hungarian Parliament in 1991 and took effect on January 1, 1992. It required managers of firms with arrears of 90 days or more to file for bankruptcy or liquidation. The law led to a wave of filings for bankruptcy and —from January 1992 through September 1993, there were 5,000 filings for bankruptcy by managers, and 16,000 filings for liquidation by creditors. The law was amended in September 1993 to remedy deficiencies noted in the first 18 months of practice. These amendments: (I) made filing for bankruptcy optional for enterprises with debts 90 days in arrears; (ii) reduced the previously required 100-percent creditor approval of a reorganization agreement to two-thirds (in value) and one-half (in number) of claims; (iii) changed the previously automatic 90-day moratorium on debt-service payments to a moratorium conditional on agreement of the above proportion of creditors; (iv) raised compensation levels for liquidators; (v) required the appointment of a trustee in reorganizations; and (vi) allowed debtors to resort to reorganization through bankruptcy every 2 years.

Some of the amendments introduced in September 1993 seem to have resulted in a sharp decrease in the number of filings (Figure 4.1). The specific amendments that may have led to the reduction in filings include: (I) the removal of the automatic trigger; (ii) the removal of the automatic moratorium on debt service (because it reduced the financial incentives to file for bankruptcy); and (iii) the requirements of a trustee in bankruptcy procedures (because it increased the financial costs for the participants). However, the decrease in the number of filings cannot be attributed entirely to the amendments. Another important factor was the announcement by the Government of a parallel Debtor Consolidation Scheme in the last quarter of 1993 (see next section). This scheme probably appeared to enterprises as an alternative and beneficial way for debt resolution, leading them to postpone or abandon plans to file for

---

[8]   As mentioned before, the large subsidies to MAV are recorded as revenues by the company. Losses would be commensurately larger (by more than 1 percent of GDP) if these subsidies were recorded as a financing item.

bankruptcy. While it is difficult to identify with accuracy the most important causes of the decrease in the number of filings for bankruptcy, the decrease is worrisome, as it indicates a slowdown in restructuring activity.

Although the number of filings for liquidation have not decreased as much as the filings for bankruptcy, long delays in the conclusion of liquidation cases are also worrisome—out of the 23,000 filings for liquidation accumulated until the end of 1994, the court had announced only 7,200, and only 2,850 had been concluded. The absence of restrictions to legal appeals has resulted in a long period between the time of filing and the appointment of a liquidator by the court, facilitating abuses and adverse resolutions (e.g., asset stripping). In addition, the new fee system (which includes a percentage of sales revenues) creates an incentive for court-appointed liquidators to slow the procedure, and accommodate manager and employee requests at the expense of creditors. As a result of all these problems, it takes about two years to conclude an average liquidation procedure, by which time many creditors (even secured ones) gain very little.

Other Initiatives. In attempting to deal with the problem of enterprise debts and losses, the Government has frequently used initiatives outside the normal bankruptcy/liquidation framework. These attempts have included the 1991 Loan Guarantee Program, the 1992 Loan Consolidation Scheme, the North-East Steel Enterprises Program, the "13+1" Program, and the 1993 Bank Consolidation Program, implemented in parallel with the 1993 Debtor Consolidation Scheme. Unfortunately, these programs were not well designed or implemented, and opened avenues for political interference and abuse; they did not significantly accelerate enterprise restructuring.

Figure 4.1 Bankruptcy and Liquidation Developments, 1992-94

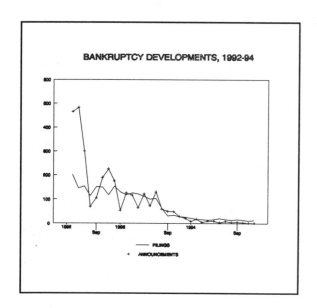 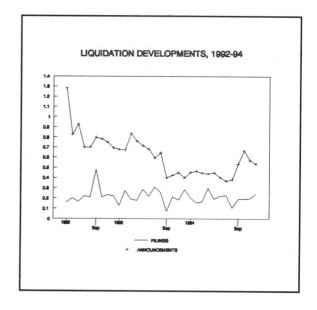

As mentioned before, the December 1993 Debtor Consolidation Scheme was the latest initiative to deal with enterprises losses and debts, and was implemented in conjunction with the 1993 Bank Consolidation Program (see next section). The 1993 Debtor Consolidation Scheme aimed at achieving out-of-court resolution of enterprise debts to the banks and state creditors (the tax and customs authorities and social security) under a conciliation process coordinated and led by the banks. The negotiations promoted by the program were expected to lead to more rapid resolutions than those achievable through ordinary bankruptcy. All enterprises with classified loans were eligible to participate, although only 2,000 effectively applied, out of a universe of 8,000 enterprises with 13,000 classified loans. The low rate of applications was partly due to the fact that several small debtors had already gone into liquidation, and that eligibility was not open-ended—the scheme attempted to support enterprises that had reasonable chances of successful restructuring.

Enterprises participated in the program through one of three schemes: accelerated, normal, and simplified. One hundred and twenty enterprises managed by AVU or AVRt participated in the first two schemes, which were initially designed to include participation by line ministries in the negotiations, and included the mandated sale of classified loans by the banks to AVU or AVRt, at their option, if the banks were the only party in the negotiations that did not approve the restructuring plans proposed by the debtors. These two features caused problems, as the participation of line ministries opened room to introduce non-commercial pressures during negotiations. Also, the option for state managers to buy loans at the net value (face value minus loan provisions) created expectations of additional bailouts among banks and enterprises. The simplified process excluded these problematic features, and provided for the type of negotiations between debtors and creditors that is common practice in market economies.

The banks appeared to take their leadership role seriously in the first stages of the program. Liquidation proceedings were initiated for a number of enterprises, and there are indications of meaningful agreements between enterprises and bank-led creditors in a significant number of cases. However, negotiations were progressively interrupted by interventions from AVU, which quickly spent all its available resources to influence the outcome of the negotiations. It also blocked several negotiations, and arbitrarily removed some enterprises from the scheme after reasonable agreements had been reached. As a result of these interventions and other delays, only 20 percent of the total value of classified loans under the program (HUF29 billion, out of a total stock of classified loans HUF150 billion) had effectively been resolved by December 1994.

The Government reviewed the Debtor Consolidation Scheme at the end of 1994, and concluded that it had not met its objectives. The final deadline of the scheme was extended to June 1995, but its two problematic features were eliminated, namely, the presence of line ministries in the negotiations, and the option for state asset management agencies to buy out loans at their net value. Although this was a step in the right direction, it is doubtful that these changes alone will fundamentally improve the credibility of the scheme, which has been greatly impaired by excessive interference and only moderate progress in debt resolution. Therefore, the Government still faces the task of setting up an efficient framework for debt and loss resolution after the expiration of the Debtor Consolidation Scheme in mid-1995.

C.   The Banking Sector

Background

The current structure of the Hungarian banking system still reflects the structure of the system established under central planning. Under that system, the NBH borrowed abroad, mobilized enterprise deposits, and provided virtually all credit to enterprises. The Hungarian Foreign Trade Bank (MKB), the National Savings Bank (OTP) and a network of rural cooperative banks, all Government directed, performed the remaining banking services (basically foreign trade and housing finance). Credit was extended primarily on the basis of the Government's assessment of an enterprise's importance in the economy, rather than its profitability and ability to service its loans.

The transformation of this system began in 1987, when the NBH established the Hungarian Credit Bank (MHB), Commercial and Credit Bank (K&H), and Budapest Bank (BB) to replace its role as financier to industry and agriculture, and gave greater autonomy to the Hungarian Trade Bank (MKB), the National Savings Bank (OTP), and the cooperatives. Under this two-tier system, banks were separated into different groups, each limited in the services it could offer. OTP and the cooperatives retained control of retail deposits, and MKB of foreign exchange transactions. The three new commercial banks were given the right to carry enterprise accounts and provide virtually all lending to the enterprise sector. In 1989 the market was opened to new entrants, paving the way for establishing new foreign joint-venture banks and small privately owned banks. Governmental agencies participated in the establishment of some of these new banks, such as Postabank, established with capital from AVU.

Current Structure

There are 41 banks in Hungary, about half of which are domestically controlled, and 255 cooperatives. At end-June 1994, the banking sector had assets of HUF2.8 trillion, loans of HUF1.3 trillion, and deposits of HUF1.6 trillion (67 percent, 31 percent, and 39 percent of GDP, respectively). The six largest banks—OTP, MHB, K&H, MKB, BB and Postabank—constitute the dominant group. They account for roughly 70 percent of the system's assets, loans and deposits. The cooperatives, which hold less than 5 percent of total assets, enjoy strong representation in rural areas. The foreign-owned and joint-venture banks have continuously increased their market share since 1990, but still make up only about 15 percent of the system's assets. The other domestically owned banks, the largest of which has less than HUF50 billion in assets (a market share of 1.5 percent), are heterogenous and have little impact on the system as a whole.

OTP, the largest bank in the system, dominates retail banking with a third of the approximately 1,050 branches in the commercial banking sector, 42 percent of the banking sector's deposits, and more than two-thirds of household deposits. Even though other banks have been able to offer retail deposits since 1987, the erosion of OTP's dominant position has taken place only slowly. Postabank (OTP's closest retail bank competitor) has recorded significant growth since its inception in 1990, but its deposit base is still relatively small—less than one-sixth of OTP's. The savings cooperatives (the second closest competitor, at least in rural areas) are also relatively small. The introduction in 1993 of deposit insurance may facilitate competition, as depositors will be able to expect the same level of safety for their deposits that up to now they have believed they could only get from OTP. Commercial bank efforts to gain access to OTP's cheaper and more stable deposit base should also lead to more competition in the retail market and a further decline in OTP's share.

The 255 savings cooperatives represent only about 5 percent of total banking assets, although they constitute a potentially valuable network for savings mobilization and lending to small enterprises, especially in rural areas. In order for the cooperatives to operate efficiently with their limited resources, the Government has determined that they should be coordinated through one organizational structure. In October 1993 the cooperatives relinquished some of their independence in return for inclusion in the bank consolidation program through the newly established National Organization Protection Fund of Savings Cooperatives (OTIVA). Under the new structure, cooperatives will receive support services and supervision, in part through a restructured and recapitalized Takarekbank.

Table 4.3: Structure and Size of the Financial Sector (June 1994)			
	Assets	Loans	Deposits
I. Market Shares (in % of Total)			
1. Domestic Banks	79.4	79.2	80.9
Large Banks	69.3	68.0	72.5
OTP	29.6	22.8	41.1
MHB	11.0	11.8	8.5
K&H	8.3	11.2	5.5
BB	5.8	8.1	4.7
MKB	8.1	6.8	7.3
Postabank	6.6	7.4	5.4
Other Banks	10.1	11.2	8.4
2. Savings Cooperatives	5.5	4.6	6.9
3. Foreign and Joint Venture Banks	15.1	12.1	10.7
4. Total Banks and Cooperatives	100	100	100
II. Total Size (percent of GDP)	67	31	39

The four large banks other than OTP and Postabank can still be characterized as wholesale banks, as they remain basically focused on mobilizing resources from, and lending to, enterprises. Their share in total lending remains high (38 percent), although it has fallen significantly recently, mostly as a result of the growth of the foreign and joint venture banks. None of these banks is individually dominant—the largest one (MHB) has less than 15 percent of total loans—and they will continue to face strong competition, from the foreign banks, OTP, and Postabank. On the other hand, these banks have demonstrated increasing interest in the retail market, and some of them may become effective in this market in the future.

Aside from the Hungarian Foreign Trade Bank (MKB), the state has maintained effective control over the five large banks that initially comprised the system (Table 4.4). Moreover, state control over these banks was strengthened through a series of recapitalizations in 1993 and 1994. State participation is much smaller in the MKB and the Postabank. The former was privatized in 1994, while the latter was born as a majority private bank. State participation in smaller banks is also substantial, partly as a result of the recent recapitalization of these banks by the state in 1993 and 1994. The Government has recently adopted a new policy, which prescribes a reduction of minimum state holdings in OTP to 25 percent, and generally relinquishes minimum state holdings in the other banks, although the state may retain a golden share in some cases.

Recapitalizations and Other Recent Developments

After the acceleration of the reforms in 1990, the Hungarian authorities became progressively aware of the critical financial situation of most Hungarian banks, particularly those created from the National Bank of Hungary. Unfortunately, the authorities did not address this problem through a well-articulated program. Instead, the banks benefitted from a series of bank recapitalizations without being submitted to any serious conditions. Therefore, this series of recapitalizations did not reward past prudent behavior, generated expectations of additional bailouts, and postponed the difficult task of bank and enterprise restructuring. The Government's current efforts to improve bank performance and the tasks that remain to be fulfilled largely reflect these misguided initial steps.

The recapitalization schemes implemented between 1991 and mid-1993 included the 1991 Consolidation Agreement, the 1992 Loan Consolidation Scheme, and the "13+1" Program. The failure of these initiatives to restore the health of the system led the Government to launch the 1993 Bank Consolidation Program. This program was intended to be a final and comprehensive solution to bank problems, and was preceded by an evaluation of their portfolios by Credit Suisse First Boston. The evaluation concluded that eight banks, including three of the five largest banks in the system, were technically insolvent and their financial position would continue to deteriorate because of the loss of interest income. A number of cooperatives were also found to be capital-deficient, and OTP was found to have lower levels of capital than desirable.

Table 4.4: Ownership Structure of the Banking Sector (September 1994)			
	State Share %	Private Domestic Share %	Private Foreign Share %
Large Banks			
OTP	80.4	19.6	-
MHB	90.2	9.8	-
K&H	85.2	14.6	0.1
MKB	28.2	29.9	41.9
BB	78.2	18.9	2.9
Postabank	16.3	68.5	15.1
Smaller Banks			
Takarekbank	87.4	12.6	-
MBFB	100.0	-	-
Mezobank	77.4	20.7	1.9
Agrobank	34.4	62.3	3.3
Dunabank	95.3	4.7	-
Corvinbank	68.4	31.6	-
InterEuropabank	4.7	68.5	26.8
Iparbank	87.0	13.0	-
Konzumbank	9.4	90.6	-

Immediate action on the insolvent banks appeared to be merited, as their negative cash flow created the risk of a liquidity crisis and contributed to the fairly high interest spreads (around 10 percent during 1993). In addition, the Government viewed solvency as crucial to maintaining public confidence in the banking system. As a result, the Government recapitalized these banks to an estimated 0 percent CAR at year-end 1993, and proceeded with two additional recapitalizations to bring the banks to 4 and 8 percent CAR in May and December 1994, respectively. The 1993 Bank Consolidation Program was implemented in coordination with the Debtor Consolidation Scheme (see preceding section) and marked a change in the Government's strategy of bank and enterprise reform—from a centralized approach, as in the 1992 consolidation program and the "13 + 1" program, toward a bank-led decentralized program.

To effect the capital infusion, the state issued 20-year bonds with flexible interest rates paid semi-annually. The total amount of state bonds issued to implement the 1993 consolidation program was HUF165 billion, more than half of the total amount of recapitalization bonds issued (Table 4.5). Each of the recapitalized banks was required to sign a Consolidation Agreement with the MoF, presumably designed to ensure their operational and financial restructuring. The banks were asked to evaluate their financial and operational positions, prepare corrective action plans, develop special work-out units, and improve key operational functions, such as loan processing and review and asset/liability management.

Although the move toward a decentralized approach, was not a negative development in itself, the Consolidation Agreements (a critical component of this type of program) were not designed and implemented with the necessary care. For one thing, the agreements were signed in the absence of reliable information that only in-depth audits could have generated. As a result, the agreements did not specify quantitative performance criteria and targets, or adequately specify remedial institutional measures. Therefore, the extent of operational and financial restructuring required was left open to interpretation. Moreover, the agreements included no sanctions for non-compliance.

This situation was aggravated by the absence of a strong bank governance. Although the MoF established a Bank Control Unit (BCU) in January 1994 to exercise shareholder rights and monitor compliance with the Consolidation Agreements, the BCU's mandate and authority were not articulated, and the unit was very lightly staffed. The duality of ownership between MoF and AVRt (which retained a minority position) complicated the exercising of governance. Finally, the ability to reform the banks was also impaired by the lack an efficient supervisory framework, caused, *inter alia*, by a serious fragmentation of supervisory responsibilities. This problem is rooted in the 1991 Banking Act, which established a dual structure involving a Bank

Table 4.5: Government's Bank Recapitalization (in HUF billion)			
1. "1992" Consolidation		98.6	
2. "13+1" Program		57.2	
3. "1993" Consolidation		165.1	
	December 1993	May 1994	December 1994
Sub-Totals	130.1	19.0	16.0
● MHB	54.8	4.0	
● K+H	33.4	5.0	
● BB	5.0	4.6	
● Takarenkbank	10.7	1.4	0.0
● Other Banks	12.4	4.0	0.0
● Cooperatives	8.8	0.0	0.0
● OTP	5.0	0.0	0.0
4. Total (1+2+3)		320.9	
In % of 1994 GDP		7.5%	

Supervisory Committee responsible for regulation and enforcement, and a State Banking Supervision (SBS) responsible for supervision. The NBH also performed some bank supervisory functions. This fragmentation created confusion and paralysis, and spread Hungary's the scarce supervisory skills even more thinly.

In sum, the Government elected in mid-1994 inherited a situation where, even though the CARs of state banks had been increased through successive recapitalizations, true CARs could still not be ascertained with precision, because of the lack of thorough audits. More importantly, although these recapitalizations averted a possible liquidity crisis and may have contributed to the decrease in spreads (from almost 10 percent in 1993 to 7 percent in 1994), they were not accompanied by credible restructuring programs, leaving the risk that the problem of insolvency would re-emerge, and that the resources would be wasted. The new Government also inherited very deficient governance and supervisory frameworks, and a Debtor Consolidation Scheme that yielded only modest results (see previous section). It is against this rather unfavorable background that the Government must redesign and implement the program of banking reform.

D.   Finalizing the Enterprise and Bank Reforms

An Agenda for Enterprise Reform

Privatization is the central element of the program for enterprise reform elaborated by the new Government. The new privatization program sets ambitious yearly privatization targets, and is expected to result in the divestiture of the bulk of the state's remaining shareholdings within three years. The program also includes large administered price increases and regulatory frameworks for electric and gas utilities, as these measures are preconditions for privatizing enterprises in these sectors. The privatization is expected to be carried out by a new agency—APVRt—which will merge the functions and resources of AVU and AVRt.

The Government's program also includes measures to rejuvenate enterprise restructuring and curtail enterprise losses. The Government has already removed the most problematic features of the Debtor Consolidation Scheme, and will not extend the deadline of the scheme. At the same time, the Government is elaborating a number of improvements in the bankruptcy and liquidation framework designed to achieve greater speed in resolving debts and minimize fraudulent practices. Finally, faster resolution of bad debts is also expected to be achieved through stricter enforcement of the bank recapitalization agreements, as the banks have pledged to work out their bad assets under such agreements. These recent actions are all commendable; faster progress in privatization and curtailing loss-making activities will imply a significant withdrawal of the state from the productive sectors of the economy, and should lead to substantial gains in productivity.

Enterprise Privatization. In its economic policy statement following the last elections, the new Hungarian Government expressed its intention to complete the privatization of most remaining state enterprises within three years, and a new privatization law was submitted to Parliament in December 1994. The law prescribes the merger of AVU and AVRt, and the centralization of privatization operations in a new Privatization Agency (APVRt), which would hold around HUF1.5 trillion of enterprise equity, the equivalent of 90 percent of total state equity holdings in enterprises or more than 25 percent of 1995 GDP (Table 4.1). APVRt will benefit from a significant broadening of the scope and depth of the privatization base, enabling it to divest HUF1.2 trillion in equity holdings over the next three years, the equivalent of 80 percent of the combined holdings of AVU and AVRt in December 1994 (Table 4.6).

The new privatization strategy favors divestiture through cash sales, but the potential amount of cash that can be raised over the next three years is much smaller than the overall divestiture target of HUF1.2 trillion. For one thing, divestiture though liquidations is estimated to reach HUF60-90 billion, or more than 5 percent of the divestiture target (Table 4.6). The final figure may actually prove larger, given the number of enterprises in dire financial conditions. In addition, total obligations to compensation coupon holders and social security funds could amount to HUF350 billion, although the Government hopes that the final amounts will be significantly smaller. Finally, the market value of these equity holdings may prove considerably lower than book value. Therefore, the amount of cash revenues that can be realistically expected is smaller than the HUF820-1,050 billion that would result from the simple deduction of liquidations, compensation coupons, and transfers from the global divestiture target, and the speed of privatization will depend partly on a realistic attitude by the Government toward prices and the potential for cash generation.[9]

The new privatization strategy includes a division of the portfolio of APVRt into three groups, and it is only in the first group that holds potential for cash generation. This first group comprises 30 to 40 large, "blue-chip" enterprises in the energy and infrastructure areas, and currently managed by

---

[9] Table 4.1 refers to book value of equity, thus comprising the book values of share capital, reserves, and retained profits. The state may be able to sell its shares at a premium in the cases where reserves are large, but the premium is likely to be much smaller than the percentage difference between equity and share capital.

AVRt.[10] The second group consists of medium-sized enterprises of lower value, mostly AVU-managed, located in other sectors of the economy. The potential for cash generation is much more limited in this group. Finally, the third group consists of small enterprises of much smaller value, also currently managed by AVU. Divestiture of these enterprise will also have to rely primarily on non-cash methods.

The Government expects to sell a significant share of enterprises in the first group to strategic foreign investors for cash, and has already taken a number of initial measures required to achieve this goal. New Electricity and Gas Supply Laws were passed by Parliament in April 1994, and the Government has finalized the regulatory framework to underpin the privatization of the power and gas distribution sectors. The two laws designate a new Energy Office in the Ministry of Industry and Trade as the regulator for these sectors, and enunciates basic pricing principles. In January 1995 the Government implemented the first price increases required to initiate privatization (average electricity and gas prices were increased by 31 percent and 21 percent respectively, and by 65 percent and 53 percent for households), and believes that additional price increases can be negotiated with foreign investors in the context of the new regulatory framework.

The Government also expects to privatize some of the best enterprises in the second group through cash sales. However, the potential for cash generation in the second group is much more limited, and will in any case require much more flexibility on the part of the new agency. APVRt will have to refrain from imposing conditions (such as minimum politically acceptable selling prices, and commitments by buyers with respect to future investments, maintenance of employment, and cleaning up past environmental damage) that appear to have previously impeded the sale of AVU enterprises. In addition, this group includes 100 to 150 enterprises with a book value of around HUF150 billion in difficult financial condition, and which AVU was unable to privatize. In this case, divestiture may have to rely more on liquidations, or swaps of shares for compensation coupons. Finally, the privatization of the smaller enterprises in the third group will be primarily self-initiated and follow a multi-track approach, including credits, installment sales, and leasing. The Government does not expect to generate significant cash revenues from the divestiture of these enterprises, and realizes from experience that most revenues are uncertain and are in any case distributed over many years.

Table 4.6: DIVESTITURE OF STATE ASSETS (In HUF Billion)			
	Total Equity	Equity Owned by State	State Equity to be Divested
1. TOTAL BOOK VALUE	2,284	1,575	1,261
LARGE	1,552	1,102	824
MATAV	181	120	75
MVM	304	304	152
Power Companies	551	259	259
MOL	264	253	189
Gas Supply	65	65	65
Other			
MEDIUM	637	409	373
SMALL	95	65	64
2. LIQUIDATIONS			60-90
3. TRANSFERS TO SSFs			50-200
4. COMPENSATION COUPONS			100-150
5. POTENTIAL CASH REVENUES			821-1,051

---

[10] The portfolio of APVRt will include MVMRt (the electric company, which will retain the electric grid); 15 power generation and distribution companies (former parts of MVMRt); MOL (the oil and gas company); 5 regional gas distribution companies; MATAV (the telecommunications company); MALEV (the national airline carrier); MAHART (the shipping company); and HUNGAROCAMION (the road haulage company). These large companies will account for more than 50 percent of all APVRt's holdings.

70

The Government reckons that it may generate HUF450-550 billion (approximately US$4 billion) in cash revenues from the privatization of all enterprises in the combined portfolios of AVU and AVRt, mostly from large enterprises located in the first group, and accounting for nearly half of the combined portfolio. This range does not seem unrealistic, as it apparently takes into account the difference between market and book values, and the possible need to transfer some shares of these "blue-chips" to compensation coupon holders and to the social security funds to honor (at least partly) a commitment previously made to these funds. However, the Government must still maintain a flexible attitude throughout the privatization process to avoid a situation in which a large number of privatization deals fails because of rigid adherence to price targets and expectations.

Enterprise Restructuring and Reduction of Losses. Enterprise restructuring should ideally be preceded by enterprise privatization, as private owners are the agents most likely to be guided by the right incentives, and thus better suited to handle restructuring. For this reason, the vigorous privatization of both enterprises and banks should enhance the prospects for successful restructuring. However, the restructuring of Hungarian enterprises and the curtailment of losses will also require complementary efforts in at least two major areas. First, there should be an effort to reduce losses in the state enterprises in the portfolios of AVU, AVRt and other SAMAs even before their privatization. Second, several enterprises that have already been privatized are still running losses and accumulating arrears with their creditors, and the same will probably happen to a number of state enterprises after their privatization. Therefore, there must be a mechanism to expedite the resolution of bad debts and screen the enterprises that are truly viable.

The best way to curtail the losses of state-owned enterprises awaiting privatization is to submit them to a tight budget constraint. In this regard, it is a positive development that the new privatization strategy favors privatization over restructuring by the state asset managers, and that creditors are increasingly reluctant to absorb payments arrears. It is equally positive that the new privatization strategy prescribes that privatization revenues should not be recycled toward state enterprises. However, the new privatization agency will command very large resources during the of the three-year privatization program, and it may continue to be submitted to pressures to recycle revenues to restructurings of doubtful quality. In addition, the losses of several state enterprises are partly due to intensive asset-stripping by their managers. Although this is itself a form of privatization, it is frequently not a desirable method, because it is inequitable, and imposes severe burdens on the creditors and ultimately on the state budget.

The state asset managers have an important role to play during the transition to privatization. Asset managers should make more intensive use of the scope for initiating self-liquidation for non-viable enterprises, through bankruptcy filings or out-of-court final settlements with creditors. Asset managers may also prevent asset-stripping and enhance enterprise performance more generally through improved governance and monitoring. More importantly, the Government should adopt clear policies on utilizing privatization revenues, and impose severe limits on financial support to enterprise restructuring. Ideally, privatization revenues should be transferred to the budget, after coverage of the operating costs of APVRt and the financial obligations incurred by AVU and AVRt as of December 1994. Remaining transfers to state enterprises managed by APVRt should be subject to an explicit and strict budgetary cap.

As suggested before, progress in restructuring enterprises will depend not only on quick privatization, and an enhanced disciplining role of state asset managers, but also on a substantial improvement in the debt- and loss-resolution mechanisms. Unfortunately, the Debtor Consolidation Scheme has been severely abused and has produced only modest results. Therefore, the Government should announce the termination of the scheme in June 1995 and introduce improvements in bankruptcy and liquidation rules and procedures. These could include: (I) abolition of the need for a trustee in bankruptcy procedures; (ii) the reintroduction of the automatic 90-day moratorium on debt service for enterprises that file for bankruptcy; (iii) severe limitations on the possibility for appeals after the filing of liquidation by creditors; (iv) changes in the system of fee remuneration of liquidators, from the current 5 percent of sales to a fixed percentage of recoveries, aimed at increasing the incentives for rapid liquidation of valuable assets. In addition, the Government should maintain a policy under which state creditors, such as the Social Security Funds, refrain from launching independent collection programs that violate the creditor seniority implied by the Bankruptcy and Liquidation Laws. Finally, the Government should enforce Recapitalization Agreements with the state-owned commercial banks, as these banks have the obligation to work out their bad assets under these agreements (see next section).

An Agenda for Bank Reform

As in the case of enterprise reform, privatization is also the central element of the program for bank reform elaborated by the new Government. A commissioner for bank privatization was appointed in December 1994 and tasked with the privatization of most state banks over the next three years. Except for the two largest commercial banks—MHB and K&H—privatization is expected to proceed fairly quickly. The two banks will need to be submitted to pre-privatization programs designed to make them attractive to strategic investors. The new commissioner for bank privatization has set up a secretariat staffed with local and foreign experts with a clear mandate to privatize the banks and ensure that the largest banks are indeed implementing pre-privatization programs conducive to early privatization. Finally, the Government's program also includes numerous improvements in the Banking, Accountancy and Securities Law, aimed, inter alia, at establishing a coherent supervisory and regulatory framework. These actions are all commendable, as they should correct a number of past misguided steps in the area of bank reform, strengthen the credibility of the program, and result finally in an efficient banking sector.

Bank Privatization. Privatization of the four smaller state banks (Dunabank, Iparbank, Konzumbank, and Mezobank) under the program has already been initiated. Unlike the four larger banks participating in the Bank Consolidation Program (MHB, K&H, BB, and Takarekbank), the CAR of the smaller banks was not raised to 8 percent in December 1994. As a result, since that date these banks have been in non-compliance with bank regulations, and have a limited period to regularize their situation. The Government intends to define the situation of these banks promptly, and plans to withdraw their licenses or even liquidate them, if it proves impossible to privatize them within this limited period.

The Government is making efforts to privatize Budapest Bank, the third largest state commercial bank. The Government is willing to allow majority ownership for foreign strategic investor, and hopes that the privatization of BB can follow the model adopted for the Foreign Trade Bank (MKB), which has been to sell a significant amount of shares to strategic foreign investors as a first step, followed by subsequent sales of shares to other investors and the public.

The Government has also announced its intention to privatize OTP during 1995; it plans to sell 20 percent of OTP's share capital to domestic and foreign financial investors through private placements. The second operation would involve sales of 5 percent of OTP's share capital through public offerings in the domestic and foreign stock exchanges. An additional 5 percent of share capital is expected to be offered to OTP's management and employees. Finally, the Government is planning to transfer around 20 percent of OTP's shares to the Social Security Funds. As a result of these four operations, the state's participation in OTP's share capital would be reduced to around 25 percent.

The privatization of the two largest state-owned commercial banks (MHB and K&H) cannot start immediately, as these two banks are still not attractive to strategic investors. However, the Government has recently increased its efforts to turn the two institutions around. The banks have recently been submitted to thorough audits and pre-privatization programs, which include spinning off the bad parts of their portfolios into subsidiaries, the resolution of a minimum share of these bad assets, and laying off of excess personnel. Institutional improvement of key areas of the banks is also planned. The full implementation of these pre-privatization programs is essential for the subsequent privatization of MHB and K&H, as potential investors will otherwise react adversely to the quality of some of the banks' clients and institutional problems.

Bank Governance. The Government's ownership position in the problem banks enables it to implement the turnaround of the two large banks and expedite the privatization of BB, OTP, and the smaller banks. It will be particularly important to exercise effective governance of the two large banks to bring them to the point of privatization. An improved governance system has already been initiated with the appointment of the bank-privatization commissioner and the establishment of a privatization secretariat in December 1994. The commissioner has hired core local staff, and the international donors are financing domestic and foreign consultants to help the commissioner complete his task. A more active governance exercise was demonstrated in December 1994 by the full replacement of MHB's management and supervisory boards.

Legal and Regulatory Framework. The required changes in the Banking Law include the elimination of the current fragmentation in responsibilities and authority within the supervisory function. Policy makers will have to choose between two principal options: transferring full powers and responsibilities to the NBH, or combining in a single supervisory agency the regulatory, enforcement, and sanction powers of the current Bank Supervisory Committee and the supervision responsibilities of SBS. The second option will require a smaller adjustment and is the more likely to be adopted by the Government. If so, it will be essential to have a representative of NBH head the board of the new agency to eliminate the current conflict of interest that arises from the dual responsibilities of the Minister of Finance (as head of the Bank Supervisory Committee and principal owner of the banks in the program) and strengthen coordination between NBH and the new agency.

The new law will also need to provide more specific definitions of the powers, responsibilities, and required qualifications of the bank management and supervisory boards. The law should delineate the enforcement process, and provide for graduated sanctions in line with the gravity of infractions, including specific personal penalties for directors, managers, and auditors who do not follow the prescriptions of the law. The new law would need to specify acceptable capital adequacy within a range linked to the risk profile of each institution. The law would need to define degrees of severity of problems and bank insolvency. The supervisory agency has to be given the flexibility to act to remedy these problems through regulatory forbearance. The law will need to provide a mechanism for temporary intervention of problem banks and define responsibility for managing bank liquidations.

Like most other Central European countries, Hungary has opted for universal banking, thereby permitting banks to invest in non-financial companies. While universal banking has many advantages, it exposes banking institutions to a number of risks, and places additional demands on bank management. These risks can be contained by segmenting banks according to risk level, and applying differential licensing, capital, and management requirements to different classes of institutions depending on their level of risk. The new banking law should empower the supervisory agency to limit bank activities by granting different licenses based on different minimum capital and capital adequacy requirements. This would be in line with the proposal being considered by the authorities to adopt a more restrictive licensing policy for a short period as a means of enhancing the franchise value of banks to be privatized.

SBS has issued regulations covering capital adequacy, loan classification, and liquidity requirements. The first two regulations need to be upgraded to international standards. The current risk weightings of off-balance-sheet short-term guarantees, loans to enterprises supported by mortgages, long-term state bonds and investments should be changed to conform to BIS standards for determining capital adequacy,. Loan classification rules should be amended to extend them to all bank assets and off-balance-sheet items, and to define in more detail the criteria to be used to classify problem debtors based on their expected ability to service their debts.

The supervisory agency should adopt audit regulations to ensure that banks undergo adequate external audits on an ongoing basis. The regulations should specify the scope and coverage of audits and auditor reporting responsibilities to the supervisory authorities. They should enhance the independence of auditors from senior management, by stating that their relationship with the banks be conducted through audit committees of the bank boards. The supervisory agency should also issue guidelines for the banks on management of banking risks, defining good banking practice in credit, foreign exchange and interest rate risk management, capital planning, and appraisal of real estate and collateral. These guidelines should over time be transformed into binding regulations.

The supervisory agency will need to adopt am active supervision model encompassing systematic and regular assessment of bank financial conditions and the quality of their management. To this end, it will need to develop a statement of its mission that defines its supervisory objectives and its strategy for achieving these goals. This strategy should set out an appropriate supervisory cycle, the mix of supervisory instruments appropriate for each bank, and a rating mechanism to define priorities. The supervisory cycle should ensure that within a maximum period of between 1 ½ to 2 years, the supervision program for each institution will include: (I) a full-scope examination; (ii) targeted follow-up visits; (iii) annual review of external audit programs, and (iv) periodic discussions of financial performance with bank management.

CHAPTER V: TOWARD GROWTH AND EUROPEAN INTEGRATION *

A.   Introduction

Hungary is committed to joining the European Union by the middle of the next decade. For Hungarians, achieving EU membership will be a major milestone in economic and political terms, as it will firmly establish Hungary as a member of the community of market-based, liberal Western democracies. However, by the time Hungary expects to join the EU, existing member countries will have reached a high degree of integration (possibly including monetary union) at high levels of per capita income. If Hungary fails to complete the transformation of its economy and reduce its very large income gap with the EU, it would create problems, not only because its population would not be enjoying more satisfactory standards of living, but also because Hungary could be seen as a burden by existing EU members. Therefore, to enhance the prospects of adhesion and reap its full benefits, more rapid growth is needed, which in turn can only be achieved by very significant policy reforms. The chapters in this report have presented the key policy options for the authorities to lay the foundations of sustainable growth. This last chapter integrates those options into a consistent macroeconomic framework, and assesses the extent to which these policies can prepare Hungary for economic integration with the EU by the middle of the next decade.

Box 5.1: The Maastricht Convergence Criteria

As the European Union prepares for monetary and economic union, member states have set up macroeconomic objectives spelled out in the Maastricht treaty. Four criteria have been set up for each member state to fulfil to achieve a high degree of macroeconomic convergence:

(i)   a high degree of price stability: a member state's price index should not exceed by more than 1.5 percentage points that of the three best performing member states in terms of price stability;

(ii)   sustainability of the government position: the ratio of general government deficit to GDP should not exceed 3 percent, and the ratio of public debt to GDP should not exceed 60 percent;

(iii)   exchange rate fluctuations: a member state's exchange rate should remain within the fluctuation margins allowed by the Exchange Rate Mechanism of the European Monetary System without severe tensions for at least two years. In particular, a member state shall not have devalued its currency bilateral central rate against any other member state for the same period;

(iv)   convergence of interest rates: a member state should have had an average nominal long-term interest rate that does not exceed by more than 2 percentage points that of, at most, the three best performing member states in terms of price stability.

For the second half of the 1990s, two broad courses of action are open to the authorities. The first is a strategy that builds on the measures already introduced by the March 1995 package (Chapter I), and that places Hungary on a high-growth path. The key elements of such a growth-oriented strategy would include full implementation of the March 1995 package, further reductions in the deficit, and major reductions in the levels of revenues and expenditures relative to GDP. This fiscal reform would be primarily achieved through the streamlining of bloated and untargeted social programs, accompanied by changes in the tax structure. Rapid privatization of state-owned enterprises and banks would constitute another important element of this growth-oriented strategy. Under this scenario, by 2005 Hungary would

---

* Bruce Courtney contributed to this chapter.

have reduced the size of its public sector to levels more commensurate with the EU average (particularly the middle-income EU countries), and would have also improved markedly its relative economic position.

Under the second strategy, the authorities would implement the minimum set of actions required to avert a foreign exchange crisis, but would not pursue deeper reforms. Under this strategy—labeled the "muddle through" or "low growth" strategy—the Government would fully implement the March 1995 program, but would fail to consolidate the fiscal reform in subsequent years. Under this strategy, there would also be less progress in privatizing enterprises and banks. As a result, the public sector would continue draining resources from the rest of the economy, and the persistence of loss-making activities at the level of enterprises and banks would also divert scarce resources from more productive uses. Therefore, although this minimum set of actions would possibly avert a foreign exchange crisis, it would not generate the improvements required to place Hungary on a higher growth path. Instead, Hungary would grow at rates comparable with the EU average, and the large income gap would not be reduced.

This chapter is structured as follows: the next section presents the scenario of high and sustainable growth. The key policy actions required for the unfolding of such a scenario are examined, and the efficiency gains that would allow Hungary to achieve higher growth rates identified. This section also present estimates of external financing requirements under the high-growth scenario. The third section presents a scenario of more limited reforms and results. The fourth section compares the two scenarios, and the fifth section concludes.

B. The High-Growth Scenario

Creating the Conditions for Higher Growth

As described in the previous chapters, the Hungarian economy still suffers from a number of structural problems that prevent it from growing at its full potential. Enterprise losses remain large as a share of GDP, and financial intermediation is still dominated by inefficient state banks that are not able to identify the best combinations of risk and return. These problems at the level of enterprises and banks imply that scarce resources continue to be diverted from more productive uses, with adverse consequences for growth. In addition, there are a number of other growth-reducing distortions generated by the large size of the state. Indeed, expenditures and revenues have remained very high as a share of GDP—60 and 53 percent of GDP, respectively—implying a massive state presence in resource allocation and distribution, and a very heavy tax burden on the emerging private sector. This heavy tax burden generally tends to reduce savings incentives and the return on capital, reducing the scope for capital accumulation and long-run growth.

The distortions caused by the tax burden are even more severe considering that payroll taxes account for nearly one-third of tax revenues, and that payroll contributions open a large wedge between take-home pay and the final cost to firms (Chapters II and III). As a result of these highly distorting taxes, formal enterprises tend to adopt technologies that discourage employment, and devote a significant amount of resources to tax evasion. When distorting payroll taxes are as high as they are in Hungary many enterprises shift their operations to the informal sector. Although the growth of the informal sector may generate some apparent benefits—as it provides employment to a large fraction of the labor force—it probably entails larger costs. First, informal enterprises congest many public services without contributing to them, which tends to decrease factor productivity in both the formal and informal sectors. Second, informal enterprises lack access to some critical public services (e.g., courts, public-sponsored training) and to capital markets due to their illegal nature, which leads to a production structure characterized by suboptimal size and capital/labor technologies. As a result of all these factors, the return on capital is depressed, and growth performance severely weakened.[1]

The high-growth scenario has been elaborated on the assumption that Hungary fully implements its enterprise, bank, and fiscal reforms (including reforming the pension system) during the next few years. The full implementation of these reforms should eliminate the structural bottlenecks that still affect Hungary's economy, and create the conditions for an increase in the levels and efficiency of fixed investment. These reforms would enable Hungary to sustain fixed investment at levels around 22-23 percent of GDP comfortably, and enjoy long-run growth rates of 4-5 percent a year, allowing the country to start catching up with EU member states at the turn of the century.[2] The relationship between investment and growth in the steady state implies a reduction of the incremental capital-output ratio (ICOR) to around 5, reflecting an improvement in efficiency that can comfortably be achieved with the reforms—successful reformers have been able to reduce ICORs to even lower levels.

In describing this scenario, it is important to discuss in greater detail the major components of the fiscal reform underlying the high-growth strategy. As mentioned before, a sharp reduction of the fiscal deficit is essential for this scenario to unfold, as a sustained recovery of fixed investment can hardly materialize when it also leads to large current account deficits and further increases in indebtedness. In the medium term the fiscal deficit must be reduced by 5-6 percent of GDP to open room for an additional increase in fixed investment of 2-3 percent of GDP while reducing the current account to the levels of foreign direct investment (FDI) and preventing further increases in net external debt. Moreover, although other policies (e.g., exchange rate policy) and factors (e.g., higher growth) could change somewhat the extent of the required fiscal correction, the magnitude of the current disequilibrium is such that it requires significant adjustments in fiscal policy over 1995-97 (see Table 5.1 and the next section).

Such a reduction in the deficit must be primarily achieved by reductions in the level of expenditures, given the need to reduce the excessive tax burden. Therefore, the reduction in expenditures must be deep enough to enable a reduction in the deficit to the envisaged levels, and also enable a reduction in the ratio of revenues to GDP to around 40 percent, which is closer to the average revenue ratios of the OECD, (although still significantly higher than the ratios of middle-income countries). Moreover, such a reduction in expenditures must be primarily driven by reductions in transfers to households, as these are the items that have grown most in recent years, and that contribute less to Hungary's growth performance. In this regard, it is important to identify the items on which most of the effort should be focused (see also the fiscal policy block in Table 5.1).

---

[1] See Loayza, N., "The Rationality of Being Informal", unpublished manuscript, the World Bank, June 1994; and "Taxation, Public Services, and the Informal Sector in a Model of Endogenous Growth", unpublished manuscript, the World Bank, October 1994; and Corsetti, G., and Schmidt-Hebbel. K., "Pension Reform and Growth", unpublished manuscript, the World Bank, May 1994. For more general analysis of policy-induced distortions and growth see, e.g., Barro, R. and Lee, J. "Losers and Winners in Economic Growth", manuscript presented at the Annual World Bank Conference in Development, May 1993; and Easterly, W., "How Much do Distortions Affect Growth?", Journal of Monetary Economics, Vol 32 (1993), pp. 187-212.

[2] The real GDP of more developed EU members grew by an average rate of 2.3 percent p.a. during the 1980-92 period (World Development Report, 1994, Table 2), whereas the real GDP of the middle-income countries in the Union (Ireland, Portugal and Spain) grew by an average rate of 3.3 percent a year during the same period. Hungary would have to grow at higher rates than these countries, as it attempts to approach the EU average from a lower base.

Table 5.1: High-Growth Scenario: Main Economic Variables, 1994-2005							
	1994	1995	1996	1997	1998	1999	2005
Real GDP growth	2.0	0.0	1.0	3.0	3.0	3.5	5.0
Real GDP per capita growth	2.3	0.3	1.6	3.5	3.5	4.0	5.4
Real Private Consumption growth	1.3	-3.0	-2.3	0.8	1.5	2.5	4.7
Real Fixed Investment growth	11.0	4.5	6.8	6.5	5.0	5.0	5.0
Real Exports GNFS growth	3.3	18.0	8.5	7.5	7.0	6.0	5.0
Inflation (GDP deflator)	19.4	27.6	22.0	15.0	8.0	6.0	5.0
Fixed Investment/GDP	19.7	20.0	20.8	21.3	21.8	22.1	22.5
Exports GNFS/GDP	24.0	29.6	31.8	33.2	34.5	35.4	36.2
Current Account (US$ million)	-3,911	-2,518	-2,014	-1,608	-1,229	-1,011	-875
Current Account/GDP	-9.5	-6.2	-4.8	-3.6	-2.6	-2.0	-1.2
FDI (US million)	1,146	1,800	2,200	2,000	1,200	1,200	1,000
Gross External Debt (US$ million)	28,521	28,994	29,169	29,358	30,163	30,804	33,475
Gross External Debt/GDP	69.6	71.4	69.9	66.5	64.8	62.4	45.0
Foreign Reserves (US$ million)	6,769	6,111	6,122	6,352	6,778	7,257	8,150
Foreign Reserves/Imports of GNFS	6.1	5.4	5.2	5.1	5.1	5.1	4.0
General Government Balance/GDP	-6.4	-3.7	-1.5	-1.2	-1.8	-1.5	-1.5
Balance Excl. Privat. Revenues/GDP	-7.2	-5.5	-4.5	-3.5	-2.2	-1.5	-1.5
General Revenues/GDP	53.1	52.6	52.6	49.2	44.8	42.8	40.0
Direct Taxes/GDP	22.0	21.8	21.8	21.2	19.4	18.3	15.0
Social Security Taxes/GDP	12.7	11.8	11.8	11.2	9.4	8.8	6.7
Indirect Taxes/GDP	17.3	18.0	18.0	18.0	18.0	18.0	18.0
Capital Revenues/GDP	0.8	1.8	3.0	2.3	0.4	0.0	0.0
General Expenditures/GDP	59.5	56.3	54.1	50.7	46.6	44.3	41.5
Wages and Salaries	8.1	7.0	6.6	6.4	6.1	6.0	6.0
Transfers	23.1	20.9	19.7	18.9	18.0	17.4	14.6
Pensions	10.3	10.0	9.8	9.6	9.0	8.7	6.5
Family/Child Allowances	4.6	3.2	2.5	2.2	2.0	1.8	1.5
Sick Pay	1.0	0.5	0.3	0.3	0.3	0.3	0.3
Unemployment	1.1	1.0	1.0	0.8	0.7	0.6	0.4
Other	6.1	6.2	6.1	6.0	6.0	6.0	6.1
Subsidies	4.5	3.8	2.7	2.6	2.4	1.8	1.6
Other	23.8	24.6	25.1	22.8	20.1	19.1	19.1
Government Debt/GDP	88.5	84.3	75.7	68.4	64.8	61.5	46.0
Gross National Savings/GDP	12.1	13.8	16.0	17.7	19.2	20.2	21.5
Government	-0.6	0.0	1.7	2.9	4.2	5.1	5.5
Private	12.6	13.8	14.3	14.8	15.0	15.1	15.9

A fast reform of the *pension system* along the lines proposed in Chapter III would result in a significant decline in the expenditures of the PAYG system—from 10 percent of GDP in 1994 to around 6.5 percent of GDP in 2005, allowing for a reduction in contribution rates to finance the first pillar. The introduction of the (fully funded) second pillar would imply a more moderate reduction in total pension expenditures and contribution rates. However, individuals would understand that contributions to the second pillar was not really a tax, but a contribution to an individual retirement account. Therefore, the pension reform would greatly reduce severe tax-induced distortions that have discouraged employment in the formal sector and driven a number of enterprises to the informal sector.

Better targeting of *family and child benefits* would allow for a substantial reduction in expenditures relative to GDP consistent with a better coverage for the needy. Reforming *sick pay* to shift primary responsibility to employers would also result in much lower expenditures. *Unemployment benefits* would also decrease in the medium term as a result of a better growth performance and restrictions in eligibility. *Social assistance* would increase somewhat to 1 percent of GDP until 2000, as the main antipoverty instrument (including support for the long-term unemployed). Increased efficiency and greater participation of the private sector would allow expenditures on *health and education* to remain constant in real terms throughout the period and decline relative to GDP.

The need to maintain a core safety net during the reforms, implies that the targeted decline in expenditures cannot rely entirely on reductions in transfers. Therefore, additional efforts are required on subsidies and government consumption. Although Hungary has relatively low agricultural subsidies, in the wake of the implementation of the Uruguay round the Government could reduce further reduce these subsidies (which account for two-thirds of the total). Also, as the social safety net is restructured to capture most of the poor, housing and pharmaceutical subsidies, presently untargeted and even regressive, could be gradually reduced. Finally, Hungary needs to trim its bloated civil service, which represents 25 percent of total employment and costs more than 8 percent of GDP. To allow for a further decline in expenditures, the scenario assumes that the wage bill falls to about 6 percent of GDP by 2005, closer to regional averages (Tables 5.1 and 5.2), through a combination of reduction in numbers and restructuring of the salary scale.

As mentioned above, the decline in expenditures generated by these measures should enable not only a reduction in the deficit to the envisaged levels, but also a commensurate decline in the tax burden. Moreover, the overall reduction in the tax burden should be complemented by efforts to change the structure of taxation away from the more distortionary taxes, such as the taxes on payrolls. Thus, the reform of the pension system would be complemented by changes in financing the health fund (from payroll taxation to general tax revenues) to enable the overall payroll tax rate to be reduced from more than 60 percent in 1994 to around 24 percent in 2005, and the share of the payroll tax in total tax revenues to decline from 32 to 19 percent during the same period. By 2005, the payroll tax would cover only the cost of the unemployment insurance and of the PAYG pension system, and the lower rate would be expected to generate significant efficiency gains.[3]

---

[3]   The switch from payroll taxes to other taxes should generate efficiency gains under reasonable assumptions for the relevant parameters. See Auerbach, A., and Kotlikoff, L., (1987), Dynamic Fiscal Policy, Cambridge University Press.

Table 5.2: The Civil Service in Selected Economies in Transition, 1993					
	Poland	Hungary	Czech Republic	Slovakia	Slovenia
Number of Employees (1,000)	2,048	1,021	743	414	144
Share of Employment (percent of total)	21.4	26.0	15.5	20.8	18.3
Wage Bill (percent of GDP)	5.9	8.6	4.2	4.7	5.5

The Transition to the New Steady State

Growth Prospects in the Transition. Growth performance is expected to be weak in 1995 (Table 5.1), due to the contraction of aggregate demand resulting from the fiscal retrenchment and the compression of real wages, and the maintenance of a tight monetary policy. Although these factors could actually result in a fall in real GDP, offsetting stimuli are expected from investment and exports, especially the latter, resulting basically in a stagnant real GDP in 1995.[4] Growth performance is expected to remain relatively weak in 1996 (at the order of 1 percent a year.), due basically to an additional fiscal contraction (involving additional cuts in personnel expenditures and in transfers to households). Growth is expected to start picking up in 1997 as a result of continuing increases in exports and investment (albeit at more moderate rates) and some recovery of private consumption. In 1998 the Government will have to adjust the budget to a projected fall in privatization revenues, and this could have a short-run adverse impact on growth. However, it is hoped that the adjustment of the current account will have been largely achieved by then, that consumption and investment will continue recovering, and growth will have acquired momentum. Under these circumstances, it would be easier to undertake an additional fiscal adjustment without disrupting short-term economic activity. Growth is projected gradually to approach its new steady-state level during the remainder of the decade.

Government Operations. As mentioned before, the high-growth scenario assumes a significant adjustment of the government deficit in the first three years to ensure that the current account deficit is reduced to the FDI levels. As shown in Table 5.1., the reduction of the fiscal deficit (excluding privatization revenues) is expected to contribute almost two-thirds of the projected improvement of the current account during the 1994-97 period. The remaining improvement is accounted for by projected increases in private savings—both households and enterprises. Such an increase in private savings (of 2.2 percent of GDP) is not unreasonable, especially given the reduction in enterprise losses that has occurred since 1992 (Chapter IV), and is expected to occur under the full implementation of the enterprise and bank reforms. However, the fact that the necessary improvement in the current account relies partly in an improvement in enterprise financial performance brings an element of uncertainty into the program. For this reason, the Government needs to stand ready to accelerate deficit reduction if performance does not improve to the required levels.

---

[4] At the time of the completion of this report, Parliament was finalizing discussion of the supplementary budget for 1995. Delays in the implementation of the supplementary budget (and the adoption of a less strict wage policy) would probably result, *inter alia*, in a higher GDP growth rate and a larger current account deficit in 1995, relative to the projections shown in Table 5.1.

Investment, Consumption, and Savings. Investment recovery is expected to be sustained in coming years, albeit at slower rates than in 1994, and to gradually increase its share in GDP to 22-23 percent. This is a reasonable assumption, as the acceleration of the privatization program, the retrenchment of the public sector, and the prospects for EU membership are likely to increase the incentives for more domestic and foreign investment and improve the scope for their financing. This increase would come exclusively from the private sector, as public investment is projected to remain constant at 4.5 percent of GDP. Consumption, both public and private, is expected to be severely reduced in 1995 and 1996,. The reduction in public consumption results directly from the fiscal adjustment, while the reduction in private consumption results from real wage compression, layoffs, and reduced transfers to households. Private consumption is projected to start recovering in 1997 as real wages recover after a sharp decline in 1995 and stability in 1996. Private savings are expected to increase by approximately 2.2 percent of GDP over 1994-97, and at a more moderate pace thereafter. During the first three years the increase in private savings would be primarily due to enterprises, as household savings ratios may actually decline, particularly in 1995, as households typically smooth consumption under temporary drops in real income. After 1997 the increase in private savings would be primarily due to households, consistent with the well-known positive empirical relationship between income growth and savings ratios.[5]

Exports and Imports. The recovery of Western Europe, the real devaluation, other measures to foster exports, and the contraction of domestic demand, are expected to lead to strong export performance in 1995. An immediate increase in exports is not unreasonable, as the expectation of a major devaluation probably led many enterprises to under-invoice exports. Export growth is projected to slow in subsequent years, but to remain above GDP growth, resulting in increase in the ratio of exports to GDP to around 35 percent by the end of the decade. Imports are expected to stabilize in 1995 as a result of the real devaluation, the temporary 8 percent import surcharge, the contraction in consumption, and stagnant GDP. Imports are projected to start recovering in 1996, and to grow at rates slightly above GDP in the following years, due to the removal of the import surcharge and the strengthening of ties with the EU.

The Current Account and Foreign Direct Investment. The current account is projected to decline to the levels of foreign direct investment in 1998, after the completion of the privatization program, and the end of the extraordinary levels of FDI associated with it. As shown in Table 5.1, the progressive nature of the fiscal adjustment implies that the current account will remain above FDI levels in 1995, but that it will fall somewhat below FDI in 1996 and 1997. The "soft landing" implicit in the scenario does require that the current account be already below the FDI levels at the end of the privatization program. Otherwise, the Government would be forced to introduce very strong corrective measures in 1998. FDI is expected to reach US$1.8 billion in 1995, of which US$0.8-0.9 billion in the context of privatization. FDI is expected to peak in 1996, when the privatization of the electricity sector will be implemented, and to decline somewhat in 1997, which is the last year of the privatization program. During the last years of the decade, FDI is projected to remain at US$1.2 billion (it could be higher in 1998 due to spill-overs from 1997). This may be a conservative estimate, given that there will be several subsequent capital increases in the enterprises that will be privatized over 1995-97, and that greenfield investments have been over US$1 billion recently.

---

[5]   Enterprises are expected to contribute much less to the increase in savings ratios after 1997, because losses would have been hopefully eliminated by that time. The correlation between savings ratios and growth is reported in Schmidt-Hebbel, K., Serven, L., and Solimano, A., (1994), "Savings, Investment and Growth in Developing Countries", Policy Research Working Paper No. 1382, The World Bank.

Financing Requirements Under the High-growth Scenario

Despite the projected decline in its current account deficits, Hungary will still face increasing financing requirements in the second half of the decade, due basically to the increase in amortization payments projected for the same period (Table 5.3). Moreover, during 1995 the financing requirements may be somewhat reduced by a decline in the level of reserves to US$6 billion (5.5 months of imports), but from 1996 on there should be some yearly buildup in reserves to maintain them at around 5 months of imports. Under the high-growth scenario, FDI is expected to cover 30-40 percent of Hungary's financing needs during the 1995-97 period, keeping the need for new flows of debt finance at around US$3.7 billion. Financial support from official creditors (primarily multilaterals) would amount to US$0.7-0.9 billion, limiting the necessary recourse to new private sources (bonds and loans) to around US$3 billion, which is smaller than the amounts borrowed in 1993 and 1994. The projected decrease in FDI after 1997 would force Hungary to resort more intensively to private sources, but by then the adjustment would have been largely completed, and the current account reduced to very moderate levels, thus strengthening Hungary's creditworthiness and its ability to borrow in private international markets.

Table 5.3: High-Growth Scenario: External Financing Requirements, 1995-2000 (in $ million)						
	1995	1996	1997	1998	1999	2000
Requirements	5,394	5,598	5,630	6,243	6,763	6,514
Current Account Deficit	2,519	2,014	1,609	1,230	1,011	1,016
o/w: Interest Payments	2,366	2,412	2,397	2,395	2,455	2,499
Amortization Payments	3,533	3,573	3,792	4,588	5,271	4,953
Reserve Build-up	-657	11	230	425	480	545
Financing	5,394	5,598	5,630	6,243	6,763	6,514
Direct Foreign Investment	1,800	2,200	2,000	1,200	1,200	1,200
Medium-Long Term Disbursements	3,798	3,656	3,839	5,241	5,751	5,491
Official Creditors	990	656	712	625	302	209
Private Creditors	2,808	3,000	3,127	4,616	5,449	5,283
Bonds	1,200	1,000	1,000	1,500	1,500	1,500
Other Private	1,608	2,000	2,127	3,116	3,949	3,783
Other net	-204	-258	-209	-199	-188	-177

C.   A Scenario of Limited Adjustment and Lower Growth

The high-growth scenario stands a reasonable chance of realization, given the Government's latest initiatives and Hungary's will to join the European Union. However, alternative scenarios under which reforms are only partly implemented can also be envisaged. One scenario that deserves careful consideration involves less than full implementation of the enterprise and bank reforms, and non-implementation of comprehensive fiscal reform. Under this scenario the Government would refrain from implementing additional fiscal corrections beyond those achieved by the March 1995 package. As a result, the fiscal deficits would remain relatively large—around 3.7 percent of GDP, and the size of the state would also remain large—the ratios of revenues and expenditures to GDP would stabilize at levels marginally lower than the high 1995 levels (Table 5.4).

Table 5.4: Partial Adjustment Scenario: Main Economic Variables, 1995-2005							
	1994	1995	1996	1997	1998	1999	2005
Real GDP Growth	2.6	0.0	1.0	1.0	1.0	1.5	2.0
Real Private Consumption Growth	1.3	-3.0	-0.7	-0.2	-0.1	0.5	1.5
Inflation (GDP deflator)	27.6	25.0	20.0	20.0	20.0	20.0	20.0
Fixed Investment/GDP	19.7	20.0	20.0	20.0	20.0	20.0	20.0
Current Account (US$ million)	-3,911	-2,518	-2,320	-2,257	-2,156	-2,110	-2355
Current Account/GDP	-9.5	-6.2	-5.6	-5.2	-4.8	-4.5	-3.9
FDI (US$ million)	1,147	1,800	1,400	1,400	1,000	1,000	1,000
Gross External Debt/GDP	69.6	71.4	72.4	72.8	74.3	75.2	73.7
General Government Balance/GDP	-6.4	-3.7	-3.7	-3.7	-3.7	-3.7	-3.7
General Revenues/GDP	53.1	52.6	52.4	52.2	51.8	51.4	49.9
General Expenditures/GDP	59.5	56.3	56.1	55.9	55.5	55.1	53.6

Under this scenario, no fundamental restructuring of social expenditures would be undertaken, beyond an increase in the retirement age with the objective of avoiding a rise in expenditures under the PAYG system. Export subsidies on agricultural products would be reduced in the context of the implementation of the Uruguay round, but other subsidies would remain constant as a share of GDP. Finally, there would be no significant cuts in government consumption beyond those achieved by the March 1995 package. The maintenance of the current welfare system would prevent a significant decline in direct taxes. In particular, payroll contributions would need to remain above 50 percent of the wage bill by the end of the projection period, implying that the size of the informal sector would remain large.

This "muddle-through" scenario implies weaker growth performance, not only because the ratio of fixed investment to GDP stabilizes at a lower level (around 20 percent of GDP), but also because the persistence of loss-making activities by enterprises and banks, the presence of a large state, and the persistence of high inflation, all imply smaller productivity gains relative to the previous scenario. Thus, growth rates would be expected to equal the EU average—around 2 percent a year (Table 5.3.)—and the large income gap between Hungary and the EU would not be closed. The current account deficit would remain higher than the levels of FDI, implying further increases in net external debt. However, to avoid a foreign exchange crisis, the current account deficit would have to be reduced at a minimum to the level consistent with the stability of the ratios of gross and net external debt to GDP (at around 70 and 60 percent, respectively). Of course, Hungary's external situation would still remain problematic, as the stability of debt ratios at these high levels would imply greater vulnerability to balance of payments shocks and changes in the perception of foreign creditors.

D.   Comparing the Two Scenarios

The two scenarios bring about very different paths for output, consumption, and the current account. Output growth is adversely affected in 1995 under both scenarios, as it is assumed that the March 1995 package is implemented in both cases. During 1996, output growth is also assumed to be equal under both scenarios—the additional decline in private consumption is assumed to be stronger under the first scenario, but that is compensated by a stronger increase in investment and exports. However, growth performance widens considerably over the medium term (Figure 5.1) as the economy starts reaping the benefits of higher investment levels and much greater gains in efficiency under the first scenario. The comprehensive fiscal reform undertaken in the first scenario contributes decisively to its higher growth performance, as the smaller fiscal deficit opens room for a greater expansion of investment, and the retrenchment of the state contributes significantly to the generation of larger efficiency gains.[7]

As mentioned before, the short-run drop in real private consumption is more pronounced under the first scenario, due to the sharper reduction of transfers to households and the maintenance of wage discipline during 1996. However, the situation reverses completely in the long run as a result of the higher levels of investment and output under the first scenario (Figure 5.2). The sharper drop of private consumption in the short run is accompanied by a faster reduction in the current account deficit under the first scenario (Figure 5.3). Moreover, the current account deficit is reduced to the levels of FDI, implying the decline in the ratios of gross and net external debt to GDP. By contrast, under the alternative scenario, the current account deficit is kept above the levels of FDI, implying that net external debt keeps growing. However, the ratio of net external debt to GDP is assumed to stabilize, which implies a limit on the ratio of the current account deficit to GDP (Figure 5.3).

The larger ratio of current account deficit to GDP under the limited adjustment scenario is accompanied by a larger share of consumption in GDP, but that does not mean that the Hungarian population is enjoying higher standards of living under this scenario. On the contrary, the higher share of consumption applies over a lower GDP, as the economy gets trapped in a low-growth equilibrium due to the lower levels and efficiency of fixed investment. Finally, the ratio of government debt to GDP declines to below 50 percent under the first scenario, and remains above the 60 percent Maastricht limit under the second scenario. Moreover, government debt declines relatively rapidly under the second scenario just because high inflation erodes the portions of the debt not related to deficit finance (e.g., bank recapitalization bonds). Therefore, Hungary would be able to nearly meet the government debt target under the Maastrich agreement, at the cost of violating the inflation target.[8]

---

[7]   The ratio of expenditures to GDP is 12 percent lower under the high-growth scenario, contributing significantly to the 3 percent a year differential in long-run growth rates between the two scenarios. This assumption is consistent with recent empirical work on growth. For instance, Barro R. and Lee J. (ibid) report that a 6 percent reduction in the ratio of expenditures to GDP translates, *ceteris paribus*, into a 1 percent increase in long-run growth rates.

[8]   If inflation followed the same path as under the first scenario, the ratio of government debt to GDP would be almost 75 percent in 2005.

Figure 5.1

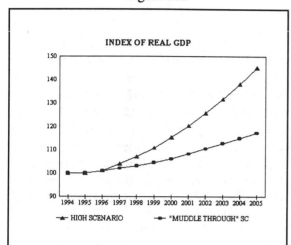

INDEX OF REAL GDP

Figure 5.2

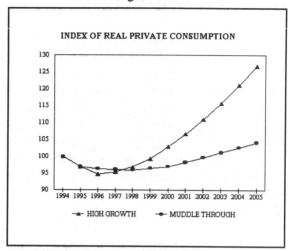

INDEX OF REAL PRIVATE CONSUMPTION

Figure 5.3

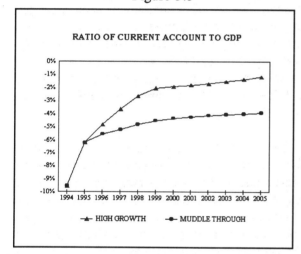

RATIO OF CURRENT ACCOUNT TO GDP

Figure 5.4

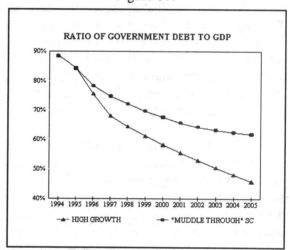

RATIO OF GOVERNMENT DEBT TO GDP

E.   The Strategic Choice Ahead

The Hungarian authorities have had no choice but to implement strong corrective macroeconomic measures during 1995 to avoid a crisis. Beyond this necessary and immediate adjustment, there may be a temptation to pursue a "muddle-through" strategy, eschewing a fundamental fiscal reform and a comprehensive divestiture of state assets. This option would appear to offer some benefits, as the social tensions of the transition would be dampened in the short run. But the strategy would also entail substantial risks and costs. Over the coming years, Hungary's debt would remain very high, and the economy would remain under constant threat of a balance of payments crisis that could be precipitated by a sudden loss of confidence by international investors. Such a crisis would restrain Hungary's access to foreign markets for many years, resulting in output losses and possibly more severe macroeconomic and political instability, thus undermining Hungary's likelihood of joining Europe. Even if Hungary's access to foreign credits is not totally restricted, the medium-term costs of such a strategy would remain high, as the absence of a full recovery of investment and the massive presence of the state in resource allocation would continue affecting Hungary's growth performance. A financial crisis would have been avoided, but incomes would remain low relative to the EU average, and the economy would not be prepared to face the challenge of full-fledged competition with other EU members.

This unfavorable scenario can be avoided, however. Building on the strong popular commitment to joining Europe, the authorities can opt for a bold strategy, and pursue a high-growth strategy centered on a radical transformation of the state and its role in the economy. They can forge a new social contract in which each Hungarian becomes primarily responsible for his or her own future, with the state providing a basic safety net for the most vulnerable, and concentrating its activities on providing goods that the private sector cannot efficiently provide. Now that the regulatory framework and the basic institutions of a market economy are in place, they can privatize state-owned enterprises and banks rapidly. They can decisively reduce the size of the state, and bolster the incentives of individuals to work, save, and invest. They can eliminate the constant threat of a financial crisis and reach the door of the EU as a different economy, ready to take on the competition within the community of European nations and the larger global economy. This is the real benefit of the fast adjustment strategy, and it is worth the challenge.

ANNEX I: THE REAL CONSOLIDATED DEFICIT [*]

---

[*] Roberto Rocha, Lawrence Bouton and Pedro Rodriguez prepared this annex.

A. Introduction

This annex provides estimates of the real deficit of the Government and NBH during the 1992-94 period. The deficit is referred to as real, or operational, (as opposed to nominal), as it excludes the inflation component of interest payments (and revenues) made by the public sector. Under reasonable assumptions about the behavior of economic agents (e.g. absence of myopia), the real deficit concept provides a more accurate measure of the true fiscal stance.[1] *Public Sector* in this case includes the General Government (i.e., the state, the Social Security Funds, the Extra Budgetary Funds, and the local authorities), and the National Bank of Hungary (NBH).

The consolidation of the Government and the NBH is particularly relevant for Hungary, as in the former regime NBH borrowed large amounts of foreign resources, and channeled these resources toward the Government and public enterprises at a low cost. In the process, NBH's net worth (the bulk of which are foreign exchange losses) became large and negative, as its stock of interest-earning assets declined relative to its stock of net foreign liabilities. NBH currently charges market rates on most of its new assets, but still has a large stock of low interest credits to the Government inherited from the previous regime,[2] and does not earn interest on its stock of foreign exchange losses, even though this stock has been recognized by the Government as its debt to the NBH.

NBH's financial situation would tend to improve as a result of two factors. First, the old stock of credits to the Government is being gradually redeemed, and replaced by higher-interest assets, primarily government securities at market rates and repurchase agreements with commercial banks. This factor tends to increase the average real interest rate on NBH assets and enhance NBH's capacity to generate resources in a non-inflationary way. Second, an ammendment to the NBH law was introduced in 1994, whereby at least 5 percent of the the stock of foreign exchange losses is to be securitized every year.[3] This securitization adds to NBH's interest income and tends to produce a similar improvement in NBH's financial position.

Despite these two positive factors, there are no clear indications that NBH's financial situation is improving. As shown in Annex Figure 1.1, the stock of interest-earning assets has continued to decline

---

[1]   The argument for the exclusion of the inflation component of the public sector's interest expenditures from the deficit definition, is that it is just a compensation given to asset holders for their nominal capital losses due to inflation. In the absence of myopia, asset holders do not channel these revenues into consumption, and such an increase in nominal expenditures does not exert additional pressure on aggregate demand. Instead, asset holders will be willing to reinvest these revenues in newly issued government securities, allowing the Government to roll over the existing stock of debt under the same conditions of price and maturity, see Blejer, M., Tanzi, V. and Teijeiro, M. (1987), "Inflation and the Measurement of Fiscal Deficits", IMF Staff Papers, Vol 34, No 4 (December); Van Wijnbergen, S. Anand, R., Chibber, A., and Rocha, R.. (1992) External Debt, Fiscal Policy and Sustainable Growth, The Johns Hopkins University Press, Baltimore; and Rocha, R. and Saldanha, F. (1992), "Fiscal and Quasi-Fiscal Deficits, Nominal and Real: Measurement and Policy Issues", The World Bank, Policy Research Working Paper, No 919 (June).

[2]   The Government also absorbed the stock of low interest credits granted to state enterprises.

[3]   If NBH experiences a decrease in net foreign liabilities greater than 5 percent of the stock of foreign exchange losses, the stock of losses is securitized by this amount.

relative to the stock of net foreign liabilities, producing some further decreases in NBH's net worth.[4] There are two possible explanation for this outcome. First, the average interest rate on NBH's assets is probably still insufficient to cover the cost of net foreign liabilities, adjusted for the depreciation of the Forint. Second, there may be still an unwarranted distribution of cash profits to the budget—if cash profits are distributed, instead of being used to cover foreign exchange losses, the final result is indeed further declines in net worth.

Annex Table 1.1. indicates that, despite the improvements achieved in the recent years, NBH's interest revenues are still insufficient to cover of the cost of foreign liabilities, including the depreciation of the Forint. Indeed, the average implicit interest rate on assets was 17.7 percent p.a. in 1994,[5] below the depreciation-adjusted cost of 23 percent p.a. in the same year (resulting from an average depreciation of 15 percent and an average interest rate on foreign liabilities of around 7.5 percent p.a.). NBH also kept distributing its small cash profits to the Government during the same period,[6] despite the continuing decline in its net worth. NBH has recorded small nominal cash profits, because the average nominal interest rate on its assets is well above the cash cost of its net foreign liabilities (depreciation-induced losses do not constitute an immediate cash cost). However, these profits should ideally be retained and rechannelled into new interest-earning assets, to prevent a decline in NBH's net worth and reduce its dependence on high nominal interest rates—and ultimately its dependence on a high rate of inflation.

Although the above analysis indicates that there is an imbalance at NBH, this imbalance is only fully revealed by examining its operations in real terms. As suggested by the discussion above, high inflation and nominal interest rates on NBH assets may give the impression of large revenues and profits in situations where the average real rate on assets is negative and the NBH is effectively transferring real resources to its debtors. Given that NBH has to pay positive real rates on its large foreign liabilities, it could be running a significant real quasi-fiscal deficit, requiring the generation of real resources for its financing (e.g., from additional foreign borrowing or from seignorage). Estimates of the real deficit of the consolidated public sector and NBH are provided below.

---

[4]   The stock of foreign exchange losses is officially accounted for as an NBH credit to the Government, although the stock does not yield any income and does not have a specified maturity. For the purposes of this analysis, the stock of foreign exchange losses is considered as a zero-value asset until its securitization (when it is replaced by a Government bond paying market rates).

[5]   The interest rates in Annex Table 1.1 are implicit, i.e., obtained by dividing interest revenues (or costs) by the geometric average of the relevant stocks. Although interest rates on Government securities and repurchase agreements increased sharply in 1993-94, such increase is reflected in implicit rates with a lag.

[6] Distribution of cash profits to the budget amounted to 0.2 percent, 0.3 percent nd 0.5 percent of GDP in 1992, 1993, and 1994, respectively.

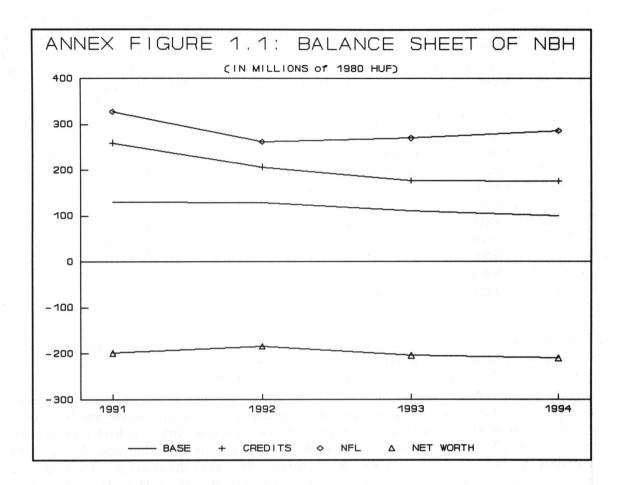

ANNEX FIGURE 1.1: BALANCE SHEET OF NBH
(IN MILLIONS of 1980 HUF)

BASE   + CREDITS   ◇ NFL   △ NET WORTH

| Annex Table 1.1: Balance Sheet and Interest Rates of NBH, 1994 a/ |||||||
| (in percent) |||||||
Implicit Interest Rate	% of Total	Asset	Liability	% of Total	Implicit Interest Rate
17.7	100.0	Total Credits	Base Money	56.9	1.8
14.9	67.2	Credits to Gov.	Currency	36.3	0.0
10.1	60.8	"Old" Credits	Reserves	20.6	5.0
22.2	32.1	Securities	Net Foreign Liabilities	163.1	7.7
10.0	-25.7	Deposits of Gov.			
23.0	32.8	Credits to Non-Gov.	Net Worth b/	-120.1	-
	100.0	Total Assets	Total Liabilities	100.0	

Notes: a/ Interest Rates are implicit averages for the year; Assets and Liabilities are as of December 1994.
       b/ Includes Foreign Exchange Losses.

B.   The Nominal Deficit of the Public Sector

The nominal deficit of the consolidated public sector is defined as:

$$D + i_B B + (i^* + \hat{E})(B^*E - NFA^*E) - i_P C_P = (\dot{H} - i_S S) - \dot{C}_P + \dot{B} + (\dot{B^*E} - \dot{NFA^*E}) \tag{1}$$

where,

D: Primary deficit of the General Government
i_B : Average interest rate on net domestic debt
B: Net public domestic debt (primarily Government securities)
i^*: Average interest rate on foreign debt
E: Exchange rate
B^* : External debt of the Government
NFA^*: Net foreign assets of the NBH
i_P: Average interest rate on NBH credits to the non-government sector
C_P : NBH credits to non-government sector
H: Stock of base money
S: Stock of bank reserves at NBH
i_S: Average interest rate on reserves
Dots stand for changes, hats for percentage variations ($\hat{x} = \dot{x}/x$), and the star superscripts indicates that the variable is expressed in foreign currency.

The 'above the line' deficit in the left hand side includes only four items once transfers between the central bank and the General Government are netted out: (i) the General Government's primary deficit; (ii) interest payments on net domestic debt held by enterprises and households; (iii) interest payments on foreign debt, net of interest received on international reserves, and adjusted for exchange rate movements; and (iv) interest receipts on NBH credits to the rest of the economy. These last two items capture the major sources of expenditure and of revenue of NBH.   The right hand side of equation 1 shows the three sources of financing: (i) net seignorage, defined as changes in base money less interests paid on reserves, and net of the credits extended to the rest of the economy; (ii) changes in the net domestic debt; and (iii) changes in the net external debt. Note that capital losses due to exchange rate depreciations are included in the definition of the deficit, but these can be easily excluded.

C.   The Real Deficit of the Public Sector

The real deficit concept excludes the inflation premium from interest payments and revenues, as it can be argued that these payments and revenues are capital items, not current items, and that their inclusion in the deficit measures would lead to a distorted assessment of the true stance of fiscal policy (to an overstatement or understatement, depending on whether the net debt position is positive or negative).   After some algebra and the application of some identities, equation (1) becomes:

$$d + r_B b + (r^* + \hat{e})(b^*e - nfa^*e) - r_P c_P = (\dot{H} - i_S S) - \dot{c}_P + \dot{b} + (\dot{b^*e} - \dot{nfa^*e}) \tag{2}$$

where lower cases such as d, b, b*, nfa*, and c_P stand for the real variables (the nominal domestic variables are deflated by the domestic price level, P and the foreign variables deflated by the foreign price level, P*), e is the real exchange rate, e = EP*/P, and r and r* are the domestic and foreign real interest rates (r = i - π and r* = i* - π*).

This equation also includes four items 'above the line': (i) the real primary deficit of the General Government; (ii) the real interest payments on domestic debt held outside NBH; (iii) the real interest payments on net foreign liabilities, adjusted for real exchange rate movements; and (iv) real interest revenues from NBH credits. Equation (2) indicates that the real deficit is also identical to the sum of: (i) net seignorage revenues,(ii) changes in real credits of NBH (a decrease in real credits to the rest of the economy add to the amount of real resources generated by the expansion of base money); (iii) real changes in net domestic debt; (iii) real changes in net external debt.

D.   Estimates of the Real Deficit of the Public Sector

Below-the-line estimates of the real deficits of the Government and the consolidated public sector are provided in Annex Table 1.2. The real government deficits were estimated at around 2.5 percent of GDP in 1992 and 1993 and at 1 percent of GDP in 1994. The improvement in the real deficit of the Government in 1994 was slightly smaller than the improvement in the primary deficit,[7] because of the increase in real interest rates during the year. The real deficits are significantly smaller than the nominal deficits because they exclude the inflation component of interest payments. The difference looks particularly large in 1994 and could be due simply to the increase in government debt, as there was no noticeable increase in inflation during that year.

The real deficits of the consolidated public sector are considerably larger than the real deficits of the Government alone, as they also capture the real quasi-fiscal deficit of the NBH. The real consolidated deficit of the public sector and the real quasi-fiscal deficit of NBH look particularly large in 1994, although this result may be partly due to errors involved in computing the foreign financing component, estimated at 3.6 percent of GDP in 1994. Such errors are, in turn, probably due to inaccurate assumptions about the currency composition of net foreign liabilities.[8]

---

[7]   The primary deficit of the General Government, excluding privatization revenues, declined from 2.3 percent of GDP in 1993 to 0.4 percent of GDP in 1994.

[8]   Information on the currency composition of foreign assets and liabilities is not available. The calculations assume a currency basket composed of US dollars, DM and Japanese Yen, whose composition was chosen so that the estimates of foreign exchange losses match the actual foreign exchange losses reported by NBH. However, this methodology may result in errors, to the extent that unreported hedging activities by NBH minimize foreign exchange losses.

Annex Table 1.2: Government Deficit (in percent of GDP)			
	1992	1993	1994
1. Nominal Government Deficit a/	6.2	7.0	7.2
2. Real Government Deficit	2.6	2.5	0.9
3. Real Consolidated Deficit	4.8	5.3	7.7
Gross Seignorage (Changes in Base Money)	3.4	0.8	1.3
Real Changes in Base Money	- 0.3	-2.6	-1.7
Inflation Tax	3.7	3.4	3.0
Interests on Reserves	0.8	0.3	0.4
Changes in Real NBH Credits to Non-Government	- 6.1	0.8	- 0.9
Changes in Real Domestic Debt Outside NBH	2.1	4.3	2.3
Changes in Real Net Foreign Liabilities	- 6.0	1.3	3.6
a/ General Government, excluding Privatization Revenues.			

The estimated real consolidated deficits averaged 5.9 percent of GDP in 1992-94, implying a substantial drainage of real resources by the Government and NBH. Gross seignorage revenues averaged 1.8 percent of GDP during the same period (net revenues were somewhat smaller), albeit with large fluctuations from year to year. These fluctuations reflect the sharp shifts in household savings and the resulting shifts in the real demand for financial assets (and ultimately in the real demand for base money).[9] A substantial volume of resources was generated by net issues of domestic debt—around 3 percent of GDP over 992-94.[10] Finally, there were large fluctuations in the foreign finance component. In 1992 this component was large and negative, reflecting the repayments of net foreign liabilities that year, whereas in 1994 most of the financing seems to have come from abroad. Finally, NBH can also channel more real resources toward the financing of the deficit by curtailing its credits to the private sector. For instance, in 1992, there was a sharp reduction in real credits to financial institutions, although the real resources generated by this credit reduction was primarily used to offset the net repayments of foreign liabilities. In 1994 a moderate amount of resources was generated through this source.

---

[9] Base money was defined as currency and Forint reserves at the NBH. Reserves in foreign exchange at the NBH were added to net foreign liabilities. Therefore, although there is a link between household savings and seignorage this link may be weakened in the cases where greater savings are primarily reflected in increasing foreign exchange deposits--an increase in the demand for foreign exchange deposits by households is reflected in a greater amount of foreign finance, as it leads to greater foreign exchange reserves at NBH, but not in an increase in seignorage.

[10] Note that the real deficit of the Government can be smaller than the real net issues of debt outside the NBH in situations where the Government is making net repayments of its real debt the NBH.

As mentioned before, the fact that most of the real consolidated deficit is due to the real quasi-fiscal deficit of NBH should come as no surprise, as NBH is the institution that effectively services the large stock of foreign liabilities of the consolidated public sector. The reduction of inflation to Western European levels will require a successful resolution of the real quasi-fiscal deficit of NBH. That may be achieved either by a direct absorption of NBH's foreign liabilities by the Government, or by a greater internal generation of resources by NBH (e.g., higher real rates on its credits to the Government, progressive securitization of its foreign exchange losses, and the retention of cash profits). In either case, the reduction of the real quasi-fiscal deficit and the real consolidated deficit will require ultimately a fiscal adjustment by the Government.

ANNEX II: PENSION REFORM [*]

_____

[*] Robert Palacios prepared this annex.

A. Description of the Hungarian Pension Model

The Hungarian Pension Model (HPM) takes the form of two large spreadsheets. The *Expenditure Module* is used to project total pension spending levels for each year between 1994 and 2000, followed by projections for the years 2005, 2010, 2015 and 2020. The *Covered Wage Bill Module* is used to project the covered wage bill for the same years. The years were chosen based on the availability of demographic data from official sources. The modules are not interactive and no endogeneity between variables exists.

Expenditure Module

Pension Spending in 1994

Pension spending is defined here as total spending on benefits arising from old age, invalidity and survivors' pensions excluding agricultural pensions. For each of the years projected, the spreadsheet shows a column for males and females for each one-year age cohort from ages 24 to 100+ corresponding to the minimum age of disability and survivor pensions of 24. For each one-year age cohort, the number of old age, disability, and survivor pensioners respectively are listed for both men and women in adjoining columns. In total, six types of pensioners—male and female old age, disability and survivors pensioners—are shown separately. The average pension for each of the six types of pensioners for each one-year age cohort is shown in another set of columns.

For 1994, the number of male and female pensioners in each one-year age cohort, by gender is taken from statistical data of the Hungarian Pension Fund. Average pension levels for each of these six types of pensioners is also taken from this source. The demographic data is taken from "Demografiai Tajekoztato Fuzetek" #14 (1993).

Pension Fund data was available only for February 1994, while demographic data was based on projections of annual averages. Although the number of pensioners in certain age categories was adjusted based on the previous years' trends, some discrepancy between the demographic and pensioner data remains. For example, the number of male pensioners over the age of 60 implies a pensioner/population ratio of about 105%, suggesting that some of the male pensioners in February probably died during the year or data errors in one or both sets of data.

Monthly pension level data from the Pension Fund for February 1994 was annualized taking into account the two retroactive increases that took place during the year. Spending on orphans benefits was calculated by annualizing the average pension to orphans and multiplying by the number of orphans in February 1994.

Multiplying the number of pensioners in each of the six gender/pension type categories by their respective average annual pensions resulted in a total pension spending projection for 1994 of 426 billion forints. Orphans benefits were estimated at about 10.8 billion forints for a total of 436.8 which corresponds very closely with the Pension Funds preliminary estimates for 1994 pension spending of 437 billion forints which includes own-right, dependents, and under-age disability pensioners. Spending on under-age disability pensions actually appears as an expenditure of the Health Fund in the Social Security Accounts. Agricultural pensions amounting to about 5.2 billion forints in 1994 are excluded. These pensions are being phased out and will be transferred to the central budget in 1995.

Pension Spending in 1995-2020

Those already receiving pensions in 1994 are assumed to continue receiving pensions in future years. In order to track the pensioner stock in future years, the percentage of each one-year age cohort receiving old age and disability pensions is carried forward into the following periods and multiplied by the demographic projection for that one-year age cohort. In addition, new old age pensioners are added at the respective male and female retirement age at the rate which prevailed in 1994. These new old age pensioners then become part of the pensioner stock and are carried through the aging of their cohort just like the rest of the pensioner stock. The rate of survivor pension eligibility is assumed to remain constant by one-year age cohort and gender.

The net increase in disability pensioners is calculated for each year. The baseline assumption for net new disability pensioners is based on the experience in between 1992 and 1994, a period during which the net increase in disability pensioners rose by approximately 30,000 each year. The rate of new disability claims has doubled since the mid-1980s and is the result of policy choices, not demographic changes.

Pension levels for the stock of old age pensioners are determined by changes in the net wage except in the scenarios which involve a shift to price indexation. In practice however, indexation is still ad hoc since increases must be cleared with Parliament and ceilings on increases are apparently negotiable. New old-age pensioners are assumed to receive the previous years' new pension adjusted for changes in the net wage. In other words, the ratio of new old-age pensions to net wages remains constant over time at 1994 levels. This assumption reflects at least two major ambiguities in the calculation of the wage base to which the pension formula is subsequently applied. First, the final two years of salary are not adjusted for either inflation or wage growth when calculating the average wage used as the base for the calculation. Second, the number of years used for the average[1] increases one year every year, which will tend to depress the base wage assuming positively sloped age-earnings profiles. Without a clear picture of the typical age-earnings profile in Hungary, the effect of these two factors is ambiguous. (To complicate matters, Hungarian age-earnings profiles are evolving toward those found in market economies and will therefore look different in the future so that 1994 data would be of limited usefulness in any case.)

Pension levels for the stock of disability and survivors pensioners are also determined by net wage changes unless otherwise stated. New disability pensioners are assumed to receive the average disability pension received by the stock of disability pensioners in any given year.

The average pension level of orphans is assumed to change with the net wage or CPI depending on indexation method and the number of orphans' benefits is assumed to remain constant throughout the projections. Because the population is stable and even declines somewhat during this period, the ratio of orphans to the population remains about constant.

The model at present ignores the effects of declining coverage on future pension spending. This is justified on several grounds: First, the period required for eligibility for disability pensions is only three years. Second, many of those who are leaving the system are too young to affect old-age pension spending by the year 2020, as they will still be below retirement age. Young persons are most likely to

---

[1] All contribution years since 1988 are used in the average.

operate outside the formal pension system. Third, those who are old enough to lose contribution credits may become eligible for a minimum pension which may not be much lower than a pension based on their own earnings would have been in any case. Finally, the unemployed and other inactive persons (like students) receive contribution credits so that eligibility will not fall commensurately.

Covered Wage Bill Module

The Covered Wage Bill in 1994

Again, the building block of the model is the one-year age cohort. The number of persons in each of these cohorts is shown by gender for each of the years projected from ages 20-100+. The 15-19 year old group is also shown for both sexes. Adjoining columns show the labor force participation rates by age group as of June of 1994 along with their respective unemployment rates. These data, taken from the Monthly Bulletin of Statistics (Kozponti Statisztikai Hivatal) were not available for each one-year age cohort but are available for the following demographic groups: males and females ages 15-19, 20-24, 30-39, 40-54 and 55+. These rates were applied to each one-year age cohort in the model to arrive at the number of labor force participants and employed persons in Hungary for 1994.

The average gross wage for the Hungarian labor force is also taken from the Monthly Bulletin of Statistics. However, it has been established that not all of this wage is subject to the payroll taxes which support the Health and Pension Funds in Hungary. Two factors are responsible for the discrepancy between the wage bill and the covered wage bill. The ceiling on taxable wages probably has a minor negative effect on the covered wage bill since probably less than 1% of workers received net wages totalling more than HUF 900,000 during 1994. A more important factor is the use of "wage-like" incomes in the remuneration package. These items which may include vacation and transportation allowances and other subsidies are paid monthly but are apparently not subject to payroll taxes (see Lutz 1994). Evidence of this can be found by calculating the wage bill implied by actual contribution revenues. By dividing total employee contributions by the rate for pensions (.06), we arrive at a 1993 figure of 1110, which is about 23% less than "Wages" in the national accounts and is approximately equal to "Wages" minus "wage-like" incomes (1096 billion HUF). IMF data suggest that the share of "wage-like" income has increased from approximately 12 percent in 1990 to almost 24 percent in 1994, presumably as a strategy for employers to avoid the extremely high social insurance taxes. A separate parameter in the model applies this factor to the average gross wage in order to arrive at the average gross covered wage.

This new average gross covered wage is then multiplied by the number of workers in each one-year age cohort after netting out the unemployed.[2] This produces an age- and sex-specific covered wage bill which can be summed to get the total covered wage bill in each projected year. Finally, a separate parameter is included to account for the rate of arrears which was experienced in 1994 and which has the effect of reducing the amount of revenues coming from the employers' share of the payroll tax. In 1994,

---

[2] The model allows for the inclusion of age-earnings profiles, but data is not yet available and changes in the labor market make them difficult to predict.

the rate of arrears was approximately five percent according to Pension Fund preliminary budget figures.[3] This is the covered wage bill which is used to calculate the implicit contribution rate for various spending scenarios.

The Covered Wage Bill from 1995-2020

The covered wage bills in future periods are determined by changes in wages, unemployment rates, labor force participation, the rate of arrears, the proportion of wage-like income in the gross wage, and demographic changes. Demographic changes are implicit in the model as assumed labor force participation rates and unemployment rates are applied to the number of men and women in each age group projected by the Hungarian authorities. As the number of persons in each age group changes, so does the number of employees who contribute to the system. Average wages grow in accordance with the assumptions under the different scenarios. Chapter III uses the assumptions for slow and fast adjustment explained in Chapter 5. Assumptions from the Ministry of Finance's medium term scenario are used for the period 1995-1997 and baseline assumptions from 1998-2020 are used in the simulations shown in Section C of this Annex (see Section C for specific assumptions).

Wage-like income share along with the rate of arrears are held constant throughout the period in the "crisis avoidance" and MoF scenarios. The "fast adjustment" scenarios include a reduction in this untaxed share of income back to the 1990 share of 12 percent. Labor force participation rates by age and gender are assumed to remain constant. In this way, the positive impact of the disability and retirement age reforms on labor force participation are not endogenized in the model. To the extent that these new members of the labor force join the ranks of the unemployed, however, there could be a negative fiscal impact due to higher unemployment payments. The "fast adjustment" scenario parameters for employment and wage growth however, are meant to capture the positive effects of falling marginal tax rates on labor and higher national savings and investment.

B.   Projections using MoF Medium-Term Assumptions

The Hungarian Ministry of Finance recently produced its medium-term scenario projections which included wage growth and employment projections through 1997. The following projections are based on those underlying parameters along with the following assumptions about the period from 1998-2020:

- Annual real wage growth of 3 percent after 1997
- The unemployment rate stabilizes in 1998-2000 and declines slightly thereafter

The figures shown below apply the individual reforms described in the text under these assumptions. The "no reform" scenario assumes that the current retirement ages, disability rates, indexation rules, benefit taxation, rate of arrears and non-wage like share of income remain as they are in 1994. The term "compression" refers to the taxation of higher income pensioners or some other equivalent reduction at the higher end of the pension distribution which results in a 2.1% overall reduction in pension spending in each subsequent period. As opposed to the "combined reforms" shown in Figure 3.4 of the text, the figure shown here refers to the combined impact of the three reforms -

---

[3] At the end of the year, employers had not paid approximately HUF 30 billion in payroll tax payments to the Health and Pension Funds combined. Along with another 60 billion in interest payments on past arrears, the total stock of arrears seems to have risen to HUF 180 billion as of January 1, 1995.

disability, taxation and retirement age increase. The effect of the indexation reform is also shown separately. It should be borne in mind that the decline of the ICR will be completely dependent on the growth of wages over and above the rate of the CPI. The last two figures show the impact of the creation of the second pillar when a) indexation is changed to the CPI and the three spending reforms are implemented and b) when a) occurs *and* the proportion of the gross wage subject to taxation is broadened. This last scenario is consistent with Figure 3.4 in the text. The fact that the ICR falls further here than in Figure 3.4 is due partly to the MoF assumptions through 1997 and partly to different real wage growth assumptions.

Annex Figure 2.1: Implicit Payroll Tax in Hungary, 1994-2020

Required Tax Rate

- No Reform
- Retirement Age Increased

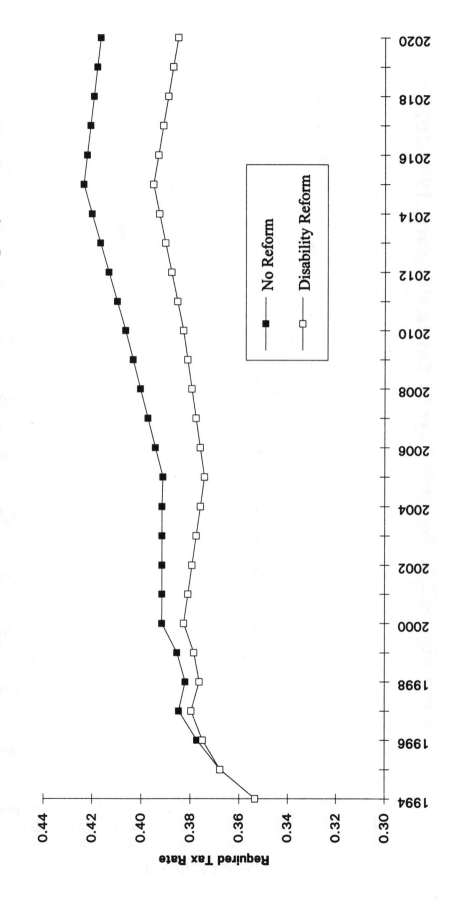

Annex Figure 2.2: Implicit Payroll Tax in Hungary, 1994-2020

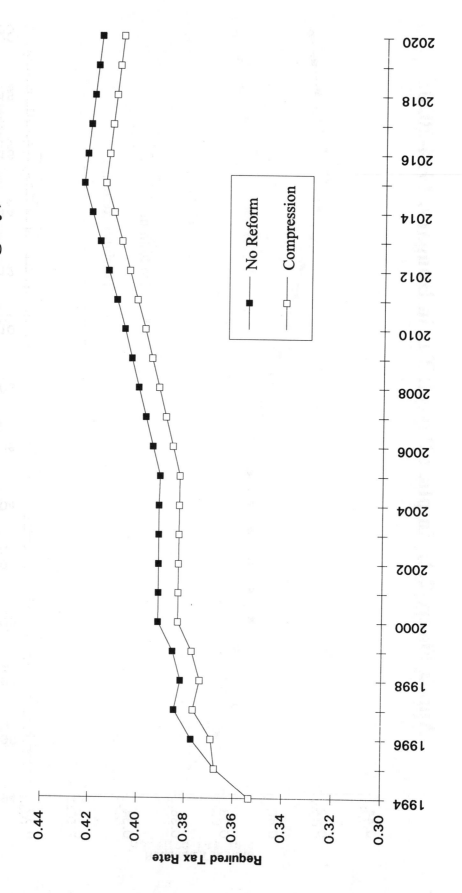

Annex Figure 2.3: Implicit Payroll Tax in Hungary, 1994-2020

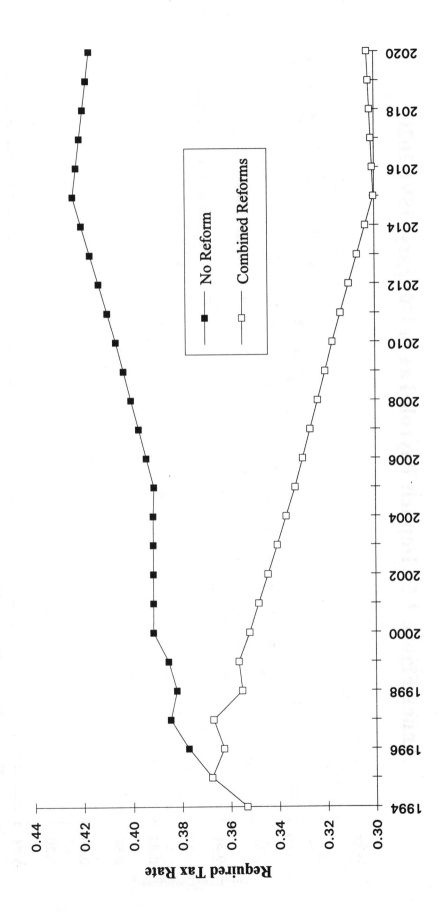

Annex Figure 2.4: Implicit Payroll Tax in Hungary, 1994-2020

Annex Figure 2.5: Implicit Payroll Tax in Hungary, 1994-2020

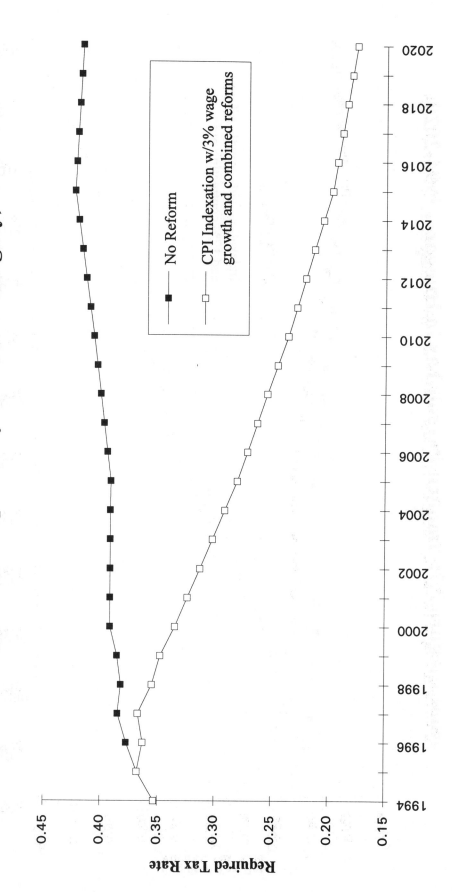

Annex Figure 2.6: Implicit Payroll Tax in Hungary, 1994-2020

Annex Figure 2.7: Implicit Payroll Tax in Hungary, 1994-2020

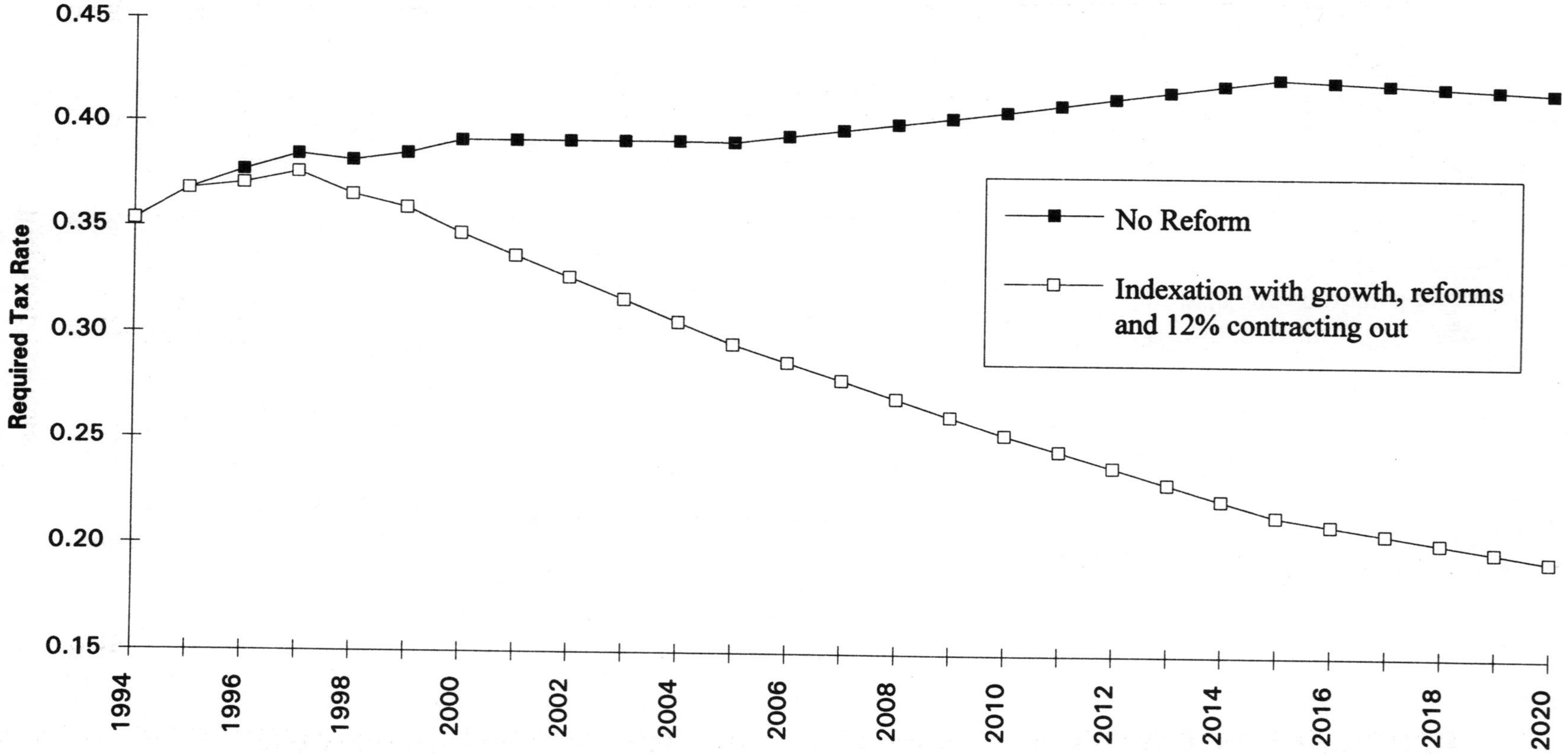

Legend:
- No Reform
- Indexation with growth, reforms and 12% contracting out

Y-axis: Required Tax Rate (0.15 to 0.45)

X-axis: 1994 to 2020

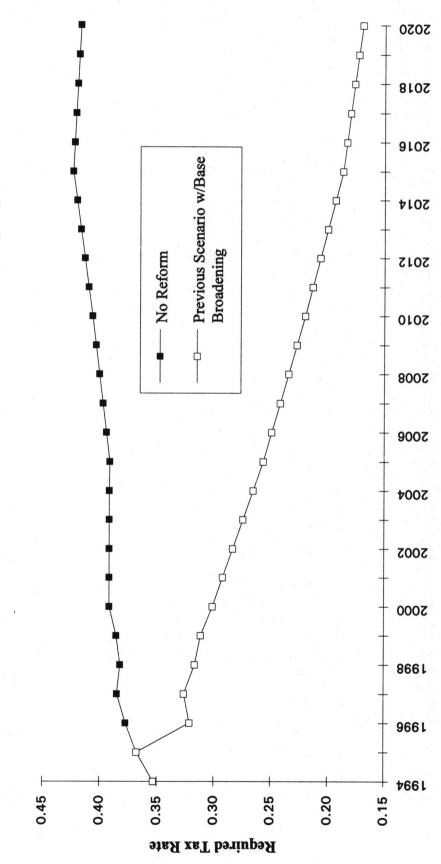

Annex Figure 2.8: Implicit Payroll Tax in Hungary, 1994-2020

C.   The Implicit Public Pension Debt

Any pension reform will be concerned with reducing the future stream of public pension spending in Hungary. There are only two ways that this can be accomplished over the next few decades. Either the pension promises being made to workers today or the pension promises which have been made to current pensioners, or both, will have to be reduced. While there are many ways to do this, the bottom line is that the present value of the pension promise will have to be reduced for some Hungarians if any reform is to take place.

More radical reforms may also involve the creation of incentives for workers with accrued rights in the old system to move to a new system. Pensioners will react to the losses they perceive in the present value of their pension promise while workers will also take into account the perceived cost of the system in terms of the payroll tax. The value of the government's pension promises, the sum of individual claims on the system under current rules, can be quantified under different assumptions regarding the discount rate, life expectancies and pension levels.

This section attempts to estimate the pension debt currently owed to workers and pensioners based on the accrued liability concept, which focuses on the current stock of pensioners and workers, ignoring future entrants into the labor force and possible changes in the future economic environment. The estimate presented here is the funding level which would be required to pay off all pension obligations in 1994. In order to make this estimate, it is necessary to divide the pension debt into two components, the accrued rights of workers and the expected benefits to be paid to current pensioners.

The Implicit Debt owed to the Current Stock of Pensioners

Table 1 below shows the population receiving pensions from the Hungarian Pension Fund as of February of 1994.[4] One striking fact found in the table is that there are almost 400,000 disability pensioners under age 60 which make up almost one-sixth of the total pensioner population. The high rate of disability pensions is largely the result of recent trends and helps explain the fact that more than one-quarter of Hungary's population of 10 million receives pensions. Another important part of the explanation lies in the ratio of female to male old age pensioners shown in the bottom row of the first two columns in the table. This ratio of more than 1.5:1 in favor of women is due not only to the advantage women hold over men in terms of life expectancy but also to the retirement age differential mentioned above. As a result, a female old age pensioner can expect a retirement lasting about 24 years while a male will live only 15 years after retirement. On the other hand, women, on average, contribute for fewer years and have lower pensions on which to live during their final years.   In order to estimate the present value of the pension annuity each of the 2.6 million pensioners in this table could expect to receive, data was collected on the average pension level by one year age cohorts for February 1994 by gender and by type of pension received. These monthly data were annualized by applying the March and October adjustments of 10 and 8 percent with respect to the February starting point. As is true in practice, these adjustments are applied in retroactive fashion to the intermittent months. The annualized pension totals are presented in the table below.

---

[4] This excludes 255,000 pensioners receiving the non-contributory agricultural pension which is gradually disappearing in any case and is funded from the central government budget.

Pension Type	Old Age		Disability		Survivors		Combined		Total
	Male	Female	Male	Female	Male	Female	Male	Female	
Annex Table 2.1: Hungarian Pension System **Stock of Pensioners, February 1994**									
Ages									
Under 60	31864	213840	212050	186723	3768	43329	247682	443892	691574
60-64	140036	221263	75642	46020	115	14292	215793	281575	497368
65+	476135	558592	113355	82637	200	168926	589690	810155	1399845
Totals	648035	993695	401047	315380	4083	226547	1053165	1535622	2588787

The annualized figures show that pensions received by men are systematically higher than those received by women. It can also be seen that disability pensions for those under the retirement age are high enough that their increasing share in the total pensioner population results in much higher spending levels. From the point of view of the pension debt, these under-age pensions are even more important given the number of years over which such pensions will have to be paid.

The value of the annuity promised these pensioners is a function of their life expectancy. It is assumed that the value of the pension would have remained constant in the future and that each type of pensioner values the pension promise by this amount multiplied by the number of years someone of his or her age could expect to live. Fortunately, data on life expectancy by one-year age cohorts for men and women were available from the Hungarian Central Statistical Office and are included here as Appendix 1.

It should be noted at this point that this method will be less accurate to the extent that pension levels are inversely related to mortality rates. This relationship, if it held, would tend to increase the value of the pension promise to pensioners at the higher end of the distribution and make it lower for those receiving the lowest pensions. In any case, actuarial tables reflecting these differences are not available.

114

Type of Pension	Males			Females		
	Old Age	Disability	Survivor	Old Age	Disability	Survivor
Age						
23	n.a.	n.a.	n.a.	n.a.	n.a.	n.a.
24	n.a.	99021	115490	n.a.	108004.2	104198
25	n.a.	108214	100672	n.a.	111236.4	92291
26	n.a.	113517	61243	n.a.	115196.1	98672
27	n.a.	116329	76844	n.a.	114818.4	97510
28	n.a.	119156	74857	n.a.	116091.6	99567
29	n.a.	122864	81294	n.a.	117392.9	102589
30	n.a.	126656	88597	n.a.	117742.7	101848
31	n.a.	125564	87422	n.a.	118778.1	102687
32	n.a.	128377	97734	n.a.	117882.6	103093
33	n.a.	130112	90808	n.a.	119589.6	104100
34	n.a.	133568	93369	n.a.	120261.2	106437
35	n.a.	132015	92263	n.a.	120527.1	107501
36	n.a.	131847	92837	n.a.	121338.6	105220
37	n.a.	136282	94754	n.a.	121828.3	106955
38	n.a.	136618	93005	n.a.	123045.6	107249
39	n.a.	138255	93523	n.a.	124556.8	107067
40	n.a.	138605	93425	n.a.	125144.4	108186
41	n.a.	140312	94936	n.a.	125746.1	109837
42	n.a.	141333	94628	n.a.	127523.1	109921
43	n.a.	143530	94600	n.a.	128208.7	110453
44	n.a.	146594	93690	n.a.	128054.8	110957
45	n.a.	149309	91382	n.a.	129258.1	111502
46	n.a.	151715	92641	n.a.	130223.5	112790
47	n.a.	156473	92319	n.a.	132000.5	113279
48	n.a.	158250	88373	n.a.	134533.1	112524
49	254025	162167	87982	174060.5	135204.7	113769
50	220178	164630	88373	151099.6	136492	115742
51	276062	170143	86988	161397.7	136589.9	115812
52	267149	173725	91927	157577.9	138562.8	118260
53	284639	174480	89605	158501.4	138940.6	117743
54	279770	177167	89899	160712.1	140115.9	118890
55	276706	179587	81266	164601.9	141235.2	122808
56	270130	180931	84036	142998.2	144075.6	128475
57	254528	181644	80748	149490.5	145852.6	131063
58	246301	180861	87114	153660.1	148203.3	132490
59	248036	182526	92151	159270.9	150665.9	131595
60	250275	182400	89717	157172.1	152191	131889
61	194755	183855	108312	157787.8	152806.6	129706
62	197693	185520	117127	156472.5	152638.7	128894
63	203052	189801	132420	155633	154079.9	129594
64	213168	189955	137192	156038.8	154009.9	128279
65	208719	190529	110789	155814.9	154443.7	127033
66	207040	188080	139458	154681.6	153926	127033

Annex Table 2.2: Annualized Value of Pensions for Men by Age and Type of Pension

Type of pension	Males			Female		
	Old Age	Disability	Survivor	Old Age	Disability	Survivor
67	202884	186709	114734	154765.5	154989.4	126796
68	200267	186947	117589	154093.9	154681.6	126390
69	197553	185604	121437	154891.4	155535.1	126390
70	193999	182903	124683	154975.4	155884.9	126152
71	192362	184499	113391	155241.2	155311.2	125242
72	197637	188304	109571	155633	155898.9	124949
73	196434	187269	125033	156052.8	156668.4	124725
74	195356	187017	123675	156906.3	157326	124921
75	192138	183603	119030	157619.9	158683.3	126390
76	204857	188262	130657	161705.5	160600.2	128586
77	205878	185604	128237	161453.7	159774.6	128377
78	205375	182302	144971	161663.6	161481.7	128363
79	200351	179489	128908	162013.4	161005.9	127635
80	194629	177712	135722	160502.2	161285.8	127397
81	191173	172311	119702	160292.4	160432.3	127425
82	186443	165791	129244	159089	159746.7	126851
83	186443	162461	122682	158585.3	161383.7	127075
84	180889	160866	115336	158473.4	159872.6	126823
85	173837	160138	122318	158263.5	159942.6	126404
86	170870	158613	118610	157480	158305.5	126530
87	168114	158907	108872	157326	158543.4	126096
88	164434	165693	106773	156850.3	159201	126432
89	164658	159355	138115	156178.7	159942.6	126740
90	164042	169429	108116	156738.4	156976.2	126012
91	160992	165707	121199	157200.1	153940	125424
92	163720	169933	152569	157102.2	153366.3	126474
93	164602	166953	113587	157018.2	146146.4	126418
94	157004	162013	115938	157018.2	176663	126040
95	164588	161803	114734	155479.1	157158.1	126544
96	164588	161803	n.a.	155479.1	157158.1	n.a.
97	164588	161803	n.a.	155479.1	157158.1	n.a.
98	164588	161803	n.a.	155479.1	157158.1	n.a.
99	164588	161803	n.a.	155479.1	157158.1	n.a.
100	164588	161803	n.a.	155479.1	157158.1	n.a.

Annex Table 2.2 (cont'd): Annualized Value of Pensions for Men by Age and Type of Pension

Another problem arises because it is impossible to ascertain the value of survivor pensions to married pensioners. This is an important problem for women married to workers or pensioners with accrued survivor rights but with none of their own. Increasingly however, the high labor force participation rate of females in Hungary will mitigate this measurement error. It seems clear however, that this problem will bias the estimates downward by ignoring some of the contingent liabilities of the system.

With these caveats in mind, the following tables show the average value of the promised annuity calculated by taking the discounted present value of each future year of benefits over the expected future lifetimes of each one-year age cohort by gender and type of pension. Table 3 uses a discount rate of 2 percent while Table 4 assumes a discount rate of 4 percent. The results highlight the importance of considering the intertemporal fiscal implications of different reform measures rather than concentrating on year-to-year budgetary impacts. For example, while the average disability pension was lower than the average old age pension in 1994, the annuity value of the disability benefit is often higher given the relatively low retirement age of those who claim to be disabled. In the long term one under-age disability pensioner is often more expensive than one old-age pensioner.[5]

---

[5] Another important policy consideration arises from the fact that the increase of under age disability reduces the number of contributors to the system and has a negative impact on the revenue as well as on the spending side of the pension equation.

Type of Pension		Males				Females		
Age		Old Age	Disability	Survivor	Old Age	Disability	Survivor	
	23	n.a.	n.a.	n.a.	n.a.	n.a.	n.a.	
	24	n.a.	2750106	3260835	n.a.	3433223	3312244	
	25	n.a.	2958308	2798642	n.a.	3495449	2900123	
	26	n.a.	3052876	1675331	n.a.	3577079	3063958	
	27	n.a.	3128511	2102106	n.a.	3521837	2990943	
	28	n.a.	3150558	2013852	n.a.	3516018	3015546	
	29	n.a.	3248596	2149453	n.a.	3509145	3066633	
	30	n.a.	3289176	2300825	n.a.	3472250	3003507	
	31	n.a.	3200486	2228286	n.a.	3454062	2986143	
	32	n.a.	3209238	2443218	n.a.	3378699	2954808	
	33	n.a.	3187551	2224670	n.a.	3376588	2939256	
	34	n.a.	3204096	2239779	n.a.	3395551	3005231	
	35	n.a.	3098161	2165265	n.a.	3350592	2988460	
	36	n.a.	3024258	2129466	n.a.	3319276	2878339	
	37	n.a.	3125998	2173435	n.a.	3277498	2877362	
	38	n.a.	3059756	2082978	n.a.	3253406	2835724	
	39	n.a.	3020094	2042879	n.a.	3234672	2780466	
	40	n.a.	2949685	1988194	n.a.	3189787	2757540	
	41	n.a.	2905422	1965824	n.a.	3143479	2745778	
	42	n.a.	2926572	1959450	n.a.	3124136	2692913	
	43	n.a.	2887971	1903448	n.a.	3075542	2649605	
	44	n.a.	2862025	1829161	n.a.	3005233	2603966	
	45	n.a.	2824012	1728388	n.a.	3033472	2616772	
	46	n.a.	2869531	1844847	n.a.	2987029	2587132	
	47	n.a.	2862228	1688722	n.a.	2956344	2537053	
	48	n.a.	2794378	1560503	n.a.	2938792	2458010	
	49	4406640	2758662	1496675	3762726	2877328	2421148	
	50	3819492	2800553	1503340	3179585	2826325	2396654	
	51	4514012	2782077	1422383	3301731	2748330	2330253	
	52	4188489	2723736	1441281	3129423	2788027	2379521	
	53	4462706	2735582	1404865	3147763	2712600	2298744	
	54	4194321	2656089	1347763	3093708	2650141	2248677	
	55	4148382	2566639	1161437	3066250	2583504	2246425	
	56	3860657	2585836	1201031	2573128	2544094	2268610	
	57	3455914	2466311	1096371	2689951	2481129	2229541	
	58	3344206	2455673	1182811	2665586	2521117	2253819	
	59	3187082	2345320	1184076	2604308	2463603	2151763	
	60	3215848	2343702	1152794	2464217	2386121	2067810	
	61	2357748	2225793	1311253	2365559	2290882	1944554	
	62	2243494	2105349	1329201	2345841	2288365	1932387	
	63	2304309	2153938	1502755	2224287	2202090	1852139	
	64	2254326	2008843	1450848	2118649	2091102	1741730	
	65	2207271	2014910	1171628	2002107	1984488	1632285	

Annex Table 2.3: Present Values of Pension Promise by Age, Gender and Type of Pension (Using Two Percent Discount Rate)

Type of Pension Age	Males			Females		
	Old Age	Disability	Survivor	Old Age	Disability	Survivor

Annex Table 2.3 (cont'd): Present Values of pension Promise by Age, Gender and Type of Pension

Age	Males Old Age	Males Disability	Males Survivor	Females Old Age	Females Disability	Females Survivor
66	2026265	1840715	1364857	1987544	1977836	1632285
67	1985595	1827295	1122888	1873630	1876340	1535018
68	1798920	1679268	1056251	1748715	1755384	1434318
69	1774537	1667203	1090814	1757766	1765070	1434318
70	1742613	1492901	1017690	1638918	1648536	1334099
71	1570104	1657274	925526	1519322	1520007	1225728
72	1613160	1536985	894347	1523157	1525758	1222853
73	1438971	1371835	915923	1401757	1407287	1120350
74	1431079	1369990	905981	1409424	1413195	1122110
75	1243516	1188277	770361	1286531	1295210	1031623
76	1325832	1218432	845613	1184571	1176474	941957.9
77	1332442	1039647	718309	1182726	1170426	940420.4
78	1150391	1021151	812046	1046285	1045108	830761.7
79	1122255	1005397	722071	1048549	1042029	826052.7
80	917375	837640	639722	899042.2	903431.2	713606.4
81	901085	812183	564208	897866.5	898650.3	713763.1
82	878793	781450	609187	749859.7	894809.9	710549.8
83	709926	618608	467139	747485.5	760675.7	598964.5
84	688775	612534	439168	746957.9	753553	597777.4
85	661923	609764	465754	602624.5	609017.8	481311.1
86	492770	457422	342058	599641	602784.3	481790.6
87	484821	458270	313973	599054.9	603690.1	480139
88	474208	477840	307921	452338	459117	364614.3
89	474854	459561	398308	450401.2	461255.7	365502
90	473079	328957	209914	452015.2	452701.2	363403.8
91	312576	321731	235315	305213.6	298883.9	243518.9
92	317873	329935	296222	305023.4	297770	245556.4
93	319585	324149	220536	304860.5	283752.2	245447.7
94	304833	314559	225100	304860.5	343002	244714.2
95	319557	314151	222764	301872.2	305132.1	245692.2
96	161361	158631	n.a.	152430.5	305132.1	n.a.
97	161361	158631	n.a.	152430.5	305132.1	n.a.
98	161361	158631	n.a.	152430.5	305132.1	n.a.
99	161361	158631	n.a.	152430.5	305132.1	n.a.
100	161361	158631	n.a.	152430.5	305132.1	n.a.

Annex Table 2.4: Present Values of Pension Promise by Age, Gender and Type of Pension
(Using Four Percent Discount Rate)

Type of Pension		Males			Females		
	Age	Old Age	Disability	Survivor	Old Age	Disability	Survivor
	23	n.a.	n.a.	0	n.a.	n.a.	n.a.
	24	n.a.	1977359	2331237	n.a.	2334780	2252508
	25	n.a.	2140089	2012749	n.a.	2389601	1982617
	26	n.a.	2222228	1212169	n.a.	2458455	2105797
	27	n.a.	2277284	1520957	n.a.	2433590	2066742
	28	n.a.	2307795	1466040	n.a.	2442909	2095184
	29	n.a.	2379608	1574482	n.a.	2451710	2142543
	30	n.a.	2424514	1695982	n.a.	2439633	2110290
	31	n.a.	2374203	1653000	n.a.	2440752	2110105
	32	n.a.	2396100	1824170	n.a.	2401362	2100088
	33	n.a.	2395511	1671886	n.a.	2413992	2101333
	34	n.a.	2423938	1694421	n.a.	2427549	2148500
	35	n.a.	2359568	1649072	n.a.	2409704	2149264
	36	n.a.	2318983	1632862	n.a.	2401628	2082593
	37	n.a.	2396996	1666577	n.a.	2385945	2094656
	38	n.a.	2362401	1608243	n.a.	2383131	2077178
	39	n.a.	2348083	1588319	n.a.	2384338	2049534
	40	n.a.	2309580	1556740	n.a.	2366267	2045614
	41	n.a.	2291233	1550261	n.a.	2347002	2050069
	42	n.a.	2307912	1545234	n.a.	2347853	2023780
	43	n.a.	2294006	1511969	n.a.	2326686	2004459
	44	n.a.	2290106	1463639	n.a.	2288794	1983188
	45	n.a.	2276503	1393294	n.a.	2310301	1992941
	46	n.a.	2313197	1505135	n.a.	2290436	1983798
	47	n.a.	2324688	1371572	n.a.	2282558	1958828
	48	n.a.	2286882	1277095	n.a.	2284871	1911070
	49	3704221	2275071	1234309	2996630	2252924	1895739
	50	3210664	2309619	1239806	2550947	2228857	1890016
	51	3751775	2312295	1182199	2668830	2183085	1850993
	52	3508722	2281689	1207369	2548830	2214617	1890128
	53	3738435	2291613	1176864	2563767	2170541	1839386
	54	3541692	2242806	1138053	2539240	2136342	1812712
	55	3502901	2184800	988649.6	2536483	2098310	1824536
	56	3286307	2201141	1022354	2145557	2082053	1856600
	57	2965841	2116571	940897.6	2242968	2046190	1838705
	58	2869974	2107441	1015080	2240691	2079167	1858727
	59	2757762	2029391	1024574	2164544	2047598	1788416
	60	*2782653*	2027991	997505.1	2064289	1998867	1732217
	61	2057217	1942082	1144114	1997482	1934425	1641985

Annex Table 2.4 (cont'd): Present Values of Pension Promise by Age, Gender and Type of Pension
(Using Four Percent Discount Rate)

Type of Pension Age	Males			Females		
	Old Age	Disability	Survivor	old Age	Disability	Survivor
62	1974092	1852537	1169589	1980832	1932299	1631711
63	2027605	1895291	1322302	1893380	1874485	1576597
64	2000599	1782745	1287553	1818210	1794569	1494741
65	1958840	1788129	1039760	1732411	1717165	1412406
66	1813766	1647675	1221721	1719810	1711409	1412406
67	1777361	1635662	1005128	1634807	1637172	1339356
68	1624349	1516309	953750.2	1538727	1544596	1262083
69	1602332	1505414	984959.3	1546691	1553118	1262083
70	1573506	1359948	927057.3	1454455	1462991	1183945
71	1430275	1496448	843100.9	1359987	1360600	1097183
72	1469497	1400105	814699.3	1363419	1365748	1094609
73	1322538	1260834	841812	1265728	1270721	1011629
74	1315284	1259138	832674.2	1272651	1276055	1013218
75	1153224	1101995	714424.2	1218834	1179863	939749.6
76	1229562	1129961	784212.2	1088722	1081280	865740
77	1235693	972960.9	672234.2	1087026	1075722	864326.9
78	1076602	955650.8	759958.4	970313.6	969221.8	770439.4
79	1050270	940907.9	675754.9	972413.1	966366.5	766072.4
80	866452.5	791144	604212	841374.7	845482.2	667833.3
81	851066.9	767100.1	532890.1	840274.4	841007.9	667980
82	830012.9	738073	575371.8	736565.6	837413.9	664972.8
83	676770	589716.8	445322.3	705993.7	718451.7	565716.9
84	656606.6	583926.8	418657.8	705495.4	711724.4	564595.6
85	631008.7	581285.8	444001.8	574480	580574.7	458832.3
86	474180.6	440166.4	329154.1	571635.8	574632.3	459289.4
87	466531.3	440981.8	302129	571077.1	575495.8	457714.9
88	456319.3	459813.9	296304.7	435273.9	441797.2	350859.5
89	456940.5	442224.3	383281.8	433410.1	443855.1	351713.7
90	455232.1	319559.4	203917.4	434963.3	435623.4	349694.6
91	303646.1	312539.6	228592.2	296494.3	290345.4	236562.1
92	308792.2	320509.4	287759.1	296309.6	289263.4	238541.3
93	310454.7	314888.3	214235.9	296151.2	275646	238435.8
94	296124.8	305572.6	218669.5	296151.2	333203.1	237723.3
95	310428.4	305176.7	216399.9	293248.3	296415.1	238673.3
96	158257.6	155580.3	n.a.	149499.1	296415.1	n.a.
97	158257.6	155580.3	n.a.	149499.1	296415.1	n.a.
98	158257.6	155580.3	n.a.	149499.1	296415.1	n.a.
99	158257.6	155580.3	n.a.	149499.1	296415.1	n.a.
100	158257.6	155580.3	n.a.	149499.1	296415.1	n.a.

D.   The Accrued Pension Rights of Workers

The second component of the government's pension obligation arises from the fact that current workers have been forced to contribute to the pension system, thereby earning the right to claim a pension.   Since 1993, vesting of these benefits occurs only after 15 years of credited years of contribution. Before 1993, the vesting period was only 10 years.

An estimate of the implicit debt owed to workers is more complex than for the pensioner population. In the end, the calculation of this debt involves political decisions and is somewhat subjective due to the fact that so-called "defined benefits" are in fact, very vaguely defined a priori.   This quantification of workers' pension rights for the purpose of paying "recognition bonds" to workers during pension privatization was achieved in Chile and is currently being attempted in Colombia, Peru and Bolivia.   The experience in these countries has been that the process involved negotiations and each country has used different methods based on local circumstances.

The reason for this subjectivity lies in the vagueness of the defined-benefit promise.   For example, two workers of the same age and income level might expect very different age-earnings profiles which, under current rules in Hungary, would lead the worker with the more favorable future earnings path to expect a much higher pension.   This picture is further complicated by the fact that age-earnings profiles as well as the distribution of labor income in general is changing rapidly in the ex-socialist countries so that past patterns cannot be assumed to apply to future retirees.

Several parameters of the pension formula change automatically on an annual basis. For example, the base wage used for the pension calculation is based on an average of earnings, which increases by one year each year.   For example, a worker retiring in 1995 can expect to have his pension calculated on the basis of the last seven years of his career (1988-1994) while someone retiring five years later will find his pension based on the average of his last 12 years (1988-1999). To make matters worse, the last two years of the wage base used in the average are not adjusted for either inflation or wage growth so that the future pension is arbitrarily affected by the inflation rate during the last two years of one's working life.

One way to deal with the problem of the uncertainties mentioned above is to assume that accrued rights should be based on the old-age pension prevalent today.   Implicitly, using the current old-age pension applies the age-earnings profile which produced the current average initial pension. It also ignores the annual changes in pension parameters mentioned above. In the case of the extension of the earnings history used in benefit determination, the omission should bias the estimates downward. The possible impacts of the changing age-earnings profile and the lack of indexation of the final two years of wages are unclear and are also ignored here.

With this in mind, the estimates made here assume that the appropriate pension level upon which to base estimates of accrued rights is the 1994 average pension for old-age pensioners aged 60 for men and 55 for women. The value used in the estimates is the average present value of the annuity for these pensioners today. It is not discounted further to reflect the fact that the pension would not have been received by the worker until he reached retirement age. If the accrued rights using this method were to be put in terms of a recognition bond it would imply a real interest rate of zero percent on such bonds. An equivalent present value would be obtained by paying a bond with a 4 percent real interest rate after having calculating the discounted the pension level for each worker by the same rate.

Just as important as determining the value of the pension to be received is the accrual rate and minimum vesting period assumed in the estimate. While the benefit formula states that 15 years of credited contribution years are necessary for vesting, in actuality many people are eligible to retire with fewer actual contribution years due to generous non-contributory periods for maternity, higher education and unemployment. Also, given that the scenario being considered is one in which accrued rights are being calculated as of today without the benefit of information regarding future contribution periods for young workers, the vesting condition may be considered negotiable. For this reason, two scenarios are presented regarding vesting conditionality. In Case 1, vesting is set at 10 years while in Case 2, there is no vesting requirement whatsoever.

In both vesting scenarios, a linear accrual rate is applied to the years of contribution of male and female workers of each one-year age cohort. Since actual contribution records are not available in any form, an assumption must be made based on the age of the worker. Here, it is assumed that workers enter the labor force at age twenty. Male workers are assumed to have been credited with contribution years in each year after age 20. Given the male retirement age of 60, each year is worth 1/40th of the annuity value of the pension. For women, who retire at age 55, each year after age 20 is worth 1/35th of the expected pension value.

A final problem arises when trying to establish the number of workers with accrued pension rights. The current labor force, including unemployed persons, can be assumed to have pension claims. However, the labor force has fallen dramatically since 1989 primarily due to two factors, increasing disability rates and the growth in the informal labor sector. Much of the drop in the formal labor force can be attributed to the second factor. If some of these workers had contributed to the system prior to 1989, an estimate based on the accrued benefits of the current labor force might understate the actual pension debt. On the other hand, it could be argued that those opting for the informal sector have already forfeited pension rights. In any case, the maximum number of workers with rights would not increase by more than five percent.

Table 5 below shows the age distribution of the labor force in Hungary as of mid-1994 by age brackets. The table summarizes a larger table showing male and female labor force participants by one year age cohorts for the same period. The total number of workers, including the registered unemployed totals approximately 4.16 million. The table shows that about 3 million workers are aged 30 or more and almost 40 percent are over age 40. Through a combination of demographic reasons, university attendance and the fact that younger workers are more likely to move to the informal sector, there are fewer workers aged 20-29 than are aged 30-39. In fact, given current rules, university students aged 20 or more are credited with contribution years in their pension histories introducing another small downward bias in the estimates, at least under the scenario in which no minimum vesting period is required.

Annex Table 2.5: Hungarian Labor Force under Retirement Age, mid-1994			
Ages	Male	Female	Total
20-24	277418	252237	529655
25-29	305012	279182	584193
30-39	660774	615205	1275979
40-54	850828	799740	1650568
55-60	114749	n.a.	114749
Totals	2208781	1946364	4155144

The linear accrual rate mentioned above is then applied to each one-year age cohort by gender and multiplied by the present value of the old-age pensions of 60 year old males and 55 year old females respectively. In Case 1, in which a ten-year vesting requirement is required, workers under age 30 are assumed not to have acquired any vested pension rights in 1994 while in Case 2, the linear accrual rate is applied in the first year of contribution, assumed here to be at age 20.

The average value of the accrued pension benefits of workers by age and gender is shown below in Table 6 which uses the pension levels derived from a 4 percent discount rate from Table 4 above. Not surprisingly, the value of the pension promise increases with the age of the worker until reaching a level which equals the value of the pensioner who has just retired. The male worker aged 59 is assumed to have contributed since age 20 so that his accrued rights are 40/40 or 1.0 times those of the 60 year old pensioner who has just retired.

The ten-year vesting requirement mentioned above as Case 1, would have the effect of changing the average accrued benefit of workers under age 30 to zero. The values for ages above 30 would remain the same. The arbitrary results of such a discrete jump in the accrual rate suggests that it would be politically difficult to draw such a line. For example, as of December 1993, Colombia's pension reform law limited pension claims to persons with more than three years of contributions to the old pension scheme. This was a negotiated cutoff line with no relation to the minimum eligibility period required by law.

124

Age	Immediate Vesting Linear Accrual Times PV 1994 avg.O.A. Pension for 60 yr. old male	Immediate Vesting Lineaɪ Accrual Times PV 1994 avg.O.A. Pension for 55 yr. old female
	Annex Table 2.6: Estimated Average Accrued Pension Benefits of Workers Under Retirement Age, by Age and Gender, Hungary, 1994 (using 4% discount)	
20	0	0
21	69566	63412
22	139133	126824
23	208699	190236
24	278265	253648
25	347832	317060
26	417398	380472
27	486964	443885
28	556531	507297
29	626097	570709
30	695663	634121
31	765230	697533
32	834796	760945
33	904362	824357
34	973929	887769
35	1043495	951181
36	1113061	1014593
37	1182628	1078005
38	1252194	1141417
39	1321760	1204829
40	1391327	1268242
41	1460893	1331654
42	1530459	1395066
43	1600026	1458478
44	1669592	1521890
45	1739158	1585302
46	1808725	1648714
47	1878291	1712126
48	1947857	1775538
49	2017424	1838950
50	2086990	1902362
51	2156556	1965774
52	2226123	2029186
53	2295689	2092599
54	2434822	2219423
55	2504388	
56	2573954	
57	2643521	
58	2713087	
59	2782653	

E.   The Total Implicit Pension Debt

In order to calculate the total debt of pensioners, the number of pensioners in each age/gender/pension type category is multiplied by the value of the pension promise under assumptions of 2 and 4 percent discount rates, respectively. In a similar fashion, the number of male and female workers by one-year age cohort is multiplied by the value of accrued pension benefits corresponding to that age and gender category. In addition to the two discount rate alternatives, the calculation of workers' accrued benefits includes Case 1 and Case 2 options for minimum vesting periods as described above.

The results are presented below in Table 7 and 8 which express the estimates as percentages of 1994 gross domestic product under the two discount rate alternatives.[6]   While the estimates are clearly sensitive to the discount rate used, both cases show an implicit pension debt twice as great as GDP. The conventional public debt, (ie., the debt owed to domestic bondholders) in Hungary by comparison, is only about two-thirds of GDP in 1994. Although the methodology used differed from the one presented here, a recent study of seven OECD countries found similar relative magnitudes. According to the results of that study, Hungary is probably closest to Italy which had the highest pension debt of the seven countries (van der Noord and Herd 1993).

Annex Table 2.7: Total Implicit Pension Debt as a Percentage of 1994 GDP Hungary 1994, Using 2 Percent Discount Rate

	% of 1994 GDP
Workers (a)	142
Pensioners	107
	249
Workers (b)	132
Pensioners	107
	239

(a) = Case 2
(b) = Case 1 (10 year vesting)

Annex Table 2.8: Total Implicit Pension Debt as a Percentage of 1994 GDP Hungary 1994, Using 4 Percent Discount Rate

	of 1994 GDP
Workers (a)	120
Pensioners	93
	213
Workers (b)	112
Pensioners	93
	204

(a) = Case 2
(b) = Case 2 (10 year vesting)

---

[6] This reflects the most recent IMF estimates of 1994 GDP as of January 1995 of 4314.5 billion HUF.

Appendix Table 2.1A: Hungarian Life Expectancy by Gender and Age		
Age	Male Life Expectancy	Female Life Expectancy
20	46.04	55.03
21	45.1	54.05
22	44.16	53.08
23	43.22	52.1
24	42.29	51.13
25	41.36	50.15
26	40.42	49.18
27	39.5	48.21
28	38.57	47.24
29	37.66	46.27
30	36.74	45.31
31	35.84	44.34
32	34.94	43.39
33	34.06	42.44
34	33.18	41.5
35	32.31	40.57
36	31.46	39.64
37	30.62	38.72
38	29.78	37.8
39	28.96	36.89
40	28.15	35.99
41	27.36	35.09
42	26.57	34.19
43	25.79	33.3
44	25.02	32.41
45	24.27	31.53
46	23.52	30.65
47	22.79	29.78
48	22.07	28.93
49	21.38	28.06
50	20.69	27.21
51	20.03	26.37
52	19.37	25.54
53	18.73	24.71
54	18.1	23.89
55	17.48	23.07
56	16.87	22.26
57	16.27	21.46
58	15.68	20.67
59	15.09	19.88

Appendix Table 2.1A (cont'd): Hungarian Life Expectancy by Gender and Age		
Age	Male Life Expectancy	Female Life Expectancy
60	14.52	19.1
61	13.95	18.33
62	13.4	17.57
63	12.86	16.81
64	12.34	16.07
65	11.83	15.35
66	11.34	14.63
67	10.86	13.93
68	10.39	13.25
69	9.93	12.58
70	9.48	11.92
71	9.04	11.28
72	8.61	10.66
73	8.17	10.05
74	7.73	9.46
75	7.29	8.88
76	6.86	8.32
77	6.46	7.81
78	6.08	7.3
79	5.71	6.81
80	5.34	6.34
81	4.99	5.89
82	4.66	5.45
83	4.33	5.03
84	4.02	4.63
85	3.73	4.25
86	3.44	3.9
87	3.18	3.56
88	2.93	3.24
89	2.69	2.95
90	2.47	2.67
91	2.26	2.42
92	2.07	2.19
93	1.89	1.97
94	1.72	1.77
95	1.56	1.59
96	1.42	1.43
97	1.29	1.27
98	1.13	1.12
99	0.94	0.94
100	0.64	0.66

Appendix Table 2.2A: Consolidated Budget of the Health Insurance Fund

HUF millions — ITEM	1992 actual	1993 preliminary	1993 actual	1994 budgeted	1994 preliminary	1995 budgeted	93/92 actual	93 act/prel	94/93 prel/act	94 prel/budg	95/94 budgeted
I Contribution revenues	209,351	234,328	245,207	276,822	284,891	333,798	117.13%	104.64%	116.18%	102.91%	120.58%
II Contributions paid by the Budget	2,600	5,800	5,800	7,000	7,000	10,400	223.08%	100.00%	120.69%	100.00%	148.57%
III Extraordinary revenues from collecting arrears	0	0	0	0	7,828	15,912					
IV Revenues from the Budget for state-financed services	0	2,500	2,500	5,500	5,500	2,500		100.00%	220.00%	100.00%	45.45%
V Other social insurance revenues	9,066	11,179	12,580	14,141	14,141	12,765	138.76%	112.53%	112.41%	100.00%	90.27%
VI Interest earned	2,503	400	464	256	256	50	18.54%	116.00%	55.17%	100.00%	19.53%
VII Returns on assets transferred by the State	0	2,216	0	7,109	7,109	500				100.00%	7.03%
VIII Revenues for replenishing the liquidity reserve	0	3,600	0	3,600	3,600	0				100.00%	
IX Transfers from the Budget for covering wage increases	1,660	2,371	2,371	0	7,410	0	142.83%	100.00%	312.53%		
X Contributions paid by the Pension Insurance Fund	32,337	38,586	38,315	45,286	48,547	56,794	118.49%	99.30%	126.70%	107.20%	125.41%
XI Asset transfer for balancing the budget	0	0	0	0	0	0					
XII Operational revenues	0	0	0	712	1,796	2,765				252.25%	388.34%
XIII Other revenues	492	0	88	6,130	6,130	535	17.89%		6965.91%	100.00%	
XIV TOTAL REVENUES	258,009	300,980	307,325	366,556	394,208	436,019	119.11%	102.11%	128.27%	107.54%	118.95%
XV In-kind provisions	156,203	185,371	186,873	225,780	243,690	270,412	119.63%	100.81%	130.40%	107.93%	119.77%
of which xv/1 *Pharmaceutical and other medication subsidies*	42,962	52,000	54,233	57,700	68,200	75,202	126.23%	104.29%	125.75%	118.20%	130.33%
xvi Cash benefits	72,895	87,750	88,581	98,870	109,260	116,301	121.52%	100.95%	123.34%	110.51%	117.63%
of which xvi/1 *Under retirement age disability pensions*	36,455	45,050	45,034	54,160	57,800	69,616	123.53%	99.96%	128.35%	106.72%	128.54%
xvi/2 *Sick pay*	28,912	34,000	35,255	34,100	41,500	34,835	121.94%	103.69%	117.71%	121.70%	102.16%
xvi *Temporarily financed provisions*	18,341	22,210	22,467	0	0	0	122.50%	101.16%			
xvii Administrative expenses shared with the Pension Insurance Fund	762	698	6,367	1,132	830	674	835.56%	912.18%	13.04%	73.32%	59.54%
xviii Administrative expenses	3,673	5,973	327	7,017	8,401	11,198	8.90%	5.47%	2569.11%	119.72%	159.58%
xix Contributions paid to the Pension Insurance Fund	22,233	26,764	27,017	30,155	33,325	36,524	121.52%	100.95%	123.35%	110.51%	121.12%
xx Replenishing reserves	5,215	3,600	1,402	3,600	3,600	0	26.88%	38.94%	256.78%	100.00%	
xxi Other expenses	421	5	16	2	2	910	3.80%	320.00%	12.50%	100.00%	45500.00%
xxii TOTAL EXPENSES (A)	279,743	332,371	333,050	366,556	399,108	436,019	119.06%	100.20%	119.83%	108.88%	118.95%
xxiii *BALANCE (A)*	*-21,734*	*-31,391*	*-25,725*	*0*	*-4,900*	*0*	*118.36%*	*81.95%*	*19.05%*		
xxiv TOTAL EXPENSES NET OF DISABILITY PENSIONS (B)	243,288	287,321	288,016	312,396	341,308	366,403	118.38%	100.24%	118.50%	109.25%	117.29%
xxv *BALANCE (B)*	*14,721*	*13,659*	*19,309*	*54,160*	*52,900*	*69,616*	*131.17%*	*141.36%*	*273.97%*	*97.67%*	*128.54%*
xxvi TOTAL EXPENSES NET OF DISABILITY PENSIONS AND TEMPORARILY FINANCED PROVISIONS (C)	224,947	265,111	265,549	312,396	341,308	366,403	118.05%	100.17%	128.53%	109.25%	117.29%
xxvii *BALANCE (C)*	*33,062*	*35,869*	*41,776*	*54,160*	*52,900*	*69,616*	*126.36%*	*116.47%*	*126.63%*	*97.67%*	*128.54%*
Pharmaceutical subsidies/total expenditures	15.36%	15.65%	16.28%	15.74%	17.09%	17.25%					
Pharmaceutical subsidies/total revenues	16.65%	17.28%	17.65%	15.74%	17.30%	17.25%					
Pharmaceutical subsidies/total revenues net of ghost revenues	16.65%	17.41%	17.65%	16.05%	17.62%	17.27%					

Appendix Table 2.2A (cont'd): Consolidated Budget of the Pension Insurance Fund

HUF millions	as of 94.11.25. ITEM	1992 actual	1993 preliminary	1993 actual	1994 budgeted	1994 preliminary	1995 budgeted	93/92 actual	93 act/prel	94/93 prel/act	94 prel/budg	95/94 budgeted
I/1	Employer's contribution	207,648	228,017	239,695	274,294	286,539	338,805	115.43%	105.12%	119.54%	104.46%	123.52%
I/2	Employee's contributions	54,146	60,840	66,652	69,810	74,010	81,321	123.10%	109.55%	111.04%	106.02%	116.49%
I/3	Contribution on unemployment benefits	10,013	15,435	12,558	18,344	9,410	12,700	125.42%	81.36%	74.93%	51.30%	69.23%
I/4	Contribution on certain social benefits	0	1,000	304	1,400	2,870	1,660		30.40%	944.08%	205.00%	118.57%
II	Revenues from arrears amnesty	na	na	na	na	10,172	19,488					
III	Late payment fees, charges	9,902	12,426	13,584	14,098	14,098	11,714	137.18%	109.32%	103.78%	100.00%	83.09%
IV	Interest earned	6,497	3,600	3,968	2,304	2,304	4,835	61.07%	110.22%	58.06%	100.00%	209.85%
V	Returns on assets transferred by the State	0	2,784	0	8,931	8,931	0				100.00%	0.00%
VI	Revenues for replenishing the liquidity reserve	0	3,600	0	3,600	3,600	3,636				100.00%	101.00%
VII	Contributions paid by the Health Insurance Fund	22,233	26,764	27,017	30,155	33,325	36,524	121.52%	100.95%	123.35%	110.51%	121.12%
VIII	Operational revenues	0	0	118	118	812	395			688.14%	688.14%	334.75%
IX	Other revenues	790	395	1,118	311	311	339	141.52%	283.04%	27.82%	100.00%	109.00%
X	TOTAL REVENUES	311,229	354,861	364,896	423,365	446,382	511,417	117.24%	102.83%	122.33%	105.44%	120.80%
XI	Own-right, old-age pensions	215,980	258,550	255,461	304,280	324,250	380,381	118.28%	98.81%	126.93%	106.56%	125.01%
XII	Dependent pensions	36,255	42,900	39,091	49,520	55,020	63,320	107.82%	91.12%	140.75%	111.11%	127.87%
XIII	Agricultural provisions	0	0	4,782	5,220	5,230	0			109.37%	100.19%	
XIV	Temporarily financed provisions	21,848	25,490	25,784	0	0	0	118.02%	101.15%			
XV	Expenses shared with the Health Insurance Fund (mailing, travel, legal)	908	802	843	918	920	1,609	92.84%	105.11%	109.13%	100.22%	175.27%
XVI	Administrative expenses	4,086	6,613	6,567	7,551	8,245	7,575	160.72%	99.30%	125.55%	109.19%	100.32%
XVII	Replenishment of the liquidity reserve	2,797	3,600	1,403	3,600	3,600	0	50.16%	38.97%	256.59%	100.00%	
XVIII	Interests and returns on investments (transferred to reserves)	6,482	0	0	0	0	0	0.00%				
XIX	Expenses of asset management	15	45	47	18	18	90	313.33%	104.44%	38.30%	100.00%	500.00%
XX	Other expenses	139	0	5	0	0	1,648	3.60%				
XXI	Payments to the Health Insurance Fund	32,337	38,586	38,315	51,416	54,677	56,794	118.49%	99.30%	142.70%	106.34%	110.46%
XXII	TOTAL EXPENSES	320,847	376,586	372,298	422,523	451,960	511,417	116.04%	98.86%	121.40%	106.97%	121.04%
XXIII	*BALANCE*	*-9,618*	*-21,725*	*-7,402*	*842*	*-5,578*	*0*	*76.96%*	*34.07%*	*75.36%*	*-662.47%*	*0.00%*
	Memorandum items											
a)	Under retirement age disability and accident provisions financed by the Health Insurance Fund	36,455	45,050	45,034	54,160	57,800	69,616	123.53%	99.96%	128.35%	106.72%	128.54%
b)	TOTAL REVENUES OF THE HEALTH INSURANCE FUND	235,776	274,216	280,308	336,401	360,883	436,019	118.89%	102.22%	128.75%	107.28%	129.61%
c)	Contribution revenues	211,951	240,128	245,207	283,822	284,891	360,110	115.69%	102.12%	116.18%	100.38%	126.88%
d)	TOTAL EXPENDITURES OF THE HEALTH INSURANCE FUND	267,511	305,607	306,033	336,401	365,783	436,019	118.84%	100.14%	119.52%	108.73%	129.61%
e)	Cash and in-kind benefits excl. jointly financed provisions	229,098	273,121	275,454	324,650	352,950	386,713	120.23%	100.85%	128.13%	108.72%	119.12%
f)	TOTAL PENSION EXPENDITURES	357,302	421,636	417,332	476,683	509,760	581,033	116.80%	98.98%	122.15%	106.94%	121.89%
g)	TOTAL PENSION REVENUES (incl. proportional HIF revenues)	344,607	395,284	406,144	477,525	503,408	581,033	117.86%	102.75%	123.95%	105.43%	121.68%
h)	*BALANCE OF THE PENSION SYSTEM*	*-12,695*	*-26,352*	*-11,188*	*842*	*-6,352*	*0*	*88.13%*	*42.45%*	*56.78%*	*-754.43%*	*0.00%*
	Total old age expenditures	284,572	340,036	337,649	410,436	439,177	500,495	118.65%	99.30%	130.07%	107.00%	121.94%
	(net of admin., financial and temporary expenses/provisions)											
	Total pension expenditures	321,027	385,086	382,683	464,596	496,977	570,111	119.21%	99.38%	129.87%	106.97%	122.71%
	(net of admin., financial and temporary expenses/provisions) PLUS under-age disability pensions)											

ANNEX III: SUMMARIZED DESCRIPTION OF THE MODEL USED IN THE PROJECTIONS [*]

---

[*] Bruce Courtney prepared this annex.

A. Introduction

This annex describes briefly the macroeconomic model underlying the projections in Chapter 5. The model is a variant of the Revised Minimum Standard Macroeconomic Model Extended (RMSM-X) and comprises three components: a consistency framework, a projection model, and a debt module.[1]

The consistency framework assembles the historical data into a flow-of-funds accounting format for the base year, which is composed of a series of identities that ensure intersectoral consistency. The projection model combines the consistency framework and a simple behavioral structure elaborated below. The debt module supplies detailed projections of debt stocks, interest payments and capital flows by creditor and borrower.

B. Description of the RMSM-X Model

The consistency framework divides the Hungarian economy into four "sectors", each with its own budget constraint. The flow-of-funds approach ensures that total sources (revenues) equals total uses (expenditures) for each sector, and that each source of funds for one sector is also a use of funds for another. This double entry accounting framework ensures consistency in the data by requiring that the budget constraints for all economic sectors be satisfied simultaneously. The core of the model can be expressed in a system of nine equations, four of which represent the budget constraint for each sector, and five of which represent equilibrium in five markets.

C. Budget Constraints

The four sectors are: (i) the General Government, including the state, local authorities, social security and other central and local extrabudgetary funds and budgetary institutions; (ii) the financial sector, including the central bank, the commercial banks, and other financial institutions; (iii) the household and enterprise sector, often called "private" sector, although it also includes public non-financial enterprises; and (iv) the external sector. The budget constraint for each sector is expressed as:

Revenue(i) - Expenditure(i) = Increase in assets(i) - Increase in liabilities(i)

Where (i) represents each of the four sectors. These budget constraints should be familiar, as they correspond to the fiscal accounts of the Government, the monetary survey of the financial institutions, the savings equation of the "private" sector, and the Balance of Payments, respectively. The relevant equations are presented below:

$$DT + IT + NTR - Cg - SUB - Tgp - i.Bgp - i.CRg - E.i.F^*g = Ig + KTgp - KRpg - \Delta Bg - \Delta CRg - E.\Delta F^*g \tag{1}$$

Equation (1) indicates that the government's current income minus its current expenditure must equal the changes in the Government's net worth. Current income includes direct (DT) and indirect (IT) taxes and current non-tax revenue (NTR). Current expenditure is defined as transfers to the private sector

[1] Greater detail is provided in World Bank (1991) "RMSM-X: An Exposition", World Bank, Washington, D.C.

(Tgp), subsidies to the private sector (SUB), government consumption (Cg), and interest payments on domestic (iBgp) and foreign ($i^*.E.F^*g$) debts, where i and i^* stand for the domestic and foreign interest rates, respectively, and E stands for the exchange rate. Changes in net worth are given by the sum of public investment (Ig) and capital transfers (KTgp) less capital revenue (KRpg), and borrowing from the private sector (ΔBg), the monetary sector (ΔCRg), and the external sector ($E\Delta F^*g$), where Δ stands for the difference operator.

$$\Delta M = \Delta CRp + \Delta CRg + E^*(\Delta R^*m - \Delta F^*m) - \Delta NOL \tag{2}$$

Equation (2) states that the change in the money supply (ΔM) is equal to credit creation ($\Delta CRp + \Delta CRg$) and net external asset accumulation $E.(\Delta R^*m - \Delta F^*m)$, minus the change in net other liabilities (ΔNOL).

$$IM - X + E.i.F^*t + E.PRpf - E.i.R^*t - E.Tfp = E.DFI + E.(\Delta F^*t - \Delta R^*t) + E.KNEI \tag{3}$$

Equation (3) states that the current account deficit must be financed by direct foreign investment (E.DFI), total net debt accumulation $E.(\Delta F^*t - \Delta R^*t)$, and net other capital inflows (E.KNEI). The current account deficit is defined as the excess of imports of good and nonfactor services (IM), interest payments ($E.i.F^*t$) and net profit remittances (E.PRpf) over exports of goods and non-factor services (X), net transfers from abroad (E.Tgp) and interest receipts ($E.i.R^*t$).

$$GDPfc + Tgp + i.Bgp + i.CRt + E.i.R^*t + E.Tfp - DT - NTR - E.i.F^*p - E.PRpf - Cp = Ip + \Delta M + \Delta Bg + KRpg + \Delta NOL - E.\Delta F^*p - KTgp - E.DFI - E.KNEI - \Delta CRp \tag{4}$$

Equation (4) states that GDP at factor cost (GDPfc = GDP - IT + SUB), transfers from the government (Tgp) and from abroad (E.Tfp) and interest income ($i.Bgp + i.CRt + E.i.R^*t$) minus direct taxes (DT), non-tax government revenue (NTR), interest payments on external debt ($E.i.F^*p$), profit remittances to foreign investors (E.PRpf), and private consumption must equal private investment (Ip), changes in money holdings (ΔM), net domestic lending ($\Delta Bg - \Delta CRp$), capital revenues of the government (KRpg) and other liabilities (ΔNOL), minus capital transfers (KTgp), foreign borrowing ($E.\Delta F^*p$), and other foreign inflows (E.DFI + E.KNEI).

D.   Market Clearing Conditions

In addition to the budget constraints, five markets, including one goods market and four asset markets are defined: (i) goods market; (ii) money market; (iii) foreign credit market; (iv) bond market; and (v) domestic credit market.

$$M^D = M^S \tag{5}$$
$$B^D = B^S \tag{6}$$
$$Fp^D + Fm^D + Fg^D = Ft^S \tag{7}$$
$$CRp^D + CRg^D = CRt^S \tag{8}$$
$$Y^S = Cp^D + Cg^D + Ip^D + Ig^D + X^D - M^D \tag{9}$$

Equations 5 - 8 describe the condition for equilibrium in the asset markets, whereas equation 9 states the condition for equilibrium in the goods market. For simplicity, we assume that the economy produces only one good that can be used for consumption and investment or sold abroad.

Walras's law implies that only eight of our nine equations are linearly independent. In order to have the system determined, we must provide rules to project all variables in equations 1 - 9 except for eight endogenous variables. A mathematical constraint requires that each of the nine equations must contain at least one endogenous variable. The choice of endogenous variables determines the model's closure and will be discussed below. The other variables are projected in 3 ways. Some are assumed exogenously. This set of variables is assumed to converge to a steady state, or to converge to a specified policy target by the end of the period. Another set of variables is determined by a few behavioral relationships discussed below, and the final group of variables is projected by technical relationships with other variables.

E. Behavioral Relationships

The relationship between investment and GDP is captured though the incremental capital to output ratio (ICOR),

$$g^F_{t+1} = (1/ICOR) * (I_t/Y) \tag{10}$$

Equation 10 states that the full employment growth rate (g^F) is determined by both the amount of investment of the previous period, as a share of output (Y), and the efficiency of this investment, as measured by the ICOR. This equation can be solved for Y, I, or the ICOR.

Imports are projected according to the following rule:

$$IM^D = (1 + \epsilon\Omega + \rho g) * IM_{t-1} \tag{11}$$

Equation 11 states that the demand for imports is determined by the growth or the real exchange rate (Ω) and income (Y) and the elasticities of imports to each.

Money demand is projected with the basic quantity theory of money:

$$M^D = k * p * Y \tag{12}$$

Where (k) is the inverse of the velocity of circulation.

The supply of foreign credit is obtained endogenously since we assume that Hungary will maintain access to external borrowing in excess of identified sources of credit. Here the interest rate on foreign borrowing is determined by:

$$i^* = i^*_{id} * F^*_{id\,t-1}/F^*_{t-1} + i^{MC} * (F^*_{t-1} - F^*_{id\,t-1})/F^*_{t-} \tag{13}$$

Equation 13 links the debt module to the projection model. In the debt module, assumptions are made on future sources of external financing and added to the stocks and flows of loans already committed. Together the new and "existing" sources are credit are "identified" and are denoted with the subscript ("id"), so that (i^*_{id}) and (F^*_{id}) are the interest rate and stock of identified debt. i^{MC} is the interest rate on unidentified debt $(F^*_{t-1} - F^*_{id\,t-1})$. The superscript MC denotes the interest rate charged by the creditors who are assumed to supply the required additional credit.

F. Model Closure

The choice of the set of eight endogenous variables determines whether the solution to the model is recursive or simultaneous. We have chosen a set which allows the model to solve recursively. We have chosen a closure rule that checks whether a particular set of policies is consistent with the stated objectives. The consistency of the policy package is determined by looking at the implied behavior of the private sector in terms of investment, consumption and foreign financing.

136

First, targets are set for inflation, real growth and foreign reserves. Second, assumptions are made on the path of fiscal policy variables. The growth equation (10) and assumptions on investment determine the ICOR and the values of Ip and Ig that are consistent with the growth target. Once Y^s is known all expenditure items can be projected, except Cp, which is determined endogenously from the goods market equilibrium equation (9). The endogenous variable in the balance of payments is ΔF^*_t. With this supply of foreign credit, we solve the foreign assets market. The money market is determined by the exogenously given paths for the price level, the level of income and the income velocity. The endogenous variable in the monetary sector is the level of domestic credit, CR_t. The credit market is then solved for the amount of credit that is given to the private sector.

To sum up, this model closure gives us the behavior of the private sector in terms of investment, consumption, and the sources and magnitude of financing, that would make the stated policies and objectives possible. By looking at whether this private sector behavior is plausible or not, we can check the consistency of a particular macroeconomic program.

STATISTICAL APPENDIX

TABLE OF CONTENTS

Table 1.1: Population and Demographic Indicators

	1960	1970	1980	1981	1982	1983	1984	1985	1986	1987	1988	1989	1990	1991	1992	1993	1994
Thousands of Persons								(thousands of persons, as of Jan. 1.)									
Male	4804.0	5003.7	5188.7	5188.1	5184.5	5177.1	5163.5	5149.3	5138.1	5126.6	5116.0	5106.7	4984.9	4972.0	4960.5	4943.4	4922.9
Female	5157.0	5318.4	5520.8	5524.7	5526.4	5523.1	5515.3	5508.1	5501.9	5494.5	5488.0	5481.9	5389.9	5383.0	5376.7	5366.8	5354.0
Urban	3954.5	4789.5	5697.5	6088.3	6126.3	6152.1	5980.1	6193.0	6218.8	6254.4	6277.8	6292.6	6417.3	6435.0	6581.5	6574.1	6557.6
Rural	6006.5	5532.6	5012.0	4624.5	4584.6	4548.1	4698.7	4464.4	4421.2	4366.7	4326.2	4296.0	3957.5	3920.0	3755.7	3736.1	3719.3
Under 15 Years of Age	2529.4	2176.5	2341.2	2356.3	2362.7	2349.8	2325.0	2298.5	2278.6	2258.3	2233.0	2202.8	2130.5	2064.0	2009.8	1958.0	1910.8
15 - 59 Years of Age	6058.9	6385.8	6538.2	6507.7	6476.2	6456.1	6442.1	6437.0	6420.5	6408.0	6406.0	6403.5	6284.5	6317.0	6347.5	6367.7	6380.5
Over 59 Years of Age	1372.7	1759.8	1830.1	1848.8	1872.0	1894.3	1911.7	1921.9	1940.9	1954.8	1965.0	1982.3	1959.8	1974.0	1980.0	1984.5	1985.6
Total	9961.0	10322.1	10709.5	10712.8	10710.9	10700.2	10678.8	10657.4	10640.0	10621.1	10604.0	10588.6	10374.8	10355.0	10337.2	10310.2	10276.9
Percent Distribution																	
Male	48.2	48.5	48.4	48.4	48.4	48.4	48.4	48.3	48.3	48.3	48.2	48.2	48.0	48.0	48.0	47.9	47.9
Female	51.8	51.5	51.6	51.6	51.6	51.6	51.6	51.7	51.7	51.7	51.8	51.8	52.0	52.0	52.0	52.1	52.1
Urban	39.7	46.4	53.2	56.8	57.2	57.5	56.0	58.1	58.4	58.9	59.2	59.4	61.9	62.1	63.7	63.8	63.8
Rural	60.3	53.6	46.8	43.2	42.8	42.5	44.0	41.9	41.6	41.1	40.8	40.6	38.1	37.9	36.3	36.2	36.2
Under 15 Years of Age	25.4	21.1	21.9	22.0	22.1	22.0	21.8	21.6	21.4	21.3	21.1	20.8	20.5	19.9	19.4	19.0	18.6
15 - 59 Years of Age	60.8	61.9	61.1	60.7	60.5	60.3	60.3	60.4	60.3	60.3	60.4	60.5	60.6	61.0	61.4	61.8	62.1
Over 59 Years of Age	13.8	17.0	17.1	17.3	17.5	17.7	17.9	18.0	18.2	18.4	18.5	18.7	18.9	19.1	19.2	19.2	19.3
Total	100.0	100.0	100.0	100.0	100.0	100.0	100.0	100.0	100.0	100.0	100.0	100.0	100.0	100.0	100.0	100.0	100.0
Per Thousand Population																	
Birth Rate	14.7	14.7	13.9	13.3	12.5	11.9	11.8	12.2	12.1	11.9	11.7	11.4	11.9	12.1	12.3	11.8	11.4
Death Rate	10.2	11.6	13.6	13.5	13.5	13.9	13.8	13.9	13.8	13.4	13.2	13.3	13.9	14.1	14.0	14.4	14.6
Rate of Natural Increase	4.5	3.1	0.3	-0.2	-1.0	-2.0	-2.0	-1.7	-1.7	-1.5	-1.5	-1.9	-2.0	-2.0	-1.7	-2.6	-3.2

Data of the Population Census after 1989 are not comparable with the 1981-89 figures.
Sources: Statistical Yearbook and Central Statistical Office.

142

Table 1.2: Employment by Sector

	1984	1985	1986	1987	1988	1989	1990	1991	1992	1993
	(thousands of persons, as of Jan. 1.)									
Agriculture	1072.0	1035.1	986.2	942.7	911.5	887.8	863.3	752.2	588.9	391.9
Industry	1907.8	1895.9	1884.0	1867.7	1842.6	1804.9	1768.0	1717.1	1499.5	1375.1
Manufacturing & Mining	1544.6	1539.5	1536.5	1526.2	1497.2	1465.6	1435.5	1388.4	1226.7	1119.3
Construction	363.2	356.4	347.5	341.5	345.4	339.3	332.5	328.7	272.8	255.8
Services	1960.2	1981.9	2022.3	2074.8	2090.7	2130.0	2163.9	2199.4	2153.4	2099.9
Transport & Communication	397.0	396.1	400.5	404.3	400.0	400.3	410.1	417.5	372.8	347.7
Trade	503.8	508.8	508.8	514.2	519.7	519.3	517.5	557.8	564.2	574.5
Water Works & Supply	77.5	78.2	78.7	79.2	79.6	78.3	75.0	66.8	59.5	51.9
Non-Material Production	981.9	998.8	1034.3	1077.1	1091.4	1132.1	1161.3	1157.3	1156.9	1125.8
Total Active Earners	4940.0	4912.9	4892.5	4885.2	4844.8	4822.7	4795.2	4668.7	4241.8	3866.9
	(percentage change)									
Agriculture	-1.0	-3.4	-4.7	-4.4	-3.3	-2.6	-2.8	-12.9	-21.7	-33.5
Industry	-2.2	-0.6	-0.6	-0.9	-1.3	-2.0	-2.0	-2.9	-12.7	-8.3
Manufacturing & Mining	-2.1	-0.3	-0.2	-0.7	-1.9	-2.1	-2.1	-3.3	-11.6	-8.8
Construction	-2.6	-1.9	-2.5	-1.7	1.1	-1.8	-2.0	-1.1	-17.0	-6.2
Services	1.2	1.1	2.0	2.6	0.8	1.9	1.6	1.6	-2.1	-2.5
Transport & Communication	1.0	-0.2	1.1	0.9	-1.1	0.1	2.4	1.8	-10.7	-6.7
Trade	1.2	1.0	0.0	1.1	1.1	-0.1	-0.3	7.8	1.1	1.8
Water Works & Supply	0.6	0.9	0.6	0.6	0.5	-1.6	-4.2	-10.9	-10.9	-12.8
Non-Material Production	1.3	1.7	3.6	4.1	1.3	3.7	2.6	-0.3	0.0	-2.7
Total Active Earners	-0.6	-0.5	-0.4	-0.1	-0.8	-0.5	-0.6	-2.6	-9.1	-8.8
	(in percent of total)									
Agriculture	21.7	21.1	20.2	19.3	18.8	18.4	18.0	16.1	13.9	10.1
Industry	38.6	38.6	38.5	38.2	38.0	37.4	36.9	36.8	35.4	35.6
Manufacturing & Mining	31.3	31.3	31.4	31.2	30.9	30.4	29.9	29.7	28.9	28.9
Construction	7.4	7.3	7.1	7.0	7.1	7.0	6.9	7.0	6.4	6.6
Services	39.7	40.3	41.3	42.5	43.2	44.2	45.1	47.1	50.8	54.3
Transport & Communication	8.0	8.1	8.2	8.3	8.3	8.3	8.6	8.9	8.8	9.0
Trade	10.2	10.4	10.4	10.5	10.7	10.8	10.8	11.9	13.3	14.9
Water Works & Supply	1.6	1.6	1.6	1.6	1.6	1.6	1.6	1.4	1.4	1.3
Non-Material Production	19.9	20.3	21.1	22.0	22.5	23.5	24.2	24.8	27.3	29.1
Total Active Earners	100.0	100.0	100.0	100.0	100.0	100.0	100.0	100.0	100.0	100.0

Sources: Statistical Yearbook and Central Statistical Office.

Table 2.1: GDP by Origin in Current Values

(Billions of Current Forint)

	1975	1980	1981	1982	1983	1984	1985	1986	1987	1988	1989	1990	1991
Manufacturing	204.4	243.4	268.3	290.0	303.8	329.7	351.9	361.0	402.3	430.3	515.6	558.1	619.5
Agriculture & Forestry	86.4	123.5	136.8	148.5	152.9	166.1	166.6	182.6	189.2	209.8	235.9	261.2	230.6
Construction	43.4	53.4	55.5	60.1	65.5	71.1	74.0	79.0	92.3	102.3	127.5	125.4	121.9
Transport & Communications	39.4	58.5	64.0	70.5	71.4	74.2	77.7	86.3	94.4	101.4	124.4	143.5	185.4
Trade & Other Material Services	69.7	77.7	82.4	86.1	95.7	108.7	120.9	134.0	158.5	157.2	195.2	312.9	359.5
Non-Material Services	57.5	89.0	96.4	103.3	112.9	125.4	140.4	154.3	173.7	262.0	311.2	395.3	522.3
GDP at factor cost	500.8	645.5	703.4	758.5	802.2	875.2	931.5	997.2	1110.4	1263.0	1509.7	1796.5	2039.2
Taxes net of subsidies	-18.1	75.5	76.5	89.4	94.2	103.3	102.2	91.6	116.0	177.4	213.1	292.8	269.2
GDP at market prices	482.7	721.0	779.9	847.9	896.4	978.5	1033.7	1088.8	1226.4	1440.4	1722.8	2089.3	2308.4

(Percent Distribution)

	1975	1980	1981	1982	1983	1984	1985	1986	1987	1988	1989	1990	1991
Manufacturing	42.3	33.8	34.4	34.2	33.9	33.7	34.0	33.2	32.8	29.9	29.9	26.7	26.8
Agriculture & Forestry	17.9	17.1	17.5	17.5	17.1	17.0	16.1	16.8	15.4	14.6	13.7	12.5	10.0
Construction	9.0	7.4	7.1	7.1	7.3	7.3	7.2	7.3	7.5	7.1	7.4	6.0	5.3
Transport & Communications	8.2	8.1	8.2	8.3	8.0	7.6	7.5	7.9	7.7	7.0	7.2	6.9	8.0
Trade & Other Material Services	14.4	10.8	10.6	10.2	10.7	11.1	11.7	12.3	12.9	10.9	11.3	15.0	15.6
Non-Material Services	11.9	12.3	12.4	12.2	12.6	12.8	13.6	14.2	14.2	18.2	18.1	18.9	22.6
GDP at factor cost	103.7	89.5	90.2	89.5	89.5	89.4	90.1	91.6	90.5	87.7	87.6	86.0	88.3
Taxes net of subsidies	-3.7	10.5	9.8	10.5	10.5	10.6	9.9	8.4	9.5	13.5	13.7	14.1	11.3
GDP at market prices	100.0	100.0	100.0	100.0	100.0	100.0	100.0	100.0	100.0	100.0	100.0	100.0	100.0

Source: Central Statistical Office.

The Hungarian Central Statistical Office has recently adopted the U.N. System of National Accounts methodology for measuring Hungary's national account data. This methodology been applied to data for 1991 through 1993. The data presented in tables 2.1-2.4 present national account data for 1975 -1991 using the former Hungarian methodology, while tables 2.5 and 2.6 present data for 1991-1994 using SNA methodology.

Table 2.2: GDP By Origin in Real Terms

(Billions of 1981 Forint)

	1975	1980	1981	1982	1983	1984	1985	1986	1987	1988	1989	1990	1991
Manufacturing	203.5	249.3	261.7	274.1	279.1	286.2	280.2	278.9	287.9	283.5	277.8	256.4	210.5
Agriculture & Forestry	118.0	131.5	136.0	151.8	151.9	159.0	152.5	157.9	153.1	165.2	163.2	155.5	142.8
Construction	43.2	53.4	54.1	53.7	55.2	52.3	49.9	49.9	53.8	50.8	55.0	43.0	36.5
Transport & Communications	52.7	61.1	63.9	64.6	64.8	66.7	66.1	68.0	71.0	72.0	77.0	71.3	63.2
Trade & Other Material Services	70.7	79.6	81.9	81.5	84.5	85.1	88.4	91.3	97.6	88.2	88.8	100.3	99.2
Non-Material Services	77.8	95.1	98.5	100.4	102.2	107.0	111.4	114.6	121.3	122.8	126.1	130.7	127.8
GDP at factor cost	565.9	670.0	696.1	726.1	737.7	756.3	748.5	760.6	784.7	782.5	788.0	757.2	680.0
Taxes net of subsidies	74.1	81.0	76.5	68.4	62.7	65.2	70.9	71.4	81.0	82.7	83.3	83.5	60.9
GDP at market prices	640.0	751.0	772.6	794.5	800.4	821.5	819.4	832.0	865.7	865.2	871.3	840.8	740.9

(percentage change)

	1980	1981	1982	1983	1984	1985	1986	1987	1988	1989	1990	1991
Manufacturing	-1.4	5.0	4.7	1.8	2.5	-2.1	-0.5	3.2	-1.5	-2.0	-7.7	-17.9
Agriculture & Forestry	3.7	3.4	11.6	0.1	4.7	-4.1	3.5	-3.0	7.9	-1.2	-4.7	-8.2
Construction	-2.7	1.3	-0.7	2.8	-5.3	-4.6	0.0	7.8	-5.6	8.3	-21.9	-15.0
Transport & Communications	0.8	4.6	1.1	0.3	2.9	-0.9	2.9	4.4	1.4	6.9	-7.3	-11.4
Trade & Other Material Services	-4.9	2.9	-0.5	3.7	0.7	3.9	3.3	6.9	-9.6	0.7	12.9	-1.1
Non-Material Services	2.6	3.6	1.9	1.8	4.7	4.1	2.9	5.8	1.2	2.7	3.6	-2.2
GDP at factor cost	-0.2	3.9	4.3	1.6	2.5	-1.0	1.6	3.2	-0.3	0.7	-3.9	-10.2
Taxes net of subsidies	2.7	-5.6	-10.6	-8.3	4.0	8.7	0.7	13.4	2.1	0.7	0.3	-27.1
GDP at market prices	0.1	2.9	2.8	0.7	2.6	-0.3	1.5	4.1	-0.1	0.7	-3.5	-11.9

Source: Central Statistical Yearbook.
The Hungarian Central Statistical Office has recently adopted the U.N. System of National Accounts methodology for measuring Hungary's national account data. This methodology been applied to data for 1991 through 1993. The data presented in tables 2.1-2.4 present national account data for 1960 -1991 using the former Hungarian methodology, while tables 2.5 and 2.6 present data for 1991-1994 using SNA methodology.

Table 2.3: GDP by Expenditure in Current Values

	1975	1980	1981	1982	1983	1984	1985	1986	1987	1988	1989	1990	1991
							(Billions of Current Forint)						
Total expenditure	518.7	736.6	788.1	841.1	879.3	947.6	1012.3	1104.2	1232.3	1413.5	1673.0	2003.5	2375.6
Government Consumption	50.2	74.1	79.1	84.2	90.9	95.3	104.6	116.0	126.3	168.5	177.7	221.8	289.3
Private Consumption	286.1	441.2	477.7	515.1	551.2	600.5	649.3	695.5	778.5	886.8	1050.4	1282.5	1605.5
Total Consumption	336.3	515.3	556.8	599.3	642.1	695.8	753.9	811.5	904.8	1055.3	1228.1	1504.3	1894.8
Gross Fixed Investment	161.0	207.7	206.7	213.9	220.1	225.4	232.1	261.2	303.5	295.6	348.4	369.6	440.9
Change in Stocks	21.4	13.6	24.6	27.9	17.1	26.4	26.3	31.5	24.0	62.6	96.5	129.6	39.9
Total Investment	182.4	221.3	231.3	241.8	237.2	251.8	258.4	292.7	327.5	358.2	444.9	499.2	480.8
Exports, GNFS	200.2	281.8	308.2	321.8	360.7	402.0	436.2	431.6	464.4	530.4	620.9	669.0	834.9
Imports, GNFS	236.2	297.4	316.4	315.0	343.5	371.1	414.8	447.0	470.3	491.7	563.5	593.0	902.0
Resource Balance	-36.0	-15.6	-8.2	6.8	17.2	30.9	21.4	-15.4	-5.9	38.7	57.4	76.0	-67.0
GDP at market prices	482.7	721.0	779.9	847.9	896.5	978.5	1033.7	1088.8	1226.4	1452.2	1730.4	2079.5	2308.4
							(Percent Distribution)						
Government Consumption	10.4	10.3	10.1	9.9	10.1	9.7	10.1	10.7	10.3	11.6	10.3	10.7	12.5
Private Consumption	59.3	61.2	61.3	60.8	61.5	61.4	62.8	63.9	63.5	61.1	60.7	61.7	69.6
Total Consumption	69.7	71.5	71.4	70.7	71.6	71.1	72.9	74.5	73.8	72.7	71.0	72.3	82.1
Gross Fixed Investment	33.4	28.8	26.5	25.2	24.6	23.0	22.5	24.0	24.7	20.4	20.1	17.8	19.1
Change in Stocks	4.4	1.9	3.2	3.3	1.9	2.7	2.5	2.9	2.0	4.3	5.6	6.2	1.7
Total Investment	37.8	30.7	29.7	28.5	26.5	25.7	25.0	26.9	26.7	24.7	25.7	24.0	20.8
Exports, GNFS	41.5	39.1	39.5	38.0	40.2	41.1	42.2	39.6	37.9	36.5	35.9	32.2	36.2
Imports, GNFS	48.9	41.2	40.6	37.2	38.3	37.9	40.1	41.1	38.3	33.9	32.6	28.5	39.1
Resource Balance	-7.5	-2.2	-1.1	0.8	1.9	3.2	2.1	-1.4	-0.5	2.7	3.3	3.7	-2.9
GDP at market prices	100.0	100.0	100.0	100.0	100.0	100.0	100.0	100.0	100.0	100.0	100.0	100.0	100.0

Source: Central Statistical Yearbook.
The Hungarian Central Statistical Office has recently adopted the U.N. System of National Accounts methodology for measuring Hungary's national account data. This methodology been applied to data for 1991 through 1993. The data presented in tables 2.1-2.4 present national account data for 1975 -1991 using the former Hungarian methodology, while tables 2.5 and 2.6 present data for 1991-1994 using SNA methodology.

Table 2.4: GDP By Expenditure in Real Terms

	1975	1980	1981	1982	1983	1984	1985	1986	1987	1988	1989	1990	1991
						(Billions of 1981 Forint)							
Government Consumption	60.4	76.1	79.6	80.4	80.6	81.6	84.9	88.9	89.2	94.1	88.2	90.5	88.0
Private Consumption	411.5	467.4	479.7	485.8	488.3	494.1	500.8	510.8	530.0	507.8	519.0	500.3	471.4
Total Consumption	471.9	543.5	559.3	566.2	568.9	575.7	585.7	599.7	619.2	601.9	607.1	590.8	559.4
Gross Fixed Investment	193.5	216.0	206.7	203.4	196.5	189.2	183.4	195.4	214.6	195.0	212.2	201.1	199.9
Change in Stocks	22.5	10.4	14.8	10.3	1.6	4.0	3.1	7.2	-5.6	7.2	-21.6	-18.8	-58.9
Total Investment	216.0	226.4	221.5	213.7	198.1	193.2	186.5	202.6	209.0	202.2	190.6	182.4	141.0
Exports, GNFS	209.4	292.5	308.2	319.1	340.4	363.0	381.9	373.4	391.2	416.4	421.6	399.2	338.3
Imports, GNFS	257.3	311.4	316.4	304.5	307.1	310.4	334.7	343.7	353.7	355.3	361.6	346.0	315.5
Resource Balance	-47.9	-18.9	-8.2	14.6	33.3	52.6	47.2	29.7	37.5	61.1	60.0	53.2	22.8
Statistical Discrepency	0.0	0.0	0.0	0.0	0.0	0.0	0.0	0.0	0.0	0.0	13.5	14.4	17.7
GDP at market prices	640.0	751.0	772.6	794.5	800.4	821.5	819.4	832.0	865.7	865.2	871.3	840.8	740.9
						(percentage change)							
Government Consumption		0.1	4.6	1.0	0.2	1.2	4.0	4.7	0.3	5.5	-6.3	2.6	-2.7
Private Consumption		0.7	2.6	1.3	0.5	1.2	1.4	2.0	3.8	-4.2	2.2	-3.6	-5.8
Total Consumption		0.6	2.9	1.2	0.5	1.2	1.7	2.4	3.3	-2.8	0.9	-2.7	-5.3
Gross Fixed Investment		-5.8	-4.3	-1.6	-3.4	-3.7	-3.1	6.5	9.8	-9.1	8.8	-5.2	-0.6
Change in Stocks		:	:	:	:	:	:	:	:	:	:	:	:
Total Investment	:	-3.4	-2.2	-3.5	-7.3	-2.5	-3.5	8.6	3.2	-3.3	-5.8	-4.3	-22.7
Exports, GNFS		0.6	5.4	3.5	6.7	6.6	5.2	-2.2	4.8	6.4	1.2	-5.3	-15.3
Imports, GNFS		-1.1	1.6	-3.8	0.9	1.1	7.8	2.7	2.9	0.5	1.8	-4.3	-8.8
GDP at market prices		0.1	2.9	2.8	0.7	2.6	-0.3	1.5	4.1	-0.1	0.7	-3.5	-11.9

Source: Central Statistical Yearbook.

The Hungarian Central Statistical Office has recently adopted the U.N. System of National Accounts methodology for measuring Hungary's national account data. This methodology been applied to data for 1991 through 1993. The data presented in tables 2.1-2.4 present national account data for 1975 -1991using the former Hungarian methodology, while tables 2.5 and 2.6 present data for 1991-1994 using SNA methodology.

Table 2.5: GDP By Origin

	1991	1992	1993	1992	1993
	(billions of current HUF)			(percentage change) (in constant 1991 prices)	
Agriculture, hunting, forestry, fishing	195.2	189.9	209.2	-16.6	-6.7
Mining and quarrying	81.8	32.2	20.1	-63.2	-44.1
Manufacturing a/	494.2	583.0	691.7	1.6	6.3
Electricity, gas,steam,water supply	90.5	102.0	123.8	-0.7	10.2
Construction	123.5	153.9	166.8	1.9	-6.4
Wholesale and retail trade b/	307.2	284.0	354.5	-18.0	-4.9
Hotels and restaurants	48.5	57.6	63.5	-4.2	-6.9
Transport, storage, communication	209.9	245.2	281.9	-4.3	-5.1
Financial intermediation	101.8	109.1	145.6	-14.6	14.8
Real estate, renting, business activities	234.8	317.3	412.3	3.9	3.8
Public administration and defence	147.1	187.4	235.8	3.6	1.4
Education	110.0	140.9	172.6	3.5	0.4
Health and social work	95.8	123.7	147.7	3.1	2.0
Other community, social sevice	58.7	98.0	115.2	30.9	-3.7
Total	2299.0	2624.2	3140.7	..	..
FISIM c/	-107.7	-100.6	-124.4	..	..
GDP at basic prices	2191.3	2523.6	3016.3	-4.0	0.1
net taxes on products	300.4	411.5	521.5	4.3	-6.8
GDP at market prices	2491.7	2935.1	3537.8	-3.0	-0.8

a/ Beginning in 1992, all activities of Hungarian Oil Company are classified to the Manufacturing sector,
   previously split among the following sectors: Mining, Manufacturing, Wholesale trade and Transport.

b/ Includes repairs of motor vehicles and household goods.

c/ Financial intermediation services indirectly measured.

Table 2.6: GDP By Expenditure

	1991	1992	1993	1994 est.	1991	1992	1993	1994 est.	1992	1993	1994 est.
	(billions of current HUF)				(in constant 1991 prices)				(percentage change) (in constant 1991 prices)		
Total Consumption	2022.7	2488.5	3126.4	3674.0	2022.7	2030.5	2127.2	2073.7	0.4	4.8	-2.5
Individual consumption	1749.3	2136.0	2617.6	3169.0	1749.3	1739.7	1762.8	1786.0	-0.5	1.3	1.3
Collective consumption 1/	273.4	352.5	508.8	505.0	273.4	290.8	364.4	287.7	6.4	25.3	-21.0
Gross fixed capital formation	516.3	577.1	661.1	850.0	516.3	502.5	511.1	570.0	-2.7	1.7	11.5
Changes in stocks	-23.1	-122.5	41.3	82.0	-23.1	-108.1	22.1	69.9	..	..	..
Gross capital formation, total	493.2	454.6	702.4	932.0	493.2	394.4	533.2	639.9	-20.0	35.2	20.0
Domestic Demand	2515.9	2943.1	3828.8	4606.0	2515.9	2424.9	2660.4	2713.6	-3.6	9.7	2.0
Exports	818.4	925.3	937.0	1242.1	818.4	835.6	750.9	851.1	2.1	-10.1	13.3
Imports a/	842.6	933.3	1228.1	1538.1	842.6	844.7	1015.7	1120.8	0.2	20.2	10.3
External trade balance	-24.2	-8.0	-291.1	-296.0	-24.2	-9.1	-264.8	-269.7	..	..	..
GDP at market prices	2491.7	2935.1	3537.7	4310.0	2491.7	2415.8	2395.6	2443.9	-3.0	-0.8	2.0

a/ Includes the import of military equipment from Russia for debt-repayment in 1993.

Table 2.7: Derivation of Profits
(In billions of forint; percent of GDP a/)

In billions of forint

	1988	1989	1990	1991	1992	Estim. 1993	Proj. 1994
Gross domestic output	3457.8	4021.6	4790.1	5305.7	5820.8	6644.3	7589.3
Less: Intermed. input	2194.8	2511.9	2993.6	3266.5	3369.8	3759.3	4173.8
GDP at factor cost	1263.0	1509.7	1796.5	2039.2	2451.0	2885.0	3415.5
Plus: Net indirect taxes	177.4	213.1	292.8	269.2	354.0	435.0	544.0
GDP at market prices	1440.4	1722.8	2089.3	2308.4	2805.0	3320.0	3959.5
Gross labor income	658.9	783.7	980.9	1207.3	1465.0	1731.0	2072.5
Indirect taxes	558.2	649.9	765.1	819.8	997.6	1202.5	1425.4
o/w social security contributions	180.3	246.6	299.5	375.9	482.5	578.1	676.4
o/w indirect taxes	377.9	403.3	465.6	443.9	515.3	624.5	749.0
o/w taxes on products	271.9	303.4	378.0	358.5	432.3	530.3	646.0
o/w taxes on production	106.0	99.9	87.6	85.4	83.0	94.2	103.0
Indirect subsidies	217.2	201.4	177.1	144.7	130.8	156.6	160.0
o/w subsidies on products	94.5	90.3	85.2	89.3	78.3	95.3	102.0
o/w subsidies on production	122.7	111.1	91.9	55.4	52.5	61.1	58.0
Gross operating surplus	440.5	490.6	520.4	426.0	473.0	542.9	621.6
Other deductions	-46.4	-36.5	-57.8	-139.0	-300.0	-245.9	-195.6
Gross profits before taxes	394.1	454.1	462.6	287.0	173.0	297.0	426.0
Less: Depreciation	132.7	154.4	163.9	185.8	348.0	415.0	499.0
Net profits before taxes	261.4	299.7	298.7	101.2	-175.0	-118.0	-73.0
o/w Profits	270.2	326.0	356.0	309.5	235.0	235.0	260.0
o/w Losses	-8.8	-26.3	-57.3	-208.3	-410.0	-353.0	-333.0
Direct taxes on income	155.5	186.3	158.1	116.6	112.4	99.8	133.2
Subsidies received after profits	2.9	3.0	2.4	2.3	..	..	..
Net profits after taxes	108.8	116.4	143.0	-13.1	..	..	..
Profit sharing	21.4	21.4	31.8	30.1	..	..	..
Retained earnings	87.4	95.0	111.2	-43.2	..	..	..

Percent of GDP

	1988	1989	1990	1991	1992	Estim. 1993	Proj. 1994
Gross domestic output	240.1	233.4	229.3	229.8	207.5	200.1	191.7
Less: Intermed. input	152.4	145.8	143.3	141.5	120.1	113.2	105.4
GDP at factor cost	87.7	87.6	86.0	88.3	87.4	86.9	86.3
Plus: Net indirect taxes	12.3	12.4	14.0	11.7	12.6	13.1	13.7
GDP at market prices	100.0	100.0	100.0	100.0	100.0	100.0	100.0
Gross labor income	45.7	45.5	46.9	52.3	52.2	52.1	52.3
Indirect taxes	38.8	37.7	36.6	35.5	35.6	36.2	36.0
o/w social security contributions	12.5	14.3	14.3	16.3	17.2	17.4	17.1
o/w indirect taxes	26.2	23.4	22.3	19.2	18.4	18.8	18.9
o/w taxes on products	18.9	17.6	18.1	15.5	15.4	16.0	16.3
o/w taxes on production	7.4	5.8	4.2	3.7	3.0	2.8	2.6
Indirect subsidies	15.1	11.7	8.5	6.3	4.7	4.7	4.0
o/w subsidies on products	6.6	5.2	4.1	3.9	2.8	2.9	2.6
o/w subsidies on production	8.5	6.4	4.4	2.4	1.9	1.8	1.5
Gross operating surplus	30.6	28.5	24.9	18.5	16.9	16.4	15.7
Other deductions	-3.2	-2.1	-2.8	-6.0	-10.7	-7.4	-4.9
Gross profits before taxes	27.4	26.4	22.1	12.4	6.2	8.9	10.8
Less: Depreciation	9.2	9.0	7.8	8.0	12.4	12.5	12.6
Net profits before taxes	18.1	17.4	14.3	4.4	-6.2	-3.6	-1.8
o/w Profits	18.8	18.9	17.0	13.4	8.4	7.1	6.6
o/w Losses	-0.6	-1.5	-2.7	-9.0	-14.6	-10.6	-8.4
Direct taxes on income	10.8	10.8	7.6	5.1	4.0	3.0	3.4
Subsidies received after profits	0.2	0.2	0.1	0.1	..	..	..
Net profits after taxes	7.6	6.8	6.8	-0.6	..	..	..
Profit sharing	1.5	1.2	1.5	1.3	..	..	..
Retained earnings	6.1	5.5	5.3	-1.9	..	..	..

a/ Data presented here do not reflect the changes in methodology adopted by the CSO in July 1994.
Sources: Central Statistical Office; Ministry of Finance.

Table 2.8: Disposable Income a/

(in billions of HUF; percentage change)

	1988	1989	1990	1991	1992	Estim. 1993	Proj. 1994
Wages	507.4	587.3	723.7	840.0	963.9	1096.8	1267.0
(Percent change)	29.5	15.8	23.2	16.1	14.8	13.8	15.5
Wage-like incomes	46.1	57.6	94.8	135.0	181.6	220.0	275.0
(Percent change)	13.9	24.7	64.7	42.4	34.5	21.1	25.0
Sales of farm products	28.2	29.2	25.5	28.6	30.3	32.8	42.0
(Percent change)	-9.1	3.5	-12.7	12.2	5.9	8.3	28.0
Incomes from self-employment	61.9	81.6	108.1	169.9	213.7	289.2	376.0
(Percent change)	-9.2	31.9	32.4	57.2	25.8	35.3	30.0
Gross labor income in cash	643.6	755.7	952.1	1173.5	1389.5	1638.8	1960.0
(Percent change)	21.1	17.4	26.0	23.3	18.4	17.9	19.6
Gross social benefits in cash	207.0	257.3	324.1	439.8	559.1	671.3	758.2
(Percent change)	27.2	24.3	26.0	35.7	27.1	20.1	12.9
o/w Pensions	130.0	156.5	202.1	262.8	322.5	389.6	460.8
o/w Family Allowances, GYES, GYED	46.0	63.8	77.7	100.0	121.1	138.1	145.6
o/w Sickpay	17.6	22.9	26.3	30.9	36.5	43.5	45.1
o/w Unemployment benefits	...	...	...	15.5	48.4	51.5	50.0
o/w Local Gov't Benefits	...	...	...	11.9	19.0	27.5	32.0
o/w Scholarships, Other	13.4	14.2	18.1	18.6	11.6	21.1	24.7
Other incomes, gross	32.1	49.5	65.8	161.6	193.3	180.0	274.3
(Percent change)	274.8	54.0	32.9	98.1	9.5	-6.9	52.4
Gross money incomes	882.7	1062.5	1342.0	1774.9	2141.9	2490.1	2992.5
(Percent change)	25.6	20.4	26.3	30.7	19.7	16.3	20.2
Taxes, soc.sec., etc	139.6	174.3	213.9	281.6	372.7	452.9	508.2
(Percent change)	15.4	24.9	22.7	22.6	25.7	21.5	12.2
o/w PIT	73.2	96.3	126.8	172.0	225.7	284.8	311.0
o/w SS contributions	45.2	53.6	64.8	78.3	90.2	101.4	117.1
o/w Other taxes and fees	...	...	...	...	7.4	13.7	15.0
o/w Infrastructural Network	19.9	23.4	22.3	31.3	31.4	33.0	42.4
o/w Implicit contributions by employees accounted as wages & salaries	1.3	1.0	...	...	18.0	20.0	22.7
Net money incomes	743.2	888.2	1128.1	1493.3	1769.2	2037.2	2484.3
(Percent change)	14.6	19.5	27.0	32.4	18.5	15.1	21.9
Labor incomes in kind	36.7	49.5	60.7	64.0	68.0	84.0	103.5
(Percent change)	-20.3	35.0	22.6	25.7	6.4	23.5	23.2
Social benefits in kind	152.2	185.3	236.1	301.7	360.0	411.0	477.2
(Percent change)	35.0	21.8	27.4	27.8	19.3	14.2	16.1
o/w Provided by Government	142.9	177.0	227.1	290.9	...	...	...
o/w Provided by Enterprises	9.3	8.4	9.0	10.7	...	...	...
Total income in kind	188.9	234.8	296.8	365.6	428.0	495.0	580.7
(Percent change)	19.0	24.4	26.4	27.4	17.1	15.7	17.3
Disposable income	932.0	1123.1	1424.9	1858.9	2197.2	2532.2	3065.0
(Percent change)	15.5	20.5	26.9	31.4	18.2	15.2	21.0
Disposable income 2/	789.1	946.1	1197.7	1568.0	1853.4	2139.7	2609.3
(Percent change)	15.5	20.5	26.9	31.4	18.2	15.2	21.0

(Share of GDP)

	1988	1989	1990	1991	1992	Estim. 1993	Proj. 1994
Wages	35.2	34.1	34.6	36.4	34.4	33.0	32.0
Wage-like incomes	3.2	3.3	4.5	5.8	6.5	6.6	6.9
Sales of farm products	2.0	1.7	1.2	1.2	1.1	1.0	1.1
Incomes from self-employment	4.3	4.7	5.2	7.4	7.6	8.7	9.5
Gross labor income in cash	44.7	43.9	45.6	50.8	49.5	49.4	49.5
Gross social benefits in cash	14.4	14.9	15.5	19.1	19.9	20.2	19.1
o/w Pensions	9.0	9.1	9.7	11.4	11.5	11.7	11.6
o/w Family Allowances, GYES, GYED	3.2	3.7	3.7	4.3	4.3	4.2	3.7
o/w Sickpay	1.2	1.3	1.3	1.3	1.3	1.3	1.1
o/w Unemployment benefits	0.0	0.0	0.0	0.7	1.7	1.6	1.3
o/w Local Gov't Benefits	0.0	0.0	0.0	0.5	0.7	0.8	0.8
o/w Scholarships, Other	0.9	0.8	0.9	0.8	0.4	0.6	0.6
Other incomes, gross	2.2	2.9	3.1	7.0	6.9	5.4	6.9
Gross money incomes	61.3	61.7	64.2	76.9	76.4	75.0	75.6
Taxes, soc.sec., etc	9.7	10.1	10.2	12.2	13.3	13.6	12.8
o/w PIT	5.1	5.6	6.1	7.5	8.0	8.6	7.9
o/w SS contributions	3.1	3.1	3.1	3.4	3.2	3.1	3.0
o/w Other taxes and fees	0.0	0.0	0.0	0.0	0.3	0.4	0.4
o/w Infrastructural Network	1.4	1.4	1.1	1.4	1.1	1.0	1.1
o/w Implicit contributions by employees accounted as wages & salaries	0.1	0.1	0.0	0.0	0.6	0.6	0.6
Net money incomes	51.6	51.6	54.0	64.7	63.1	61.4	62.7
Labor incomes in kind	2.5	2.9	2.9	2.8	2.4	2.5	2.6
Social benefits in kind	10.6	10.8	11.3	13.1	12.8	12.4	12.1
o/w Provided by Government	9.9	10.3	10.9	12.6	...	...	...
o/w Provided by Enterprises	0.6	0.5	0.4	0.5	...	...	...
Total income in kind	13.1	13.6	14.2	15.8	15.3	14.9	14.7
Disposable income	64.7	65.2	68.2	80.5	78.3	76.3	77.4
Disposable income 2/	55.0	55.3	57.6	67.9	66.1	64.4	65.9

(Share of disposable income)

	1988	1989	1990	1991	1992	Estim. 1993	Proj. 1994
Wages	54.4	52.3	50.8	45.2	43.9	43.3	41.3
Wage-like incomes	5.0	5.1	6.7	7.3	8.3	8.7	9.0
Sales of farm products	3.0	2.6	1.8	1.5	1.4	1.3	1.4
Incomes from self-employment	6.6	7.3	7.6	9.1	9.7	11.4	12.3
Gross labor income in cash	69.1	67.3	66.8	63.1	63.2	64.7	63.9
Gross social benefits in cash	22.2	22.9	22.7	23.7	25.4	26.5	24.7
o/w Pensions	13.9	13.9	14.2	14.1	14.7	15.4	15.0
o/w Family Allowances, GYES, GYED	4.9	5.7	5.5	5.4	5.5	5.5	4.8
o/w Sickpay	1.9	2.0	1.8	1.7	1.7	1.7	1.5
o/w Unemployment benefits	0.0	0.0	0.0	0.8	2.2	2.0	1.6
o/w Local Gov't Benefits	0.0	0.0	0.0	0.6	0.9	1.1	1.0
o/w Scholarships, Other	1.4	1.3	1.3	1.0	0.5	0.8	0.8
Other incomes, gross	3.4	4.4	4.6	8.7	8.8	7.1	8.9
Gross money incomes	94.7	94.6	94.2	95.5	97.5	98.3	97.6
Taxes, soc.sec., etc	15.0	15.5	15.0	15.2	17.0	17.9	16.6
o/w PIT	7.8	8.6	8.9	9.3	10.3	11.2	10.1
o/w SS contributions	4.8	4.8	4.5	4.2	4.1	4.0	3.8
o/w Other taxes and fees	0.0	0.0	0.0	0.0	0.3	0.5	0.5
o/w Infrastructural Network	2.1	2.1	1.6	1.7	1.4	1.3	1.4
o/w Implicit contributions by employees accounted as wages & salaries	0.1	0.1	0.0	0.0	0.8	0.8	0.7
Net money incomes	79.7	79.1	79.2	80.3	80.5	80.5	81.1
Labor incomes in kind	3.9	4.4	4.3	3.4	3.1	3.3	3.4
Social benefits in kind	16.3	16.5	16.6	16.2	16.4	16.2	15.6
o/w Provided by Government	15.3	15.8	15.9	15.7	...	...	...
o/w Provided by Enterprises	1.0	0.7	0.6	0.6	...	...	...
Total income in kind	20.3	20.9	20.8	19.7	19.5	19.5	18.9
Disposable income	100.0	100.0	100.0	100.0	100.0	100.0	100.0
Disposable income 2/	84.7	84.2	84.1	84.3	84.4	84.5	85.1

Sources: Data provided by the Hungarian authorities and World Bank staff estimates.
a/ Data presented here do not reflect the changes in methodology adopted by the CSO in July 1994.

Table 3.1: Consolidated Balance of Payments
(US$ Millions)

	1982	1983	1984	1985	1986	1987	1988	1989	1990	1991	1992	1993	1994
Exports (FOB)	9038	8978	9090	8578	9198	9966	9989	10494	9127	9697	10098	8094	7613
Imports (FOB)	8628	8544	8310	8130	9663	9887	9406	9450	8599	9333	10101	11341	11248
Trade Balance	410	434	780	448	-465	79	583	1044	528	364	-3	-3247	-3635
Travel net	261	263	269	259	366	537	154	-159	399	540	587	440	503
Travel credit	399	411	433	460	603	787	884	984	983	1038	1251	1182	925
Travel debit	138	148	164	201	237	250	730	1143	584	498	664	742	1428
Investment Income net	-1113	-775	-850	-867	-991	-1027	-1093	-1394	-1428	-1324	-1216	-1131	-1286
Investment Income credit	119	132	159	205	261	243	238	231	267	309	420	456	661
Investment Income debit	1232	907	1009	1072	1252	1270	1331	1625	1695	1633	1636	1587	1947
Freight and Insurance net	-313	-234	-219	-239	-313	-390	-376	-365	-173	-88	-116	-107	-176
Foreign Investment Income net	0	0	0	0	0	0	0	0	-24	-32	-45	-56	-117
Other Services net	187	108	24	-83	-9	65	96	203	213	22	215	-72	-97
Government Expenditure net	-29	-32	-31	-38	-28	-46	-54	-30	72	63	78	-17	-12
Private Transfers net	63	56	66	65	78	105	118	130	786	866	859	732	909
Current Account Balance	-534	-180	39	-455	-1363	-677	-572	-571	373	411	359	-3458	-3911
Direct Foreign Investment	0	0	0	0	6	2	14	187	337	1459	1471	2329	1097
Medium & Long-Term Assets (net)	-528	-177	-48	-225	-127	-154	-95	-95	-52	-55	-893	237	36
Medium & Long-Term Liabilities (net)	581	119	1361	1915	1013	1086	503	1200	-33	772	-787	3039	1325
Disbursements	1835	1654	3284	4567	4165	3422	2595	3110	2198	3114	2291	6309	5429
Repayments (-)	1254	1535	1923	2652	3152	2336	2092	1910	2231	2342	3078	3270	4104
Net Short-Term Capital	-529	702	-1046	-629	495	-698	246	-153	-824	-668	610	459	960
Short-Term Assets (net)	-352	-252	-203	-199	307	-166	0	-137	-324	123	466	-164	189
Short-Term Liabilities (net)	-177	954	-843	-430	188	-532	246	-16	-500	-791	144	623	771
Changes in Net Reserves (- = increase)	1010	-464	-306	-606	-24	441	-96	-568	199	-1919	-760	-2606	493
1. Net Credit from the IMF	237	355	436	-90	-48	-354	-133	-158	-148	887	-9	29	-163
Purchases	237	355	436	0	0	0	222	66	175	963	109	79	0
Repurchases	0	0	0	90	48	354	355	224	323	76	118	50	163
2. Other Reserve Changes	773	-819	-742	-516	24	795	37	-410	347	-2806	-751	-2635	656

Source: National Bank of Hungary.

Table 3.2: Balance of Payments in Convertible Currency
(US$ Millions)

	1982	1983	1984	1985	1986	1987	1988	1989	1990	1991	1992	1993	1994
Exports (FOB)	4831	4832	4916	4188	4186	5051	5505	6447	6408	9258	10028	8094	7613
Imports (FOB)	4163	4059	4025	4060	4668	5014	5016	5910	6070	9069	10076	11341	11248
Trade Balance	668	773	891	128	-482	37	489	537	338	-189	-48	-3247	-3635
Travel net	180	167	165	147	199	367	41	-349	347	560	590	440	503
Travel credit	264	256	268	281	364	553	670	738	824	1006	1231	1182	925
Travel debit	84	89	103	134	165	186	629	1087	477	446	641	742	1428
Investment Income net	-1118	-758	-816	-833	-963	-988	-1076	-1387	-1451	-1331	-1216	-1131	-1286
Investment Income credit	79	97	128	186	252	235	230	218	233	297	420	456	661
Investment Income debit	1197	855	944	1019	1215	1223	1306	1605	1684	1628	1636	1587	1947
Freight and Insurance net	-222	-164	-154	-156	-237	-309	-299	-309	-164	-80	-116	-107	-176
Foreign Investment Income net	0	0	0	0	0	0	0	0	-24	-32	-45	-56	-117
Other Services net	164	38	-47	-149	-54	-36	1	2	325	37	222	-72	-97
Government Expenditure net	-32	-38	-37	-44	-32	-52	-75	-57	18	63	78	-17	-12
Private Transfers net	61	53	63	61	74	102	115	126	734	861	859	732	909
Current Account Balance	-299	71	65	-846	-1496	-879	-804	-1437	123	267	324	-3458	-3911
Direct Foreign Investment	0	0	0	0	6	2	14	187	337	1459	1471	2329	1097
Medium & Long-Term Assets (net)	-510	-185	-43	-240	-79	-84	-26	32	-76	-57	-146	237	36
Medium & Long-Term Liabilities (net)	467	27	1341	1933	1180	1192	701	1350	88	770	-885	3039	1325
Disbursements	1702	1523	3102	4513	4099	3362	2551	3090	2186	3104	2095	6309	5429
Repayments (-)	1235	1496	1761	2580	2919	2170	1850	1740	2098	2334	2980	3270	4104
Net Short-Term Capital	-709	574	-1049	-389	493	-778	288	-44	-893	-617	5	459	960
Short-Term Assets (net)	-500	-229	-223	-199	298	-177	-3	-137	-324	141	-152	-164	189
Short-Term Liabilities (net)	-209	803	-826	-190	195	-601	291	93	-569	-758	157	623	771
Changes in Net Reserves (- = increase)	1051	-487	-314	-458	-104	547	-173	-88	421	-1822	-769	-2606	493
1. Net Credit from the IMF	237	355	436	-90	-48	-354	-133	-158	-148	898	-9	29	-163
Purchases	237	355	436	0	0	0	222	66	175	973	109	79	0
Repurchases	0	0	0	90	48	354	355	224	323	75	118	50	163
2. Other Reserve Changes	814	-842	-750	-368	-56	901	-40	70	569	-2720	-760	-2635	656
Exchange Rate (Ft/US$, Average)	37	43	48	50	46	47	50	59	63	75	79	92	105

Source: National Bank of Hungary.

Table 3.3: Balance of Payments in Nonconvertible Currency
(US$ Millions)

	1982	1983	1984	1985	1986	1987	1988	1989	1990	1991	1992	1993	1994
Exports (FOB)	4207	4146	4174	4390	5012	4915	4484	4047	2719	439	70	..	..
Imports (FOB)	4465	4485	4285	4070	4995	4873	4390	3540	2529	264	25	..	..
Trade Balance	-258	-339	-111	320	17	42	94	507	190	175	45	..	..
Travel net	81	96	104	112	167	170	113	190	52	-20	-3	..	..
Travel credit	135	155	165	179	239	234	214	246	159	32	20	..	..
Travel debit	54	59	61	67	72	64	101	56	107	52	23	..	..
Investment Income net	5	-17	-34	-34	-28	-39	-17	-7	23	7	0	..	..
Investment Income credit	40	35	31	19	9	8	8	13	34	12	0	..	..
Investment Income debit	35	52	65	53	37	47	25	20	11	5	0	..	..
Freight and Insurance net	-91	-70	-65	-83	-76	-81	-77	-56	-9	-8	0	..	..
Other Services net	23	70	71	66	45	101	95	201	-112	-15	-7	..	..
Government Expenditure net	3	6	6	6	4	6	21	27	54	0	0	..	..
Private Transfers net	2	3	3	4	4	3	3	4	52	5	0	..	..
Current Account Balance	-235	-251	-26	391	133	202	232	866	250	144	35	..	..
Direct Foreign Investment	0	0	0	0	0	0	0	0	0	0	0	..	..
Medium & Long-Term Assets (net)	-18	8	-5	15	-48	-70	-69	-127	24	2	-747	..	..
Medium & Long-Term Liabilities (net)	114	92	20	-18	-167	-106	-198	-150	-121	-9	98	..	..
Disbursements	133	131	182	54	66	60	44	20	12	0	196	..	..
Repayments (-)	19	39	162	72	233	166	242	170	133	9	98	..	..
Net Short-Term Capital	180	128	3	-240	2	80	-42	-109	69	-51	605	..	..
Short-Term Assets (net)	148	-23	20	0	9	11	3	0	0	-18	618	..	..
Short-Term Liabilities (net)	32	151	-17	-240	-7	69	-45	-109	69	-33	-13	..	..
Change in Reserves	-41	23	8	-148	80	-106	77	-480	-222	-86	9	..	..

(-) = increase
Source: National Bank of Hungary.

154

Table 3.4: International Reserves and Other Foreign Assets
(US$ Millions at end of period)

	1982	1983	1984	1985	1986	1987	1988	1989	1990	1991	1992	1993	1994
International Reserves	1000.0	1622.0	2069.0	3017.1	3227.2	2448.6	2178.2	2292.4	1969.4	4723.3	4427.6	6781.3	6780.6
Convertible Currencies	942.0	1577.0	2026.0	2792.5	3053.0	2159.2	1976.3	1725.3	1166.5	4017.3	4380.1	6736.1	6768.8
Gold	146.0	346.0	466.0	639.9	750.6	525.1	509.7	479.1	97.1	82.6	32.6	44.6	42.2
Foreign Exchange	796.0	1231.0	1560.0	2152.6	2302.4	1634.1	1466.6	1246.2	1069.4	3934.7	4347.5	6691.5	6726.6
Nonconvertible Currencies	58.0	45.0	43.0	224.6	174.2	289.4	201.9	567.1	802.9	706.0	47.5	45.2	11.8
Other Foreign Assets	2402.0	2604.0	2792.0	3538.5	3666.9	4265.2	4161.6	4433.6	4757.3	4602.2	5185.5	3549.7	3372.4
Convertible Currencies	2007.0	2175.0	2408.0	3116.4	3185.9	3741.7	3659.9	3764.6	4165.5	4086.4	4005.7	2897.4	2816.7
Short-Term	1114.0	1280.0	1569.0	1968.2	1854.1	2276.5	2201.4	2355.3	2739.9	2605.9	2597.5	1952.6	1649.7
Medium- and Long-Term	893.0	895.0	839.0	1148.2	1331.8	1465.2	1458.5	1409.3	1425.6	1480.5	1408.2	944.8	1167.0
Nonconvertible Currencies	395.0	429.0	384.0	422.1	481.0	523.5	501.7	669.0	591.8	515.8	1179.8	652.3	555.7
Short-Term	79.0	111.0	93.0	107.5	110.4	97.8	68.5	169.4	108.1	117.0	79.1	17.5	17.8
Medium- and Long-Term	316.0	318.0	291.0	314.6	370.6	425.7	433.2	499.6	483.7	398.8	1100.7	634.8	537.9

Source: National Bank of Hungary.

Table 3.5: Commodity Pattern of External Trade

	1986	1987	1988	1989	1990	1991	1992	1993 a/	1994
(Value, in millions of Forint)									
Exports:									
Energy	7519	8054	10145	12883	14239	13005	22374	27458	37000
Materials, Semi-finished & Spares	122770	137375	166454	207951	228907	290375	296060	296454	411500
Machinery	126322	128594	133558	137060	121400	96038	100898	114216	146900
Industrial Consumer Goods	67332	73620	79833	89699	99751	173034	221876	206719	301300
Agriculture and Processed Foods	82262	84965	102335	123731	139339	191822	202358	175068	232000
Total	406205	432608	492325	571324	603636	764274	843566	819915	1128700
Imports:									
Energy	78053	67401	59768	57573	75262	127972	127934	146730	168700
Materials, Semi-finished & Spares	192342	209224	235972	264717	252089	318745	322356	388308	566200
Machinery	73466	79670	76982	94620	96805	173629	180488	312852	359200
Industrial Consumer Goods	50763	55650	54496	69073	79404	185710	196060	246045	338300
Agriculture and Processed Foods	30381	32012	33677	37524	41361	49587	51666	68556	104700
Total	425005	443957	460895	523507	544921	855643	878504	1162491	1537100
(Value, share of total)									
Exports:									
Energy	1.9	1.9	2.1	2.3	2.4	1.7	2.7	3.3	3.3
Materials, Semi-finished & Spares	30.2	31.8	33.8	36.4	37.9	38.0	35.1	36.2	36.5
Machinery	31.1	29.7	27.1	24.0	20.1	12.6	12.0	13.9	13.0
Industrial Consumer Goods	16.6	17.0	16.2	15.7	16.5	22.6	26.3	25.2	26.7
Agriculture and Processed Foods	20.3	19.6	20.8	21.7	23.1	25.1	24.0	21.4	20.6
Total	100.0	100.0	100.0	100.0	100.0	100.0	100.0	100.0	100.0
Imports:									
Energy	18	15	13	11	14	15	15	13	11
Materials, Semi-finished & Spares	45	47	51	51	46	37	37	33	37
Machinery	17	18	17	18	18	20	21	27	23
Industrial Consumer Goods	12	13	12	13	15	22	22	21	22
Agriculture and Processed Foods	7	7	7	7	8	6	6	6	7
Total	100	100	100	100	100	100	100	100	100
(Volume, percentage change)									
Exports:									
Energy	4.7%	-2.8%	30.2%	-2.5%	-18.6%	-11.6%	79.9%	9.4%	..
Materials, Semi-finished & Spares	-0.9%	6.4%	6.3%	7.6%	3.8%	6.4%	-2.2%	-8.5%	..
Machinery	-2.5%	1.3%	4.4%	-9.1%	-17.4%	-42.7%	-9.6%	3.3%	..
Industrial Consumer Goods	-1.2%	5.1%	4.2%	-0.2%	1.0%	-1.9%	17.1%	-15.8%	..
Agriculture and Processed Foods	-5.5%	0.7%	10.6%	1.9%	-4.3%	9.0%	-8.0%	-27.2%	..
Total	-2.2%	3.3%	6.8%	0.3%	-4.1%	-4.9%	1.0%	-13.1%	..
Imports:									
Energy	1.0%	-1.8%	0.8%	-2.7%	17.2%	-13.7%	-5.1%	14.6%	..
Materials, Semi-finished & Spares	1.9%	1.8%	3.7%	-2.3%	-13.3%	-6.9%	-10.1%	9.0%	..
Machinery	1.2%	4.0%	-6.3%	7.7%	-8.7%	22.5%	-9.4%	52.7%	..
Industrial Consumer Goods	11.5%	5.7%	-5.6%	11.2%	3.4%	47.7%	-4.3%	15.7%	..
Agriculture and Processed Foods	5.5%	6.0%	-4.5%	-1.3%	10.2%	-5.2%	-2.3%	17.7%	..
Total	2.6%	2.4%	-0.3%	1.1%	-5.2%	5.5%	-7.6%	20.9%	..

Source: Statistical Yearbook of External Trade.

a/ In 1993 includes military technology item as reimbursement for state debt of the former Soviet Union.

Table 3.6: Value of External Trade by Trading Partners

	1985	1986	1987	1988	1989	1990	1991	1992	1993 b/	1994
	(in millions of US$)									
Exports:										
Eastern European Countries a/	3960.1	4361.0	4230.0	3883.4	3425.9	2707.1	1980.9	2081.4	2033.8	2052.5
European Union Countries	1295.0	1533.6	1852.8	2189.7	2384.3	3088.7	4659.4	5326.7	4139.9	5490.2
Other	3012.0	2955.2	3115.8	3626.0	3795.1	3791.8	3546.6	3297.0	2733.2	3232.4
Total	8267.1	8849.8	9198.6	9699.1	9605.3	9587.6	10186.9	10705.1	8906.9	10775.1
Imports:										
Eastern European Countries a/	3466.6	4115.2	3937.2	3439.2	2916.5	2408.4	2537.5	2612.3	3538.2	3257.2
European Union Countries	1711.3	2167.9	2367.9	2347.0	2557.1	2683.4	4681.8	4734.1	5023.7	6654.9
Other	2668.4	2980.3	3142.8	3329.6	3345.6	3555.0	4162.8	3732.5	3968.4	4760.9
Total	7846.3	9263.4	9447.9	9115.8	8819.2	8646.8	11382.1	11078.9	12530.3	14673.0
Balance:										
Eastern European Countries a/	493.5	245.8	292.8	444.2	509.4	298.7	-556.6	-530.9	-1504.4	-1204.7
European Union Countries	-416.3	-634.3	-515.1	-157.3	-172.8	405.3	-22.4	592.6	-883.8	-1164.7
Other	343.6	-25.1	-27.0	296.4	449.5	236.8	-616.2	-435.5	-1235.2	-1528.5
Total	420.8	-413.6	-249.3	583.3	786.1	940.8	-1195.2	-373.8	-3623.4	-3897.9
	(share of total)									
Exports:										
Eastern European Countries a/	47.9	49.3	46.0	40.0	35.7	28.2	19.4	19.4	22.8	19.0
European Union Countries	15.7	17.3	20.1	22.6	24.8	32.2	45.7	49.8	46.5	51.0
Other	36.4	33.4	33.9	37.4	39.5	39.5	34.8	30.8	30.7	30.0
Total	100.0	100.0	100.0	100.0	100.0	100.0	100.0	100.0	100.0	100.0
Imports:										
Eastern European Countries a/	44.2	44.4	41.7	37.7	33.1	27.9	22.3	23.6	28.2	22.2
European Union Countries	21.8	23.4	25.1	25.7	29.0	31.0	41.1	42.7	40.1	45.4
Other	34.0	32.2	33.3	36.5	37.9	41.1	36.6	33.7	31.7	32.4
Total	100.0	100.0	100.0	100.0	100.0	100.0	100.0	100.0	100.0	100.0

Source: Central Statistical Office.

a/ The Eastern European countries are comprised of Albania, Bulgaria, Czech and Slovak Republic, Poland, Romania and the Successor States of the Former Soviet Union.

b/ Includes the value of military technology items worth US$713.4 million delivered in reimbursement for state debt of the former Soviet Union.

Table 4.1: External Debt
(US$ Millions, at end of period)

	1982	1983	1984	1985	1986	1987	1988	1989	1990	1991	1992	1993	1994
Total	11516.0	12126.0	12216.0	15105.4	17928.6	20530.3	20185.1	20750.9	21504.5	22812.2	21654.8	24565.9	28525.9
Convertible Currencies	10216.0	10746.0	10983.0	13955.0	16907.2	19583.7	19602.6	20390.2	21269.5	22657.6	21437.7	24560.2	28521.1
Short-Term	3261.0	3904.0	2977.0	3018.9	3493.8	3102.7	3363.0	3306.5	2940.5	2177.2	2286.2	2005.2	2396.7
Medium- & Long-Term	6955.0	6842.0	8006.0	10936.1	13413.4	16481.0	16239.6	17083.7	18329.0	20480.4	19151.5	22555.0	26124.4
By type of credit:													
Financial Loans	9155.0	9208.0	9428.0	12175.2	15084.4	17508.8	17469.1	18060.0	17586.9	18135.3	16211.0	19990.3	23776.8
Trade-related Credits	661.0	1144.0	1125.0	1318.5	1432.8	1652.4	1625.9	1762.6	1979.5	1776.6	2011.1	2557.2	2487.6
Intergovernmental Credits	5.0	4.0	3.0	2.0	1.2	0.4	0.0	0.0	472.5	1511.4	1445.9	2012.7	2256.7
Other	396.0	390.0	428.0	459.2	388.8	422.4	507.6	567.6	1230.6	1234.2	1769.6	0.0	0.0
NonConvertible Currencies	1300.0	1380.0	1233.0	1150.4	1021.4	946.6	582.5	360.7	235.0	154.6	217.1	5.7	4.8
Short-Term	250.0	368.0	317.0	105.7	111.0	183.6	119.8	86.6	79.9	38.0	15.8	5.6	4.8
Medium- & Long-Term	1050.0	1012.0	916.0	1044.7	910.4	763.0	462.7	274.1	155.1	116.6	201.3	0.1	0.0
By type of credit:													
Financial Loans	251.0	366.0	313.0	133.3	140.5	210.5	136.1	88.4	70.6	34.8	13.0	3.2	2.8
Trade-related Credits	39.0	30.0	24.0	0.2	0.0	0.0	0.0	0.0	0.0	0.0	0.0	2.4	1.9
Intergovernmental Credits	974.0	948.0	863.0	1009.3	872.6	728.3	438.5	260.2	139.9	104.2	190.1	0.1	0.1
Other	35.0	36.0	32.0	7.7	8.2	8.0	7.9	12.2	24.5	15.6	14.0	0.0	0.0
Memorandum Items:													
Stock of foreign Direct Investment in Hungary													
In Convertible Currencies	..	..	..	..	6.0	8.0	23.0	215.1	569.0	2107.3	3423.8	5575.9	7086.8
In Non-convertible Currencies	..	..	..	..				8.3	24.5	15.6	14.0	9.3	8.5

Source: National Bank of Hungary.

Table 5.1: General Government Accounts, 1988-94
(Billions of Forint)

	1988	1989	1990	1991	1992	1993	Estim. 1994
REVENUES	892.9	1019.0	1204.2	1292.1	1619.8	1942.2	2289.7
Tax Revenues	764.4	859.5	994.3	1048.1	1196.6	1473.9	1693.0
Income taxes	193.7	233.0	283.9	303.2	293.6	355.0	398.9
o/w Enterprises	127.4	138.8	157.1	131.2	72.7	70.7	92.6
o/w Individuals a/	66.3	94.2	126.8	172.0	220.9	284.3	306.3
Indirect taxes	388.5	382.5	423.9	419.9	506.9	645.3	746.7
o/w Domestic	304.3	290.7	312.0	344.9	406.7	520.4	598.7
o/w VAT	123.0	135.1	146.8	149.5	175.7	286.7	343.5
o/w Excises	83.9	95.6	108.2	137.3	166.7	148.2	172.0
o/w Other	97.4	60.0	57.0	58.1	64.3	85.5	83.2
o/w Foreign	84.2	91.8	112.0	75.0	100.2	124.9	148.0
Social Security Contributions	182.3	243.9	286.5	325.0	396.1	473.6	547.4
o/w Employers	137.1	190.3	221.7	245.3	300.3	348.8	408.5
o/w Employees	45.2	53.6	64.8	79.7	95.8	124.8	138.9
Nontax Revenues	128.5	159.5	209.9	244.0	423.2	468.3	596.7
EXPENDITURES	892.3	1041.5	1194.5	1345.6	1778.1	2177.4	2565.2
Wages and Salaries	122.9	141.6	158.7	209.7	249.6	304.6	348.5
Other Goods and Services	179.6	208.6	231.3	200.1	263.4	512.8	447.2
Subsidies on Products	79.6	123.2	116.5	130.3	87.7	92.1	93.1
o/w Subsidies on Domestic Products	76.8	121.1	116.5	130.3	87.7	92.1	93.1
o/w Subsidies on Imports	2.8	2.1	--	--	--	--	--
Subsidies on Production	106.9	83.8	82.4	54.5	74.8	59.7	101.1
Social Benefits in Cash	196.3	245.5	309.2	417.3	529.7	609.1	761.3
o/w Pensions	130.0	156.5	202.5	260.7	305.5	344.4	442.3
o/w Family Allowances, GYES, GYED	48.9	67.9	82.4	107.7	129.6	126.6	199.7
o/w Sickpay	17.4	21.1	24.3	29.0	28.9	35.3	41.4
o/w Unemployment benefits	--	--	--	19.9	47.4	74.8	45.9
o/w Local Gov't Benefits	...	...	...	0.0	18.3	28.0	32.0
Social Benefits in Kind	75.4	85.3	136.7	95.2	174.1	188.4	235.5
Interest Payments	22.5	41.3	62.9	95.0	172.4	165.0	292.1
Capital Expenditures	109.1	112.2	96.8	143.5	226.4	245.7	286.4
o/w Fixed Capital Formation	88.6	101.2	74.7	102.3	177.2	188.5	215.9
o/w Capital Transfers	20.5	11.0	22.1	41.2	49.2	57.2	70.5
Primary Balance	23.1	18.8	72.6	41.5	14.1	-70.2	16.6
Overall Balance	0.6	-22.5	9.7	-53.5	-158.3	-235.2	-275.5
Memorandum items:							
Gross Domestic Product old meth.	1435.2	1710.8	2079.5	2308.4	2805.0	3320.0	3959.5
Gross Domestic Product new meth.	...	...	...	2491.7	2935.1	3537.7	4310.0
Privatization Revenues	...	...	...	0.0	23.5	11.6	35.0
Government Debt	...	...	1411.9	1878.8	2331.2	3192.2	3815.6
o/w FX Loss-Related (non-interest bearing)	...	...	519.2	777.9	888.9	1182.0	1440.1
o/w Other	...	...	892.7	1100.9	1442.3	2010.2	2375.5
o/w credit consolidation	...	...	...	...	...	285.6	335.1
o/w other	...	...	892.7	1100.9	1442.0	1724.6	2040.5

a/ Includes interest withholding tax from 1992.

Table 5.2: GENERAL GOVERNMENT ACCOUNTS, 1988-94
(Percent of GDP)

	1988	1989	1990	1991 a/	1992	1993	Est. 1994
REVENUES	62.2	59.6	57.9	51.9	55.2	54.9	53.1
Tax Revenues	53.3	50.2	47.8	42.1	40.8	41.7	39.3
Income taxes	13.5	13.6	13.7	12.2	10.0	10.0	9.3
o/w Enterprises	8.9	8.1	7.6	5.3	2.5	2.0	2.1
o/w Individuals b/	4.6	5.5	6.1	6.9	7.5	8.0	7.1
Indirect taxes	27.1	22.4	20.4	16.9	17.3	18.2	17.3
o/w Domestic	21.2	17.0	15.0	13.8	13.9	14.7	13.9
o/w VAT	8.6	7.9	7.1	6.0	6.0	8.1	8.0
o/w Excises	5.8	5.6	5.2	5.5	5.7	4.2	4.0
o/w Other	6.8	3.5	2.7	2.3	2.2	2.4	1.9
o/w Foreign	5.9	5.4	5.4	3.0	3.4	3.5	3.4
Social Security Contributions	12.7	14.3	13.8	13.0	13.5	13.4	12.7
o/w Employers	9.6	11.1	10.7	9.8	10.2	9.9	9.5
o/w Employees	3.1	3.1	3.1	3.2	3.3	3.5	3.2
Nontax Revenues	9.0	9.3	10.1	9.8	14.4	13.2	13.8
EXPENDITURES	62.2	60.9	57.4	54.0	60.6	61.5	59.5
Wages and Salaries	8.6	8.3	7.6	8.4	8.5	8.6	8.1
Other Goods and Services	12.5	12.2	11.1	8.0	9.0	14.5	10.4
Subsidies on Products	5.5	7.2	5.6	5.2	3.0	2.6	2.2
o/w Subsidies on Domestic Products	5.4	7.1	5.6	5.2	3.0	2.6	2.2
o/w Subsidies on Imports	0.2	0.1	0.0	0.0	0.0	0.0	0.0
Subsidies on Production	7.4	4.9	4.0	2.2	2.5	1.7	2.3
Social Benefits in Cash	13.7	14.4	14.9	16.7	18.0	17.2	17.7
o/w Pensions	9.1	9.1	9.7	10.5	10.4	9.7	10.3
o/w Family Allowances, GYES, GYED	3.4	4.0	4.0	4.3	4.4	3.6	4.6
o/w Sickpay	1.2	1.2	1.2	1.2	1.0	1.0	1.0
o/w Unemployment benefits	0.0	0.0	0.0	0.8	1.6	2.1	1.1
o/w Local Gov't Benefits	0.0	0.0	0.0	0.0	0.6	0.8	0.7
Social Benefits in Kind	5.3	5.0	6.6	3.8	5.9	5.3	5.5
Interest Payments	1.6	2.4	3.0	3.8	5.9	4.7	6.8
Capital Expenditures	7.6	6.6	4.7	5.8	7.7	6.9	6.6
o/w Fixed Capital Formation	6.2	5.9	3.6	4.1	6.0	5.3	5.0
o/w Capital Transfers	1.4	0.6	1.1	1.7	1.7	1.6	1.6
Primary Balance	1.6	1.1	3.5	1.7	0.5	-2.0	0.4
Overall Balance	0.0	-1.3	0.5	-2.1	-5.4	-6.6	-6.4
Memorandum items:							
Privatization Revenues	0.0	0.0	0.0	0.0	0.8	0.3	0.8
Government Debt	0.0	0.0	67.9	75.4	79.4	90.2	88.5
o/w FX Loss-Related (non-interest bearing)	0.0	0.0	25.0	31.2	30.3	33.4	33.4
o/w Other	0.0	0.0	42.9	44.2	49.1	56.8	55.1
o/w credit consolidation	0.0	0.0	0.0	0.0	0.0	8.1	7.8
o/w other	0.0	0.0	42.9	44.2	49.1	48.7	47.3

a/ Because of the change in methodology of recorded GDP in 1991- 1993 one should be cautious in
   comparing 1990 to 1991.

b/ Includes interest withholding tax from 1992.

Table 5.3: GENERAL GOVERNMENT ACCOUNTS, 1988-94
(Billions of 1991 Forint)

	1988	1989	1990	1991	1992	Estim. 1993	Budget 1994
REVENUES	1672.1	1604.7	1510.9	1292.1	1333.2	1315.2	1298.3
Tax Revenues	1431.5	1353.5	1247.6	1048.1	984.9	998.1	960.0
Income taxes	362.7	366.9	356.2	303.2	241.7	240.4	226.2
o/w Enterprises	238.5	218.6	197.1	131.2	59.8	47.9	52.5
o/w Individuals a/	124.2	148.3	159.1	172.0	181.8	192.5	173.7
Indirect taxes	727.4	602.4	531.9	419.9	417.2	437.0	423.4
o/w Domestic	569.8	457.8	391.4	344.9	334.7	352.4	339.5
o/w VAT	230.4	212.7	184.2	149.5	144.6	194.1	194.8
o/w Excises	157.0	150.6	135.8	137.3	137.2	100.4	97.5
o/w Other	182.4	94.5	71.5	58.1	52.9	57.9	47.2
o/w Foreign	157.7	144.6	140.5	75.0	82.5	84.6	83.9
Social Security Contributions	341.3	384.1	359.5	325.0	326.0	320.7	310.4
o/w Employers	256.7	299.7	278.2	245.3	247.2	236.2	231.6
o/w Employees	84.6	84.4	81.3	79.7	78.9	84.5	78.8
Nontax Revenues	240.6	251.2	263.3	244.0	348.3	317.1	338.3
EXPENDITURES	1671.0	1640.2	1498.7	1345.6	1463.5	1474.4	1454.5
Wages and Salaries	230.1	223.0	199.1	209.7	205.4	206.3	197.6
Other Goods and Services	336.3	328.5	290.2	200.1	216.8	347.2	253.6
Subsidies on Products	149.1	194.0	146.2	130.3	72.2	62.4	52.8
o/w Subsidies on Domestic Products	143.8	190.7	146.2	130.3	72.2	62.4	52.8
o/w Subsidies on Imports	5.2	3.3	0.0	0.0	0.0	0.0	0.0
Subsidies on Production	200.2	132.0	103.4	54.5	61.6	40.4	57.3
Social Benefits in Cash	367.6	386.6	388.0	417.3	436.0	412.5	431.7
o/w Pensions	243.4	246.5	254.1	260.7	251.4	233.2	250.8
o/w Family Allowances, GYES, GYED	91.6	106.9	103.4	107.7	106.7	85.7	113.2
o/w Sickpay	32.6	33.2	30.5	29.0	23.8	23.9	23.5
o/w Unemployment benefits	0.0	0.0	0.0	19.9	39.0	50.7	26.0
o/w Local Gov't Benefits	0.0	0.0	0.0	0.0	15.1	19.0	18.1
Social Benefits in Kind	141.2	134.3	171.5	95.2	143.3	127.6	133.5
Interest Payments	42.1	65.0	78.9	95.0	141.9	111.7	165.6
Capital Expenditures	204.3	176.7	121.5	143.5	186.3	166.4	162.4
o/w Fixed Capital Formation	165.9	159.4	93.7	102.3	145.8	127.6	122.4
o/w Capital Transfers	38.4	17.3	27.7	41.2	40.5	38.7	40.0
Primary Balance	43.3	29.6	91.1	41.5	11.6	-47.5	9.4
Overall Balance	1.1	-35.4	12.2	-53.5	-130.3	-159.2	-156.2
Memorandum items:							
Privatization Revenues	0.0	0.0	0.0	0.0	19.3	7.9	19.8
Government Debt	0.0	0.0	1771.5	1878.8	1918.7	2161.6	2163.6
o/w FX Loss-Related (non-interest bearing)	0.0	0.0	651.4	777.9	731.6	800.4	816.6
o/w Other	0.0	0.0	1120.1	1100.9	1187.1	1361.2	1347.0
o/w credit consolidation	0.0	0.0	0.0	0.0	0.0	193.4	190.0
o/w other	0.0	0.0	1120.1	1100.9	1186.9	1167.8	1157.0

a/ Includes interest withholding tax from 1992.

Table 5.4: General Government Fiscal Data in Selected Countries
(in percent of GDP)

	Austria 1991	Denmark 1990	Finland 1990	France 1992	Germany 1991	Ireland 1990	Netherlands 1992	Norway 1990	Portugal 1990	Spain 1990	Sweden 1992	U.K. 1991	Hungary 1989	Hungary 1992
TOTAL REVENUE	48.2%	57.5%	45.0%	46.8%	46.7%	42.1%	54.4%	58.6%	39.6%	36.4%	65.6%	41.3%	59.6%	55.2%
Tax revenue	40.9%	48.1%	37.9%	41.5%	40.1%	35.2%	46.5%	45.2%	34.1%	33.2%	55.4%	35.2%	50.2%	40.8%
Income Taxes	11.1%	28.3%	8.8%	6.9%	12.6%	13.3%	14.7%	16.1%	9.0%	10.6%	21.6%	13.4%	13.6%	10.0%
Individual	9.1%	25.5%	7.6%	5.4%	9.4%	11.4%	11.6%	12.0%	5.6%	7.5%	1.2%	10.3%	8.1%	2.5%
Enterprises	2.0%	2.8%	1.2%	1.5%	3.2%	1.9%	3.1%	4.1%	3.5%	3.1%	20.4%	3.2%	5.5%	7.5%
Social Security Contr.	13.1%	1.5%	3.6%	18.0%	15.7%	5.3%	18.4%	11.2%	9.8%	11.6%	16.9%	6.0%	14.3%	13.5%
Payroll taxes	1.9%	0.3%	0.0%	0.5%	0.0%	0.5%	0.0%	0.0%	0.0%	0.0%	2.0%	0.0%	--	--
Property Taxes	1.1%	2.0%	1.0%	1.2%	0.9%	1.7%	1.7%	1.3%	0.2%	2.0%	1.4%	3.0%	--	--
Dom.taxes on g.&s.	12.2%	16.0%	14.2%	10.9%	11.0%	11.5%	10.5%	16.0%	13.3%	8.4%	13.1%	11.4%	17.0%	13.9%
VAT a/	5.9%	9.0%	0.0%	7.4%	5.1%	7.3%	7.2%	8.5%	6.5%	4.4%	8.4%	6.6%	7.9%	6.0%
Excises a/	1.9%	3.8%	4.4%	2.4%	2.9%	3.2%	2.6%	5.8%	4.7%	2.0%	3.9%	4.0%	5.6%	5.7%
Others b/	4.4%	3.2%	9.8%	1.0%	3.0%	1.0%	0.7%	1.7%	2.1%	2.1%	0.8%	0.7%	3.5%	2.2%
Taxes on Intl. Trade	0.5%	0.0%	0.3%	0.0%	0.0%	3.0%	0.0%	0.2%	0.8%	0.5%	0.3%	0.0%	5.4%	3.4%
Other taxes c/	0.9%	0.0%	10.0%	4.1%	-0.2%	0.0%	1.2%	0.4%	1.0%	0.1%	0.0%	1.4%	0.0%	0.0%
Non-tax revenues	7.0%	8.4%	5.9%	4.6%	6.3%	4.7%	7.1%	13.0%	3.4%	2.9%	9.8%	4.9%	9.3%	13.6%
Capital Revenues	0.3%	0.8%	1.2%	0.4%	0.3%	0.5%	0.8%	0.4%	0.6%	0.4%	0.4%	0.6%	0.0%	0.8%
Grants	0.0%	0.1%	0.0%	0.3%	0.0%	1.7%	0.0%	0.0%	1.5%	0.0%	0.0%	0.5%	--	--
TOTAL EXPENDITURE & LENDING MINUS REPAYMENTS	52.8%	58.4%	45.3%	50.9%	48.3%	44.4%	56.3%	57.1%	42.9%	40.6%	59.8%	41.3%	60.9%	60.6%
Total Expenditure	51.8%	58.1%	44.3%	50.7%	47.5%	44.4%	56.4%	56.7%	44.0%	40.1%	60.0%	42.9%	60.9%	60.6%
Current Expenditure	45.6%	55.2%	40.1%	46.2%	43.2%	41.2%	52.6%	53.2%	39.2%	34.1%	58.0%	39.0%	54.3%	52.9%
Expenditure on g&s.	18.7%	26.2%	22.8%	15.9%	20.7%	15.8%	15.2%	22.0%	15.6%	14.5%	24.8%	20.4%	20.5%	17.5%
Wages and salaries	9.3%	17.5%	13.3%	10.2%	10.3%	9.4%	9.8%	13.9%	11.6%	10.4%	17.5%	10.5%	8.3%	8.5%
Other goods and services	9.4%	8.7%	9.4%	5.7%	10.3%	6.4%	5.5%	8.1%	4.0%	4.1%	7.3%	9.9%	12.2%	9.0%
Interest Payments	4.3%	6.5%	1.4%	3.4%	2.9%	8.2%	6.8%	3.9%	8.2%	3.5%	4.9%	3.6%	2.4%	5.9%
Subsidies & curr. transf.	22.7%	22.6%	15.9%	26.8%	19.6%	17.2%	30.6%	27.3%	15.5%	16.0%	28.3%	15.0%	31.4%	29.5%
Subsidies d/	2.2%	1.9%	...	1.4%	...	1.1%	1.1%	5.9%	2.1%	1.2%	2.8%	0.7%	12.1%	5.5%
Transfers to nonprofit institutions & households d/	16.9%	7.2%	...	22.6%	...		22.9%	17.6%	12.4%	13.0%	21.5%	11.4%	19.3%	24.0%
Capital Expenditure	5.3%	2.9%	4.2%	4.6%	4.0%	3.1%	3.8%	3.5%	5.0%	6.0%	2.0%	3.9%	6.6%	7.7%
Capital Transfers	2.2%	0.9%	0.5%	0.9%	1.3%	1.0%	0.8%	0.0%	1.2%	1.3%	0.2%	1.2%	0.6%	1.7%
Lending minus Repayments	1.9%	0.3%	1.0%	0.2%	0.7%	0.0%	0.0%	0.4%	-1.1%	0.5%	-0.2%	-1.6%	0.0%	0.0%

Sources: Government Finance Statistics, 1993 and World Bank staff estimates.
a/ Central government only.
b/ Includes local government taxes not specified as VAT or excises.
c/ Includes nonclassified local taxes for Finland and France.
d/ Central government only for Western European countries.

Table 5.5: Personal Incomes and Taxes, 1989-94 a/
(Billions of Forint; Percent of GDP)

	1989	1990	1991	1992	1993	Budget 1994	Percentage change				
							90/89	91/90	92/91	93/92	94/93
INCOMES											
Household Incomes	1,122.0	1,645.5	2,140.5	2,569.9	2,979.8	3,435.9	46.7%	30.1%	20.1%	16.0%	15.3%
o/w Fringe benefits b/	-56.7	-93.3	-135.0	-181.6	-220.0	-287.5	64.6%	44.7%	34.5%	21.1%	30.7%
o/w Other incomes	-1,065.3	-1,552.2	-2,005.5	-2,388.3	-2,759.8	-3,148.4	45.7%	29.2%	19.1%	15.6%	14.1%
Household Cash Incomes	887.0	1,324.9	1,774.9	2,141.9	2,483.3	2,898.7	49.4%	34.0%	20.7%	15.9%	16.7%
o/w Non-taxable cash incomes	-228.0	-473.1	-776.8	-904.9	-1,112.6	-1,300.2	107.5%	64.2%	16.5%	23.0%	16.9%
o/w Taxable cash incomes	-659.0	-851.8	-998.1	-1,237.0	-1,370.7	-1,598.5	29.3%	17.2%	23.9%	10.8%	16.6%
o/w interest income	30.0	40.0	60.0	100.0	100.0	110.0	33.3%	50.0%	66.7%	0.0%	10.0%
o/w dividend and other non-progressively taxed incomes	18.0	30.0	40.0	50.0	50.0	50.0	66.7%	33.3%	25.0%	0.0%	0.0%
o/w progressively taxed incomes	611.0	781.8	898.1	1,087.0	1,220.7	1,438.5	28.0%	14.9%	21.0%	12.3%	17.8%
TAXES											
Nonprogressive Taxes Paid	9.6	14.0	20.0	30.0	30.0	21.0	45.8%	42.9%	50.0%	0.0%	-30.0%
o/w Interest income taxes	-6.0	-8.0	-12.0	-20.0	-20.0	-11.0	33.3%	50.0%	66.7%	0.0%	-45.0%
o/w Dividend and other non-progressively taxed incomes	-3.6	-6.0	-8.0	-10.0	-10.0	-10.0	66.7%	33.3%	25.0%	0.0%	0.0%
Progressive Taxes Paid	89.0	126.5	162.8	195.3	254.6	284.1	42.1%	28.7%	20.0%	30.4%	11.6%
INCOMES											
Household Incomes	65.8%	79.1%	86.4%	89.1%	85.1%	82.3%					
o/w Fringe benefits b/	3.3%	4.5%	5.5%	6.3%	6.3%	6.9%					
o/w Other incomes	62.4%	74.6%	81.0%	82.8%	78.8%	75.4%					
Household Cash Incomes	52.0%	63.7%	71.7%	74.2%	70.9%	69.4%					
o/w Non-taxable cash incomes	13.4%	22.7%	31.4%	31.4%	31.8%	31.1%					
o/w Taxable cash income	38.6%	40.9%	40.3%	42.9%	39.1%	38.3%					
o/w interest income	1.8%	1.9%	2.4%	3.5%	2.9%	2.6%					
o/w dividend and other non-progressively taxed incomes	1.1%	1.4%	1.6%	1.7%	1.4%	1.2%					
o/w progressively taxed incomes	35.8%	37.6%	36.3%	37.7%	34.9%	34.4%					
TAXES											
Nonprogressive Taxes Paid	0.6%	0.7%	0.8%	1.0%	0.9%	0.5%					
o/w Interest income taxes	0.4%	0.4%	0.5%	0.7%	0.6%	0.3%					
o/w Dividend and other non-progressively taxed incomes	0.2%	0.3%	0.3%	0.3%	0.3%	0.2%					
Progressive Taxes Paid	5.2%	6.1%	6.6%	6.8%	7.3%	6.8%					
Memorandum item:											
Taxable Cash Incomes/Household Incomes	58.7%	51.8%	46.6%	48.1%	46.0%	46.5%					
Taxes/Household Incomes	8.8%	8.5%	8.5%	8.8%	9.6%	8.9%					
Gross Domestic Product	1706.0	2080.9	2476.7	2885.6	3502.6	4177.3	(percentage change)				
							22.0%	19.0%	16.5%	21.4%	19.3%

Sources: Ministry of Finance and World Bank staff estimates.
a/ Using the old national accounts methodology of tables 2.1-2.4.
b/ Paid both in cash and in kind.

Table 5.6: Calculation of Household Income Taxes, 1989-94 a/
(Billions of Forint; Percent of GDP)

	1989	1990	1991	1992	1993	Budget 1994	90/89	91/90	92/91	93/92	94/93
							Percentage change				
Incomes subject to nonprogressive taxation	48.0	70.0	100.0	150.0	150.0	160.0	45.8%	42.9%	50.0%	0.0%	6.7%
o/w interest income	-30.0	-40.0	-60.0	-100.0	-100.0	-110.0	33.3%	50.0%	66.7%	0.0%	10.0%
o/w taxes paid	6.0	8.0	12.0	20.0	20.0	11.0	33.3%	50.0%	66.7%	0.0%	-45.0%
o/w dividend and other non-progressively taxed incomes	-18.0	-30.0	-40.0	-50.0	-50.0	-50.0	66.7%	33.3%	25.0%	0.0%	0.0%
o/w taxes paid	3.6	6.0	8.0	10.0	10.0	10.0	66.7%	33.3%	25.0%	0.0%	0.0%
Incomes subject to progressive taxation	611.0	781.8	898.1	1087.0	1220.7	1438.5	28.0%	14.9%	21.0%	12.3%	17.8%
Less: Allowances	52.4	67.4	30.2	61.0	48.3	152.3	28.6%	-55.2%	102.0%	-20.8%	215.3%
o/w employee allowance	-42.6	-49.7	--	--	--	--					
o/w donations to foundations	-0.2	--	--	-2.0	-2.5	-1.0					
o/w disabled allowance	-0.2	-0.6	-1.3	-1.5	-1.5	-1.5					
o/w public utility contributions	--	--	--	--	--	--					
o/w trade union dues	-2.9	-3.6	-4.9	-10.9	-22.0	-22.0					
o/w child allowances	-5.0	-6.5	-11.3	-29.2	--	--					
o/w proprietors' investments	-0.3	--	--	--	--	--					
o/w investment & privatization allowances	--	-6.5	-10.9	-7.3	-8.0	-8.5					
o/w incentives and rewards	-1.2	--	--	--	--	--					
o/w Solidarity Fund contributions	--	--	-1.6	--	--	--					
o/w allowances for local taxes paid	--	--	-0.2	-0.7	-1.5	-2.0					
o/w intellectual incomes allowances	--	--	--	-9.3	-12.0	-12.5					
o/w Pension Fund contributions	--	--	--	--	--	-104.0					
o/w unidentified	--	-0.5	0.0	-0.1	-0.8	-0.8					
Equals: Taxable incomes	558.6	714.4	867.9	1026.0	1172.4	1286.2	27.9%	21.5%	18.2%	14.3%	9.7%
Gross progressive tax liability	94.3	132.7	179.1	199.6	272.1	300.1	40.7%	35.0%	11.4%	36.3%	10.3%
Less: Tax credits	5.3	6.2	16.3	4.3	17.5	16.0	17.0%	162.9%	-73.6%	307.0%	-8.6%
o/w employee credit	--	--	-10.9	--	-7.0	-9.5					
o/w child credit	--	--	--	--	-6.0	-4.0					
o/w pension credits	-3.8	-5.5	-4.6	-3.6	-4.0	-4.0					
o/w saving for housing	-0.2	-0.3	-0.3	-0.3	-0.3	-0.3					
o/w pension & insurance premiums	-0.3	-0.4	-0.5	-0.4	-0.2	-0.2					
o/w utility investments	-1.0	--	--	--	--	--					
o/w other credits	--	--	--	--	--	-2.0					
Equals: Net progressive tax liability	89.0	126.5	162.8	195.3	254.6	284.1	42.1%	28.7%	20.0%	30.4%	11.6%
Memorandum items:											
Allowances/Incomes subject to progressive taxation	8.6%	8.6%	3.4%	5.6%	4.0%	10.6%					
Tax credits/Gross progressive tax liability	5.6%	4.7%	9.1%	2.2%	6.4%	5.3%					
Average tax rate on incomes subject to nonprogressive taxation	20.0%	20.0%	20.0%	20.0%	20.0%	13.1%					
Average tax rate on gross incomes subject to progressive taxation	14.6%	16.2%	18.1%	18.0%	20.9%	19.7%					
Average tax rate on taxable incomes subject to progressive taxation	15.9%	17.7%	18.8%	19.0%	21.7%	22.1%					

a/ Using the old national accounts methodology of tables 2.1-2.4.
Sources: Ministry of Finance and World Bank staff estimates.

Table 5.7: Enterprise Profit Tax Liabilities,
Payments and Reliefs, 1988-1994 a/
millions of Forint; Shares of GDP)

	1988	Budget 1989	1989	Budget 1990	1990	Budget 1991	1991	Budget 1992	1992	Budget 1993	Expected 1993 b/	Budget 1994 c/
Taxable Profits	237406	267135	302453	324380	337913	370775	250470	367427	200473	275379	189147	233860
o/w Financial enterprises	43500	28600	54411	38400	67907	62000	46084	92600	29025	52900	5050	19600
o/w Nonfinancial enterprises	193906	238535	248042	285980	270006	308775	204386	274827	171448	222479	184097	214260
Tax Liabilities	96048	115370	121288	116281	108796	125313	67847	120607	63074	84921	47418	66978
o/w Financial enterprises	18900	14100	25707	15540	24724	26930	14778	41000	12742	18680	1600	7100
o/w Nonfinancial enterprises	77148	101270	95581	100741	84072	98383	53069	79607	50332	66241	45818	59878
Tax Reliefs	11928	17588 d/	26773 d/	16960	28077	21880	30218	20484	33222	21310	28241	17956
o/w Financial enterprises	1	.. d/	1118 d/	800	2175	1200	3432	2000	2558	1200	420	700
o/w Nonfinancial enterprises	11638	17588 d/	25655 d/	16160	25902	20680	26786	18484	30664	20110	27821	17256
Taxes/Profits	40.5%	43.2%	40.1%	35.8%	32.2%	33.8%	27.1%	32.8%	31.5%	30.8%	25.1%	28.6%
o/w Financial enterprises	43.4%	49.3%	47.2%	40.5%	36.4%	43.4%	32.1%	44.3%	43.9%	35.3%	31.7%	36.2%
o/w Nonfinancial enterprises	39.8%	42.5%	38.5%	35.2%	31.1%	31.9%	26.0%	29.0%	29.4%	29.8%	24.9%	27.9%
Reliefs/(Taxes+Reliefs)	11.0%	13.2%	18.1%	12.7%	20.5%	14.9%	30.8%	14.5%	34.5%	20.1%	37.3%	21.1%
o/w Financial enterprises	1.5%	...	4.2%	4.9%	8.1%	4.3%	18.8%	4.7%	16.7%	6.0%	20.8%	9.0%
o/w Nonfinancial enterprises	13.1%	14.8%	21.2%	13.8%	23.6%	17.4%	33.5%	18.8%	37.9%	23.3%	37.8%	22.4%
Tax Revenues (cash basis)	107988	133200	116486	123500	129776	128000	111272	126000	58515	70000	57097	63800
o/w Financial enterprises	20553	16500	13636	17500	34985	27000	33934	41000	-5549	16000	1350	4500
o/w Nonfinancial enterprises	87435	116700	102850	106000	94791	101000	77338	85000	64064	54000	55747	59300
Memorandum items:												
Statutory Tax Rate	various	50+4%	50+4%	40.0%	40.0%	40.0%	40.0%	40.0%	40.0%	40.0%	40.0%	36.0%
					(ratios to GDP) a/							
Taxable Profits	16.5%	16.3%	17.7%	15.8%	16.2%	14.7%	10.9%	12.1%	7.6%	8.7%	5.7%	5.9%
o/w Financial enterprises	3.0%	1.7%	3.2%	1.9%	3.3%	2.5%	2.0%	3.1%	1.1%	1.7%	0.2%	0.5%
o/w Nonfinancial enterprises	13.5%	14.6%	14.5%	13.9%	13.0%	12.3%	8.9%	9.1%	6.5%	7.1%	5.5%	5.4%
Tax Liabilities	6.7%	7.0%	7.1%	5.7%	5.2%	5.0%	2.9%	4.0%	2.4%	2.7%	1.4%	1.7%
o/w Financial enterprises	1.3%	0.9%	1.5%	0.8%	1.2%	1.1%	0.6%	1.4%	0.5%	0.6%	0.0%	0.2%
o/w Nonfinancial enterprises	5.4%	6.2%	5.6%	4.9%	4.0%	3.9%	2.3%	2.6%	1.9%	2.1%	1.4%	1.5%
Tax Reliefs	0.8%	1.1%	1.6%	0.8%	1.4%	0.9%	1.3%	0.7%	1.3%	0.7%	0.9%	0.5%
o/w Financial enterprises	0.0%	...	0.1%	0.0%	0.1%	0.0%	0.1%	0.1%	0.1%	0.0%	0.0%	0.0%
o/w Nonfinancial enterprises	0.8%	1.1%	1.5%	0.8%	1.2%	0.8%	1.2%	0.6%	1.2%	0.6%	0.8%	0.4%
Tax Revenues (cash basis)	7.5%	8.1%	6.8%	6.0%	6.2%	5.1%	4.8%	4.2%	2.2%	2.2%	1.7%	1.6%
o/w Financial enterprises	1.4%	1.0%	0.8%	0.9%	1.7%	1.1%	1.5%	1.4%	-0.2%	0.5%	0.0%	0.1%
o/w Nonfinancial enterprises	6.1%	7.1%	6.0%	5.2%	4.6%	4.0%	3.4%	2.8%	2.4%	1.7%	1.7%	1.5%

Source: Ministry of Finance and World Bank staff estimates.
a/ Accrual basis; excluding the National Bank of Hungary (NBH), using old national accounts methodology.
b/ Accrual figures are expected outturn, while cash figures are actual outturn.
c/ Excludes minimum tax revenues.
d/ Includes reliefs granted for profit surtax.

Table 5.8: Distribution of Value Added Taxes on Household Consumption, 1988-94
(in percent)

Consumption Group	1988				1992				1993 Budget				1993 Actual				1994 Budget			
	0	0.25	0.15	Exempt	0	0.25	0.15	Exempt	0	0.06	0.25	Exempt	0	0.06	0.25	Exempt	0	0.1	0.25	Exempt
Food	87	13	-	-	80	20	-	-	-	82	18	-	-	82	18	-	-	82	18	-
Consumption goods	-	100	-	-	-	100	-	-	-	-	100	-	-	-	100	-	-	-	100	-
Clothes	1	99	-	-	2	98	-	-	-	2	98	-	-	2	98	-	-	2	98	-
Technical goods	-	100	-	-	-	100	-	-	-	-	100	-	-	-	100	-	-	-	100	-
Vehicles	-	100	-	-	-	100	-	-	-	-	100	-	-	-	100	-	-	-	100	-
Chemical goods	-	100	-	-	-	100	-	-	-	-	100	-	-	-	100	-	-	-	100	-
Furniture	-	100	-	-	-	100	-	-	-	-	100	-	-	-	100	-	-	-	100	-
Cultural goods	34	66	-	-	35	65	-	-	-	35	65	-	-	35	65	-	-	35	65	-
Fuel for vehicles	99	1	-	-	98	2	-	-	-	-	100	-	-	-	100	-	-	-	100	-
Fuel for heating	99	1	-	-	100	-	-	-	-	100	-	-	-	100	-	-	100	-	-	-
Therapeutic goods	100	-	-	-	100	-	-	-	25	75	-	-	25	75	-	-	25	75	-	-
Other goods	40	60	-	-	40	60	-	-	-	35	65	-	-	35	65	-	-	35	65	-
Elec., water, gas, and central heating	100	-	-	-	100	-	-	-	35	65	-	-	-	100	-	-	-	100	-	-
Household services	-	-	-	-	-	75	-	25	-	-	75	25	-	-	75	25	-	-	75	25
Trans. & communic.	-	-	-	-	86	-	14	-	-	88	-	12	-	88	-	12	-	88	-	12
Other services	-	-	-	-	15	20	35	30	-	40	30	30	-	40	30	30	-	40	30	30
Total cur. cons.	-	-	-	-	46	45	5	4	2	37	57	4	1	38	57	4	1	38	57	4
Housing pur., build	-	-	-	-	25	70	4	1	-	-	99	1	-	-	99	1	1	-	99	1
Total consumption	40	51	5	4	45	46	5	4	2	36	58	4	1	37	58	4	1	37	58	4

Sources: Ministry of Finance and World Bank staff estimates.

Table 5.9: Value Added Tax and Excise Tax, 1994-95

	1994	1995 Budget	1994	1995 Budget	1994	1995 Budget
	(Billions of forint)		(Share of total)		(Share of GDP)	
Value Added Tax	343.5	429.0	100.0	100.0	8.0	7.8
Foodstuffs	52.6	70.7	15.3	16.5	1.2	1.3
Consumer essentials	34.0	38.8	9.9	9.0	0.8	0.7
Clothing	27.5	30.7	8.0	7.2	0.6	0.6
Other goods	105.5	121.5	30.7	28.3	2.4	2.2
Services	58.4	82.8	17.0	19.3	1.4	1.5
House construction	3.0	17.5	0.9	4.1	0.1	0.3
Other purchases	65.0	71.0	18.9	16.6	1.5	1.3
Less timing adjustments	-2.5	-4.0	-0.7	-0.9	-0.1	-0.1
Excises	172.0	190.0	100.0	100.0	4.0	3.5
Tobacco	39.2	43.5	22.8	22.9	0.9	0.8
Coffee	2.4	2.4	1.4	1.3	0.1	0.0
Alcoholic drinks	28.0	30.2	16.3	15.9	0.6	0.5
Petrol	64.5	74.8	37.5	39.4	1.5	1.4
Diesel	37.0	38.3	21.5	20.2	0.9	0.7
Other petrolium products	0.5	0.6	0.3	0.3	0.0	0.0
Other items	1.7	2.4	1.0	1.3	0.0	0.0
Less timing adjustments	-1.3	-2.2	-0.8	-1.2	0.0	0.0

Source: Ministry of Finance.

Table 5.10: Subsidy Reduction Program, 1988-94 a/
(Billions of Forint)

	1988	1989	1990	1991	1992	1993	Estimate 1994	Budget 1995
Consumer Subsidies	65.9	69.1	64.3	79.7	62.2	76.2	96.0	103.7
Milk and dairy products	5.2	5.2	3.9	3.5	--	--	--	--
Household energy	20.6	21.3	20.1	19.7	--	--	--	--
Local transportation	12.8	12.3	3.5	6.1	7.5	8.3	10.5	12.5
Railway transportation	1.5	1.8	2.4	4.2	6.2	6.2	6.6	7.9
Other transportation	1.2	1.2	1.7	3.5	5.5	7.3	9.8	11.5
Water supply and sewage	6.7	8.0	5.2	3.4	--	--	--	--
Pharmaceutical subsidies b/	17.9	19.3	27.6	39.3	43.0	54.3	69.0	71.7
Other	0.0	0.0	0.0	0.0	0.0	0.1	0.1	0.1
Housing Sector Subsidies	30.7	87.2	104.4	94.4	101.6	92.4	94.3	119.3
Pre-1989 housing loans	19.1	63.9	52.1	42.5	41.4	23.7	31.6	34.7
Post-1989 housing loans	--	12.2	22.6	25.3	28.7	32.7	29.6	40.0
Maintenance subsidy	11.1	8.6	--	--	--	--	--	--
Early loan repayment	--	--	--	2.8	1.1	2.0	2.0	2.9
Inst. rental housing support	--	--	4.0	2.2	1.7	1.3	1.6	1.7
Grants	0.5	2.5	25.7	21.6	28.7	32.7	29.5	40.0
Producer Subsidies	148.5	129.4	107.4	59.6	60.3	62.4	102.0	86.2
CMEA price equalization b/	57.7	43.7	40.1	--	--	--	--	--
Coal production	5.7	0.4	1.8	--	--	--	--	--
Other mining	2.0	2.2	2.5	--	0.4	0.3	0.5	0.3
Miner's wage subsidy	--	--	--	2.6	2.3	2.8	2.8	2.3
Agriculture sector	43.0	42.1	36.1	38.2	32.4	44.8	62.5	57.5
Current production	24.1	23.6	12.8	11.4	2.2	2.2	5.9	6.5
Milk production	5.7	1.9	0.0	--	--	--	--	--
Beef production	1.8	0.4	0.3	--	--	--	--	--
Fertilizer	4.8	4.0	1.1	--	--	--	--	--
Protein feed	0.6	3.0	0.0	--	--	--	--	--
Price supplements	4.5	--	--	--	--	--	--	--
Disadvantaged areas	5.3	6.7	3.7	5.9	0.6	--	--	--
Interest rate subsidy	0.0	2.1	2.4	--	--	--	--	--
Other	1.4	5.5	5.3	5.5	1.6	2.2	5.9	6.5
Agricultural market subsidies	--	--	--	--	7.3	17.1	6.7	7.5
Export subsidy	18.9	18.5	23.3	26.8	22.9	25.5	40.0	35.0
Agricultural production subsidies	--	--	--	--	--	--	9.9	8.5
Invervention Fund	11.9	11.0	0.0	1.5	0.5	0.2	--	--
Railway subsidy	4.5	4.9	4.0	2.4	8.2	4.0	25.9	15.0
Other transportation	0.6	--	1.2	--	--	--	--	--
Trade Policy Fund	3.5	5.0	3.7	5.0	3.2	2.9	--	--
Other (culture, etc.)	2.0	2.1	1.9	1.6	1.9	1.5	2.3	1.6
Investment subsidies	17.6	18.0	16.1	8.3	11.4	5.9	8.0	9.5
Budgetary grants	7.5	6.7	5.9	8.3	11.4	5.9	8.0	9.5
SDI equity allocations	10.1	11.3	10.2	0.0	0.0	0.0	0.0	0.0
Total	245.1	285.7	276.1	233.7	224.2	230.9	292.3	309.2
Share of GDP (percent)	(17.1)	(16.7)	(13.3)	(9.4)	(7.6)	(6.5)	(6.8)	(5.6)
Memorandum item:								
Gross Domestic Product old meth.	1435.2	1710.8	2079.5	2308.4	2805.0	3320.0	3959.5	--
Gross Domestic Product new meth.	...	...	...	2491.7	2935.1	3537.7	4310.0	5500.0

Source: Ministry of Finance.
NA = not available
a/ Accrual basis.
b/ Cash basis.

Table 5.11: Excise Revenues in Selected Countries

	Austria 1991	Belguim 1991	Denmark 1991	Finland 1991	France 1991	Germany 1991	Ireland 1991	Italy 1991	Netherlands 1991	Norway 1991	Portugal 1991	Sweden 1991	U.K. 1991	Simple Average	Hungary 1993 a/
								(Share of total)							
Excises	100.0	100.0	100.0	100.0	100.0	100.0	100.0	100.0	100.0	100.0	100.0	100.0	100.0	100.0	100.0
Consumer goods	44.5	40.7	37.3	52.6	22.8	39.3	50.8	7.4	30.4	28.4	23.0	32.9	47.9	35.2	33.4
o/w tobacco	25.0	24.6	17.0	14.3	13.7	25.2	23.1	3.7	15.0	9.9	18.1	10.4	26.4	17.4	18.1
o/w coffee	--	0.6	0.6	--	--	2.8	--	0.9	--	--	0.8	--	--	0.4	0.9
o/w alcohol	8.4	15.6	15.3	32.2	8.0	9.4	26.7	2.1	12.4	13.7	3.9	21.9	21.2	14.7	14.3
o/w others	11.1	--	4.4	6.1	1.0	2.0	1.1	0.7	3.1	4.8	0.1	0.7	0.3	2.7	--
Petroleum products	45.4	59.3	23.3	30.6	68.0	60.7	36.1	73.1	42.8	46.9	63.3	31.7	46.7	48.3	62.9
o/w benzin	...	...	...	...	...	...	...	...	...	...	...	...	...	...	34.6
o/w diesel fuel	...	...	...	...	...	...	...	...	...	...	...	...	...	...	18.0
o/w others b/	...	...	...	...	...	...	...	...	...	...	...	...	...	...	10.4
Other products c/ d/	10.1	--	39.4	16.8	9.2	--	13.0	19.5	26.8	24.7	13.7	35.4	5.4	16.5	3.7
o/w electricity	--	--	11.1	--	4.5	--	--	9.8	--	8.1	--	1.6	--	2.7	0.0
o/w motor vehicle	--	--	21.6	10.7	--	--	12.6	--	20.0	9.9	13.7	2.9	5.4	7.4	3.5
o/w other	10.1	--	6.6	6.1	4.7	--	0.4	9.7	6.8	6.7	--	30.9	--	6.3	0.2
								(Share of GDP)							
Excises	2.5%	2.2%	4.8%	4.4%	2.6%	2.8%	6.1%	3.2%	2.6%	6.1%	5.0%	3.8%	4.0%	3.9%	4.8%
Consumer goods	1.1%	0.9%	1.8%	2.3%	0.6%	1.1%	3.1%	0.2%	0.8%	1.7%	1.1%	1.3%	1.9%	1.4%	1.6%
o/w tobacco	0.6%	0.5%	0.8%	0.6%	0.4%	0.7%	1.4%	0.1%	0.4%	0.6%	0.9%	0.4%	1.1%	0.7%	0.9%
o/w coffee	--	--	--	--	--	0.1%	--	--	--	--	--	--	--	--	--
o/w alcohol	0.2%	0.3%	0.7%	1.4%	0.2%	0.3%	1.6%	0.1%	0.3%	0.8%	0.2%	0.8%	0.9%	0.6%	0.7%
o/w others	0.3%	--	0.2%	0.3%	--	0.1%	0.1%	0.1%	0.1%	0.3%	--	--	--	0.1%	0.0%
Petroleum products	1.1%	1.3%	1.1%	1.3%	1.7%	1.7%	2.2%	2.4%	1.1%	2.9%	3.1%	1.2%	1.9%	1.8%	3.0%
o/w benzin	...	...	...	...	...	...	...	...	...	...	...	...	...	...	1.7%
o/w diesel fuel	...	...	...	...	...	...	...	...	...	...	...	...	...	...	0.9%
o/w others b/	...	...	...	...	...	...	...	...	...	...	...	...	...	...	0.5%
Other products c/ d/	0.2%	--	1.9%	0.7%	0.2%	--	0.8%	0.6%	0.7%	1.5%	0.7%	1.4%	0.2%	0.7%	0.2%
o/w electricity	--	--	0.5%	--	0.1%	--	--	0.3%	--	0.5%	--	0.1%	--	0.1%	--
o/w motor vehicle	--	--	1.0%	0.5%	--	--	0.8%	--	0.5%	0.6%	0.7%	0.1%	0.2%	0.3%	0.2%
o/w other	0.2%	--	0.3%	0.3%	0.1%	--	--	0.3%	0.2%	0.4%	--	1.2%	--	0.2%	--

Sources: OECD Revenue Statistics 1965-1992 and Ministry of Finance.

a/ Differs from strict excise data in Tables 1-5 by including earmarked excises for Road Fund and motor vehicle taxes.
b/ Includes earmarked excises for Road Fund for Hungary.
c/ Includes cash/accrual difference of - Ft 2.01 billion for Hungary.
d/ Includes tax on energy consumption equivalent to 29 percent of all excise for Sweden.

Table 5.12: Customs Duties and Statistical Fees, 1991-93

	1991	1992	1993
Customs Duties	8.7%	7.0%	7.6%
o/w ex-CMEA partners a/	4.6%	4.4%	4.0%
o/w other countries	9.7%	7.9%	8.6%
Statistical Fees	2.5%	2.4%	2.8%
o/w ex-CMEA partners a/	3.0%	2.5%	2.8%
o/w other countries	2.4%	2.3%	2.8%
Total Duties and Fees	11.2%	10.7%	10.4%
o/w ex-CMEA partners a/	7.6%	6.9%	6.7%
o/w other countries	12.1%	10.3%	11.3%
Memorandum items:			
Dutiable imports	100.0%	100.0%	100.0%
o/w ex-CMEA partners a/	19.3%	25.0%	20.4%
o/w other countries	80.7%	75.0%	79.6%

a/ Excluding former East Germany.
Source: Ministry of Finance.

Table 5.13: Local Government Revenues, 1990-95 a/
(Billions of HUF; percent of GDP)

	1990	1991	1992	Estim. 1993	Budget 1994	1995
REVENUES	300.5	385.5	508.5	577.9	646.3	713.2
Own Sources	62.1	80.7	142.9	161.1	171.1	197.0
Taxes	6.7	0.0	17.3	32.0	36.5	39.0
Fees	7.1	16.2	9.3	10.5	8.0	11.5
Privatization	0.0	0.0	0.0	4.4	6.8	7.0
Other capital revenues	0.0	0.0	0.0	44.6	54.5	63.0
Institutional revenues	29.4	40.9	41.1	54.2	55.0	58.0
Other Revenues	18.9	23.6	75.2	15.4	10.3	18.5
Transfers and Shared Revenues	238.4	304.8	365.6	416.8	475.2	516.2
Personal income tax	74.5	47.0	63.0	49.0	61.3	93.6
Motor vehicle tax	0.0	0.0	2.3	2.5	2.6	3.3
Social security transfers	50.6	67.1	80.8	91.6	94.2	99.0
State budget transfers	113.3	190.7	219.5	256.6	307.1	307.3
VAT refunding	0.0	0.0	0.0	9.9	5.0	6.0
CBI tranfers	0.0	0.0	0.0	4.8	2.5	4.0
EBF transfers	0.0	0.0	0.0	2.4	2.5	3.0
(in percent of GDP)						
REVENUES	14.5	15.5	17.3	16.3	15.0	13.0
Own Sources	3.0	3.2	4.9	4.6	4.0	3.6
Taxes	0.3	0.0	0.6	0.9	0.8	0.7
Fees	0.3	0.7	0.3	0.3	0.2	0.2
Privatization	0.0	0.0	0.0	0.1	0.2	0.1
Other capital revenues	0.0	0.0	0.0	1.3	1.3	1.1
Institutional revenues	1.4	1.6	1.4	1.5	1.3	1.1
Other Revenues	0.9	0.9	2.6	0.4	0.2	0.3
Transfers and Shared Revenues	11.5	12.2	12.5	11.8	11.0	9.4
Personal income tax	3.6	1.9	2.1	1.4	1.4	1.7
Motor vehicle tax	0.0	0.0	0.1	0.1	0.1	0.1
Social security transfers	2.4	2.7	2.8	2.6	2.2	1.8
State budget transfers	5.4	7.7	7.5	7.3	7.1	5.6
VAT refunding	0.0	0.0	0.0	0.3	0.1	0.1
CBI tranfers	0.0	0.0	0.0	0.1	0.1	0.1
EBF transfers	0.0	0.0	0.0	0.1	0.1	0.1

a/ Figures are shown on a gross basis and differ from tables 5.1 and 5.2 which net out intergovernment tranfers.
Sources: Ministry of Finance and World Bank staff estimates.

Table 5.14: Local Government Expenditures, 1990-95 a/
(Billions of HUF; percent of GDP)

	1990	1991	1992	1993	Estim. 1994	Budget 1995
Total Expenditures	256.7	306.4	389.4	597.5	664.8	714.7
Current Expenditure	201.1	242.9	293.2	489.3	546.5	594.7
Wages and salaries	89.1	110.7	146.6	166.3	192.0	205.4
Other goods and services	107.1	114.2	126.4	276.7	304.5	324.5
o/w Social security contributions	38.3	49.6	59.5	74.8	89.5	92.5
Subsidies and other transfers	4.9	18.0	20.2	43.5	44.0	57.8
Interest	0.0	0.0	0.0	2.8	6.0	7.0
Capital Expenditures	55.6	63.5	96.2	108.2	118.3	120.0
Fixed capital formation	46.7	63.5	81.3	89.0	97.5	101.0
Capital transfers	8.9	0.0	14.9	19.2	20.8	19.0
(in percent of GDP)						
Total Expenditures	12.3	12.3	13.3	16.9	15.4	13.0
Current Expenditure	9.7	9.7	10.0	13.8	12.7	10.8
Wages and salaries	4.3	4.4	5.0	4.7	4.5	3.7
Other goods and services	5.2	4.6	4.3	7.8	7.1	5.9
o/w Social security contributions	1.8	2.0	2.0	2.1	2.1	1.7
Subsidies and other transfers	0.2	0.7	0.7	1.2	1.0	1.1
Interest	0.0	0.0	0.0	0.1	0.1	0.1
Capital Expenditures	2.7	2.5	3.3	3.1	2.7	2.2
Fixed capital formation	2.2	2.5	2.8	2.5	2.3	1.8
Capital transfers	0.4	0.0	0.5	0.5	0.5	0.3

/ Figures are shown on a gross basis and differ from tables 5.1 and 5.2 which net out intergovernment tranfers.
Sources: Ministry of Finance and World Bank staff estimates.

Table 6.1: Monetary Survey
(Billions of Forint at end of period)

	1984	1985	1986	1987	1988	1989	1990	1991	1992 d/	1993 d/	1994 d/ e/
Net Foreign Liabilities a/	280.7	325.2	574.5	728.3	834.6	1019.4	1024.3	1134.5	1109.8	1346.6	1774.4
Convertible	..	..	578.0	733.3	834.6	1053.0	1079.9	1185.8	1113.1	1351.4	1776.2
Nonconvertible	..	..	-3.5	-5.0	..	-33.6	-55.6	-51.3	-3.3	-4.8	-1.8
Domestic Credit	767.8	825.9	1121.9	1262.7	1338.3	1550.4	1721.8	1846.4	2074.6	2402.4	2800.5
General Government, Net	209.0	216.4	511.6	589.6	629.7	724.7	730.4	852.5	1142.2	1371.5	1587.2
SDI b/	197.2	194.7	146.7	180.0	208.2	237.8	254.5	0.0	0.0	0.0	0.0
Other Official Entities	5.1	6.8	8.1	11.1	15.9	18.2	23.1	24.8	13.3	22.9	99.7
Local Governments	5.1	6.0	7.3	10.9	15.7	18.2	21.9	22.9	13.0	22.7	48.9
Financial Institutions	0.0	0.8	0.8	0.2	0.2	0.0	1.2	1.9	0.3	0.2	50.8
Non-government sector	553.7	602.7	602.2	662.0	692.7	807.5	968.3	969.1	919.1	1008.0	1113.6
Enterprises	374.1	397.7	367.1	389.9	382.8	475.3	594.3	705.4	635.4	676.2	786.2
Households	179.6	205.0	230.0	265.2	296.9	313.5	330.0	202.3	209.1	239.7	222.1
Small Entrepreneurs	0.0	0.0	5.1	6.9	13.0	18.7	44.0	61.4	68.6	85.7	92.8
Other c/	0.0	0.0	0.0	0.0	0.0	0.0	0.0	0.0	6.0	6.4	12.5
Other Assets, Net	-19.8	14.8	31.6	118.4	176.4	243.6	306.3	643.8	778.6	960.7	1262.9
Net Domestic Assets	748.0	840.7	1153.5	1381.1	1514.7	1794.0	2028.1	2490.2	2853.2	3363.1	4063.4
Broad Money	443.0	488.5	544.1	599.4	620.3	707.2	909.9	1168.9	1500.9	1758.7	1995.7
Currency Outside Banks	105.4	116.7	..	..	164.4	180.5	209.8	260.2	322.4	371.3	411.5
Other Deposits	29.3	26.1	..	..	33.0	73.4	98.5	152.3	171.9	191.7	187.8
Household Deposits	206.6	229.0	252.8	261.3	284.2	273.3	323.9	432.0	582.4	696.0	872.8
Enterprise Deposits	101.7	116.7	135.0	158.9	138.7	180.0	277.7	324.4	424.2	499.7	523.6
Bonds & Savings Notes	24.3	27.0	34.9	53.4	59.8	67.4	93.9	186.8	242.5	257.8	293.3
Savings Notes	..	..	22.1	25.3	30.3	32.3	35.6	48.6	74.5	83.2	87.9
Certificate of Deposits	..	..	..	..	6.6	13.4	32.4	82.3	91.0	91.7	91.9
Other Bonds	..	..	..	..	22.9	21.7	25.9	55.9	77.0	82.9	113.5

Sources: Hungarian authorities and IMF.

a/ At current exchange rate. They exclude from December 31, 1992 the stock of ruble claims (HUF 48.3) which were taken over by the state.

b/ State Development Institution. This was incorporated in the budget as of January 1991.

c/ Before December 31, 1992 these were recorded partly under local governments and partly under enterprise credits. Now classified as "non-profit organizations".

d/ From December 31,1992 due to changes in classification, the stock of credit to the enterprise sector cannot be fully compared to earlier data. The change in classification also affects the stock of enterprise deposits, deposits fo small entrepreneurs (in the Other Deposits category) and thus the stock of Broad Money. Also, from December 31, 1992 data reflect the impact of the credit and bank consolidation.

e/ Preliminary data.

173

Table 6.2: Financing of the Economy

	1990	1991	1992	1993	1994 Prelim.
	(Flows, in billions of HUF)				
Net Foreign Liabilities	4.9	110.2	-24.7	236.8	427.8
Convertible	26.9	105.9	-72.7	238.3	424.8
Nonconvertible	-22.0	4.3	48.0	-1.5	3.0
Domestic Credit	171.4	124.6	228.2	327.8	398.1
General Government, Net	5.7	122.1	289.7	229.3	215.7
Other Official Entities	4.9	1.7	-11.5	9.6	76.8
Local Governments	3.7	1.0	-9.9	9.7	26.2
Financial Institutions	1.2	0.7	-1.6	-0.1	50.6
Non-government sector	160.8	0.8	-50.0	88.9	105.6
Enterprises	119.0	111.1	-70.0	40.8	110.0
Households	16.5	-127.7	6.8	30.6	-17.6
Small Entrepreneurs	25.3	17.4	7.2	17.1	7.1
Other	0.0	0.0	6.0	0.4	6.1
Other Assets, Net	62.7	337.5	134.8	182.1	302.2
Net Domestic Assets	234.1	462.1	363.0	509.9	700.3
Broad Money	202.7	259.0	332.0	257.8	237.0
Currency Outside Banks	29.3	50.4	62.2	48.9	40.2
Other Deposits	25.1	53.8	19.6	19.8	-3.9
Household Deposits	50.6	108.1	150.4	113.6	176.8
Enterprise Deposits	97.7	46.7	99.8	75.5	23.9
	0.0	0.0	0.0	0.0	0.0
Bonds & Savings Notes	26.5	92.9	55.7	15.3	35.5
Savings Notes	3.3	13.0	25.9	8.7	4.7
Certificate of Deposits	19.0	49.9	8.7	0.7	0.2
Other Bonds	4.2	30.0	21.1	5.9	30.6
	(Flows, in percent of GDP)				
Net Foreign Liabilities	0.2	4.4	-0.8	6.7	9.9
Convertible	1.3	4.3	-2.5	6.7	9.9
Nonconvertible	-1.1	0.2	1.6	0.0	0.1
Domestic Credit	8.2	5.0	7.8	9.3	9.2
General Government, Net	0.3	4.9	9.9	6.5	5.0
Other Official Entities	0.2	0.1	-0.4	0.3	1.8
Local Governments	0.2	0.0	-0.3	0.3	0.6
Financial Institutions	0.1	0.0	-0.1	0.0	1.2
Non-government sector	7.7	0.0	-1.7	2.5	2.5
Enterprises	5.7	4.5	-2.4	1.2	2.6
Households	0.8	-5.1	0.2	0.9	-0.4
Small Entrepreneurs	1.2	0.7	0.2	0.5	0.2
Other	0.0	0.0	0.2	0.0	0.1
Other Assets, Net	3.0	13.5	4.6	5.1	7.0
Net Domestic Assets	11.3	18.5	12.4	14.4	16.2
Broad Money	9.7	10.4	11.3	7.3	5.5
Currency Outside Banks	1.4	2.0	2.1	1.4	0.9
Other Deposits	1.2	2.2	0.7	0.6	-0.1
Household Deposits	2.4	4.3	5.1	3.2	4.1
Enterprise Deposits	4.7	1.9	3.4	2.1	0.6
Bonds & Savings Notes	1.3	3.7	1.9	0.4	0.8
Savings Notes	0.2	0.5	0.9	0.2	0.1
Certificate of Deposits	0.9	2.0	0.3	0.0	0.0
Other Bonds	0.2	1.2	0.7	0.2	0.7

Source: National Bank of Hungary.

Table 7.1: Price Indices of the Industrial Sector

	1980	1981	1982	1983	1984	1985	1986	1987	1988	1989	1990	1991	1992 a/	1993	1994
							(1980=100)								
Producer Price Index	100.0	106.3	111.2	117.3	122.4	128.5	131.2	135.8	142.2	164.1	200.2	265.5	296.0	328.0	365.1
Domestic Sales	100.0	107.1	112.6	118.4	122.7	128.2	131.0	135.9	141.5	160.4	199.3	262.9	287.3	317.5	349.9
Sales Prices of External Trade	100.0	104.1	106.4	112.3	118.9	124.0	125.9	130.9	138.7	164.0	184.3	240.0	276.5	311.0	357.7
							(percentage change)								
Producer Price Index	15.3	6.3	4.5	5.6	4.3	5.0	2.1	3.5	4.7	15.4	22.0	32.6	11.5	10.8	11.3
Domestic Sales	19.4	7.1	5.1	5.2	3.6	4.5	2.2	3.7	4.1	13.4	24.2	31.9	9.3	10.5	10.2
Sales Prices of External Trade	..	4.1	2.2	5.5	5.9	4.3	1.5	4.0	6.0	18.2	12.4	30.2	15.2	12.5	15.0

Source: Central Statistical Office.

a/ Data beginning in 1992 are determined by the new "Standard Industrial Classification".

Table 7.2: Consumer Price Index by Main Groups of Expenditure

	1980	1981	1982	1983	1984	1985	1986	1987	1988	1989	1990	1991	1992	1993	1994
	(1980=100)														
Foodstuffs	100.0	103.4	108.4	113.8	127.6	135.7	138.4	151.1	175.0	206.0	278.5	339.6	405.4	523.8	646.4
Beverages, Tobacco	100.0	102.6	116.0	123.8	130.0	132.2	139.1	157.8	180.4	200.5	262.0	327.8	392.0	464.9	541.2
Clothing	100.0	106.0	111.8	118.8	131.9	146.3	160.1	175.6	210.7	249.1	307.1	405.7	499.0	582.3	676.0
Fuel, Household Energy	100.0	99.8	109.7	115.1	120.7	146.0	151.1	160.9	181.5	202.1	257.9	466.9	668.7	804.4	898.5
Durable Consumer Goods	100.0	101.1	103.2	111.2	117.3	123.6	131.1	134.1	145.5	171.2	206.8	272.3	311.2	345.5	386.2
Other Industrial Articles	100.0	109.0	115.9	126.8	136.0	144.0	151.0	160.4	186.5	228.3	294.2	422.0	536.7	652.7	776.7
Services	100.0	106.5	114.2	125.7	135.8	148.4	161.6	176.2	207.1	241.5	303.3	430.4	542.2	672.9	809.5
Total	100.0	104.6	111.8	119.9	129.9	139.0	146.3	158.9	183.6	214.8	276.9	373.8	459.8	563.2	669.1
	(percentage change)														
Foodstuffs	13.4	3.4	4.8	5.1	12.1	6.3	2.0	9.2	15.8	17.7	35.2	21.9	19.4	29.2	23.4
Beverages, Tobacco	1.7	2.6	13.1	6.7	5.0	1.7	5.2	13.5	14.3	11.1	30.7	25.1	19.6	18.6	16.4
Clothing	5.0	6.6	5.5	6.3	11.0	10.9	9.4	9.7	20.0	18.2	23.3	32.1	23.0	16.7	16.1
Fuel, Household Energy	21.4	-0.2	10.0	4.9	4.9	20.9	3.5	6.5	12.8	11.4	27.6	81.0	43.2	20.3	11.7
Durable Consumer Goods	13.2	1.1	2.1	7.8	5.5	5.3	6.1	2.3	8.5	17.6	20.8	31.7	14.3	11.0	11.8
Other Industrial Articles	9.5	9.0	6.4	9.3	7.3	5.9	4.9	6.2	16.3	22.4	28.9	43.4	27.2	21.6	19.0
Services	7.0	6.5	7.2	10.1	8.0	9.3	8.9	9.0	17.5	16.6	25.6	41.9	26.0	24.1	20.3
Total	9.1	4.6	6.9	7.3	8.3	7.0	5.3	8.6	15.5	17.0	28.9	35.0	23.0	22.5	18.8

Source: Central Statistical Office.

Table 8.1: Main Economic Indicators, High-Growth Scenario

	1994	1995	1996	1997	1998	1999	2000	2001	2002	2003	2004	2005
General Government					(in percent of GDP)							
Overall Balance	-6.4	-3.7	-1.5	-1.2	-1.8	-1.5	-1.5	-1.5	-1.5	-1.5	-1.5	-1.5
Expenditures	59.5	56.3	54.1	50.7	46.6	44.2	42.7	42.0	41.7	41.4	41.0	40.6
Revenues	53.1	52.6	52.6	49.5	44.8	42.7	41.2	40.5	40.2	39.9	39.5	39.1
Gross Debt	88.5	84.3	75.6	68.1	64.6	61.3	58.3	55.6	53.0	50.5	48.1	45.9
					(percentage change)							
GDP	2.0	0.0	1.0	3.0	3.0	3.5	4.0	4.2	4.5	4.8	5.0	5.0
Total Consumption	-2.5	-4.1	-2.6	0.5	1.0	2.1	3.2	3.7	4.1	4.4	4.7	4.7
Private Consumption	1.3	-3.0	-2.3	0.8	1.5	2.5	3.7	3.7	4.0	4.3	4.7	4.7
Government Consumption	-21.0	-3.0	-2.3	0.8	1.5	2.5	3.7	3.7	4.0	4.3	4.7	4.7
Gross Fixed Investment	11.5	4.5	6.8	6.5	5.0	5.0	5.0	5.0	5.0	5.0	5.0	5.0
Exports GNFS (volume)	13.3	18.0	8.5	7.5	7.0	6.0	5.2	5.0	5.0	5.0	5.0	5.0
Imports GNFS (volume)	10.3	-0.9	2.1	3.5	3.4	3.8	4.2	4.4	4.5	4.4	4.4	4.4
GDP deflator	19.4	27.6	22.0	15.0	8.0	6.0	5.0	4.5	4.5	4.5	4.5	4.5
					(in millions of US$)							
Merchandise Exports	7613	9121	10075	11140	12224	13297	14375	15486	16657	17868	19168	20563
Merchandise Imports	11248	11370	11849	12705	13555	14516	15606	16710	17900	19090	20367	21730
Trade Balance	-3635	-2250	-1774	-1565	-1332	-1219	-1230	-1225	-1244	-1222	-1199	-1167
(% of GDP)	-8.9	-5.5	-4.3	-3.5	-2.9	-2.5	-2.3	-2.2	-2.1	-1.9	-1.7	-1.6
Current Account Balance	-3911	-2519	-2014	-1609	-1230	-1011	-1016	-1020	-1031	-992	-946	-875
(% of GDP)	-9.5	-6.2	-4.8	-3.6	-2.6	-2.0	-1.9	-1.8	-1.7	-1.5	-1.4	-1.2
Direct Foreign Investment	1146	1800	2200	2000	1200	1200	1200	1000	1000	1000	1000	1000
Net liabilities (incl. ST and IMF)	1933	473	175	189	805	642	711	783	369	92	319	396
Net other capital flow	176	-412	-350	-350	-350	-350	-350	-350	-350	-350	-350	-350
Net change in reserves (- = decrease)	656	657	-11	-230	-425	-480	-545	-413	12	250	-23	-171
Stock of Reserves	6769	6112	6122	6352	6778	7258	7803	8216	8204	7954	7977	8149
(months of Imports GNFS)	6.1	5.4	5.2	5.1	5.1	5.1	5.1	5.0	4.7	4.3	4.0	3.8
Gross External Debt	28521	28994	29169	29358	30163	30804	31515	32298	32667	32759	33078	33474
(% of GDP)	69.6	71.4	69.9	66.5	64.8	62.4	59.8	57.3	54.1	50.7	47.7	45.0
Debt Service Ratio a/	59.2	46.9	43.4	40.8	42.0	42.8	38.2	31.9	33.4	32.3	33.8	27.6

a/ Total debt service in percent of exports of Goods and Services.

Table 8.2: Main Economic Indicators, Muddle-Through Scenario

	1994	1995	1996	1997	1998	1999	2000	2001	2002	2003	2004	2005
General Government					*(in percent of GDP)*							
Overall Balance	-6.4	-3.7	-3.7	-3.7	-3.7	-3.7	-3.7	-3.7	-3.7	-3.7	-3.7	-3.7
Expenditures	59.5	56.3	56.1	55.8	55.5	55.1	54.7	54.4	54.1	54.0	53.8	53.6
Revenues	53.1	52.6	52.4	52.1	51.8	51.4	51.0	50.7	50.4	50.3	50.1	49.9
Gross Debt	88.5	84.3	78.2	74.8	72.1	69.6	67.6	65.7	64.3	63.3	62.5	61.9
					(percentage change)							
GDP	2.0	0.0	1.0	1.0	1.0	1.5	1.5	2.0	2.0	2.0	2.0	2.0
Total Consumption	-2.5	-4.1	-0.5	0.0	0.1	0.7	0.7	1.5	1.6	1.6	1.6	1.6
Private Consumption	1.3	-3.0	-0.7	-0.2	-0.1	0.5	0.5	1.3	1.5	1.5	1.5	1.4
Government Consumption	-21.0	-8.1	0.2	0.6	0.9	1.5	1.4	2.0	2.0	2.0	2.0	2.0
Gross Fixed Investment	11.5	4.5	1.8	1.8	1.0	1.5	1.5	2.0	2.0	2.0	2.0	2.0
Exports GNFS (volume)	13.3	18.0	5.0	3.5	3.5	3.5	3.5	3.3	3.0	3.0	3.0	3.0
Imports GNFS (volume)	10.3	-0.9	1.2	1.2	1.0	1.5	1.5	2.0	2.0	2.0	2.0	2.0
GDP deflator	19.4	27.6	25.0	20.0	20.0	20.0	20.0	20.0	20.0	20.0	20.0	20.0
					(in millions of US$)							
Merchandise Exports	7613	9121	9753	10384	11030	11720	12463	13201	13929	14657	15424	16231
Merchandise Imports	11248	11370	11749	12294	12803	13397	14023	14664	15313	15951	16617	17310
Trade Balance	-3635	-2250	-1996	-1909	-1773	-1676	-1560	-1463	-1384	-1294	-1193	-1080
(% of GDP)	-8.9	-5.5	-4.8	-4.4	-4.0	-3.6	-3.2	-2.9	-2.6	-2.3	-2.1	-1.8
Current Account Balance	-3911	-2519	-2320	-2257	-2156	-2110	-2111	-2154	-2191	-2244	-2308	-2356
(% of GDP)	-9.5	-6.2	-5.6	-5.2	-4.8	-4.5	-4.4	-4.2	-4.1	-4.1	-4.0	-3.9
Direct Foreign Investment	1146	1800	1400	1400	1000	1000	1000	1000	1000	1000	1000	1000
Net liabilities (incl. ST and IMF)	1933	473	1229	1284	1761	1757	1774	1702	1350	1222	1519	1689
Net other capital flow	176	-412	-350	-350	-350	-350	-350	-350	-350	-350	-350	-350
Net change in reserves (- = decrease)	656	657	41	-77	-255	-297	-313	-198	191	372	138	17
Stock of Reserves	6769	6112	6070	6147	6401	6698	7012	7210	7018	6646	6508	6491
(months of Imports GNFS)	6.1	5.4	5.2	5.1	5.1	5.1	5.1	5.0	4.6	4.2	4.0	3.8
Gross External Debt	28521	28994	30223	31507	33268	35025	36800	38502	39851	41074	42593	44282
(% of GDP)	69.6	71.4	72.4	72.8	74.3	75.2	75.9	75.8	75.1	74.3	73.9	73.7
Debt Service Ratio a/	59.2	46.9	45.6	46.6	51.5	55.2	51.6	44.8	48.9	52.2	55.7	50.9

a/ Total debt service in percent of exports of Goods and Services.

Distributors of World Bank Publications

ARGENTINA
Carlos Hirsch, SRL
Galeria Guemes
Florida 165, 4th Floor-Ofc. 453/465
1333 Buenos Aires

Oficina del Libro Internacional
Alberti 40
1082 Buenos Aires

**AUSTRALIA, PAPUA NEW GUINEA,
FIJI, SOLOMON ISLANDS,
VANUATU, AND
WESTERN SAMOA**
D.A. Information Services
648 Whitehorse Road
Mitcham 3132
Victoria

AUSTRIA
Gerold and Co.
Graben 31
A-1011 Wien

BANGLADESH
Micro Industries Development
  Assistance Society (MIDAS)
House 5, Road 16
Dharmondi R/Area
Dhaka 1209

BELGIUM
Jean De Lannoy
Av. du Roi 202
1060 Brussels

BRAZIL
Publicacoes Tecnicas Internacionais
  Ltda.
Rua Peixoto Gomide, 209
01409 Sao Paulo, SP

CANADA
Le Diffuseur
151A Boul. de Mortagne
Boucherville, Québec
J4B 5E6

Renouf Publishing Co.
1294 Algoma Road
Ottawa, Ontario K1B 3W8

CHINA
China Financial & Economic
  Publishing House
8, Da Fo Si Dong Jie
Beijing

COLOMBIA
Infoenlace Ltda.
Apartado Aereo 34270
Bogota D.E.

**COSTA RICA, BELIZE, GUATE
-MALA, HONDURAS,
NICARAGUA, PANAMA**
Chispas Bookstore
75 Meters al Norte del Hotel Balmoral
en calle 7
San Jose

COTE D'IVOIRE
Centre d'Edition et de Diffusion
  Africaines (CEDA)
04 B.P. 541
Abidjan 04 Plateau

CYPRUS
Center of Applied Research
Cyprus College
6, Diogenes Street, Engomi
P.O. Box 2006
Nicosia

CZECH REPUBLIC
National Information Center
P.O. Box 668
CS-113 57 Prague 1

DENMARK
SamfundsLitteratur
Rosenoerns Allé 11
DK-1970 Frederiksberg C

EGYPT, ARAB REPUBLIC OF
Al Ahram
Al Galaa Street
Cairo

The Middle East Observer
41, Sherif Street
Cairo

FINLAND
Akateeminen Kirjakauppa
P.O. Box 23
FIN-00371 Helsinki

FRANCE
World Bank Publications
66, avenue d'Iéna
75116 Paris

GERMANY
UNO-Verlag
Poppelsdorfer Allee 55
53115 Bonn

GREECE
Papasotiriou S.A.
35, Stournara Str.
106 82 Athens

HONG KONG, MACAO
Asia 2000 Ltd.
46-48 Wyndham Street
Winning Centre
7th Floor
Central Hong Kong

HUNGARY
Foundation for Market Economy
Dombovari Ut 17-19
H-1117 Budapest

INDIA
Allied Publishers Private Ltd.
751 Mount Road
Madras - 600 002

INDONESIA
Pt. Indira Limited
Jalan Borobudur 20
P.O. Box 181
Jakarta 10320

IRAN
Kowkab Publishers
P.O. Box 19575-511
Tehran

IRELAND
Government Supplies Agency
4-5 Harcourt Road
Dublin 2

ISRAEL
Yozmot Literature Ltd.
P.O. Box 56055
Tel Aviv 61560

R.O.Y. International
P.O. Box 13056
Tel Aviv 61130

Palestinian Authority/Middle East
Index Information Services
P.O.B. 19502 Jerusalem

ITALY
Licosa Commissionaria Sansoni SPA
Via Duca Di Calabria, 1/1
Cas.lla Postale 552
50125 Firenze

JAMAICA
Ian Randle Publishers Ltd.
206 Old Hope Road
Kingston 6

JAPAN
Eastern Book Service
Hongo 3-Chome, Bunkyo-ku 113
Tokyo

KENYA
Africa Book Service (E.A.) Ltd.
Quaran House, Mfangano St.
P.O. Box 45245
Nairobi

KOREA, REPUBLIC OF
Daejon Trading Co. Ltd.
P.O. Box 34
Yeoeida
Seoul

MALAYSIA
University of Malaya Cooperative
  Bookshop, Limited
P.O. Box 1127, Jalan Pantai Baru
59700 Kuala Lumpur

MEXICO
INFOTEC
Apartado Postal 22-860
14060 Tlalpan, Mexico D.F.

NETHERLANDS
De Lindeboom/InOr-Publikaties
P.O. Box 202
7480 AE Haaksbergen

NEW ZEALAND
EBSCO NZ Ltd.
Private Mail Bag 99914
New Market
Auckland

NIGERIA
University Press Limited
Three Crowns Building Jericho
Private Mail Bag 5095
Ibadan

NORWAY
Narvesen Information Center
Book Department
P.O. Box 6125 Etterstad
N-0602 Oslo 6

PAKISTAN
Mirza Book Agency
65, Shahrah-e-Quaid-e-Azam
P.O. Box No. 729
Lahore 54000

Oxford University Press
5 Bangalore Town
Sharae Faisal
P.O. Box 13033
Karachi-75350

PERU
Editorial Desarrollo SA
Apartado 3824
Lima 1

PHILIPPINES
International Book Center
Suite 720, Cityland 10
Condominium Tower 2
Ayala Avenue, H.V. dela
  Costa Extension
Makati, Metro Manila

POLAND
International Publishing Service
Ul. Piekna 31/37
00-577 Warszawa

PORTUGAL
Livraria Portugal
Rua Do Carmo 70-74
1200 Lisbon

SAUDI ARABIA, QATAR
Jarir Book Store
P.O. Box 3196
Riyadh 11471

SINGAPORE, TAIWAN
Gower Asia Pacific Pte Ltd.
Golden Wheel Building
41, Kallang Pudding, #04-03
Singapore 1334

SLOVAK REPUBLIC
Slovart G.T.G. Ltd.
Krupinska 4
P.O. Box 152
852 99 Bratislava 5

SOUTH AFRICA, BOTSWANA
Oxford University Press
  Southern Africa
P.O. Box 1141
Cape Town 8000

SPAIN
Mundi-Prensa Libros, S.A.
Castello 37
28001 Madrid

Libreria Internacional AEDOS
Consell de Cent, 391
08009 Barcelona

SRI LANKA & THE MALDIVES
Lake House Bookshop
P.O. Box 244
100, Sir Chittampalam A.
  Gardiner Mawatha
Colombo 2

SWEDEN
Fritzes Customer Service
Regeringsgatan 12
S-106 47 Stockholm

Wennergren-Williams AB
P.O. Box 1305
S-171 25 Solna

SWITZERLAND
Librairie Payot
Case postale 3212
CH 1002 Lausanne

Van Diermen Editions Techniques
P.O. Box 465
CH 1211 Geneva 19

TANZANIA
Oxford University Press
Maktaba Street
P.O. Box 5299
Dar es-Salaam

THAILAND
Central Books Distribution Co. Ltd.
306 Silom Road
Bangkok

TRINIDAD & TOBAGO, JAMAICA
Systematics Studies Unit
#9 Watts Street
Curepe
Trinidad, West Indies

UGANDA
Gustro Ltd.
1st Floor, Room 4, Geogiadis Chambers
P.O. Box 9997
Plot (69) Kampala Road
Kampala

UNITED KINGDOM
Microinfo Ltd.
P.O. Box 3
Alton, Hampshire GU34 2PG
England

ZAMBIA
University Bookshop
Great East Road Campus
P.O. Box 32379
Lusaka

ZIMBABWE
Longman Zimbabwe (Pte.) Ltd.
Tourle Road, Ardbennie
P.O. Box ST 125